Resilience in Healthcare Leadership

Resilience in Healthcare Leadership

Practical Strategies and Self-Assessment Tools for Identifying Strengths and Weaknesses

Alan T. Belasen, PhD

Routledge
Taylor & Francis Group
A PRODUCTIVITY PRESS BOOK

First published 2022
by Routledge
605 Third Avenue, New York, NY 10158

and by Routledge
2 Park Square, Milton Park, Abingdon, Oxon, OX14 4RN
Routledge is an imprint of the Taylor & Francis Group, an informa business

ISBN: 9781032042046 (hbk)
ISBN: 9781032042015 (pbk)
ISBN: 9781003190929 (ebk)

DOI: 10.4324/9781003190929

Typeset in Garamond
by Deanta Global Publishing Services, Chennai, India

This book is dedicated to my brother Shalom Charlie Belasen for his courage and resilience.

Contents

Foreword

When I entered the healthcare field, I vividly remember one of our vice presidents telling me that the industry was on the precipice of transformational change. I had just been hired to develop a management development program for a premiere medical center in New York City. With an avuncular tone, he explained that to succeed in my role—to help managers grow—I had to understand the complex environmental factors facing the industry.

The vice president then ticked off the list of developments:

> Patients are getting older and sicker. New medical techniques are changing how and where care is provided. Emerging policies on reimbursement and financing are constricting revenue streams, making budget forecasting trickier. Hospitals are facing unprecedented pressure to find efficiencies, ramping up the need for economy of scale initiatives. Patient satisfaction is becoming an increasingly important metric for evaluating the quality of a hospital stay. A gigantic change is underway in terms of how we record, manage, store, and transfer patient data. Insurance companies are increasingly calling the shots about how we do our business and how much can be spent on providing care. More and more, regulatory bodies are requiring hospitals to focus on quality and to employ metrics to support claims about their performance.

He concluded with a sigh, saying,

> And then there's politics. The left wants policies that cover every person living in the country. The right calls this "socialism" and says it will bankrupt the country. How can you have an intelligent discussion about health policy with each side digging in intransigently?

Sound familiar?

Well, that was 40 years ago! In all that time, nothing has changed and everything has changed.

I often think about the fine line between permanence and change in healthcare. As I rose through the management ranks from vice president of human resources to chief of operations, and for many years since as a consultant focusing on strategic planning and as program director of an MBA in healthcare leadership at SUNY, I marvel at healthcare leaders who find the right balance between stability and adaptability. Rootedness provides continuity. But stability alone is not sufficient in an ever-fluctuating world. Navigating change while leveraging strengths, ever mindful of mission and continuous pursuit of quality—this must go hand-in-hand with stabilizing a culture and promoting trustful relations between the organization and those who come for care, those who work there, and all others with a vested interest. No organization succeeds by sitting still. And it cannot evolve effectively without having earned the goodwill, confidence, and support of stakeholders.

The literature on management effectiveness is replete with skills deemed critical to leading a healthcare organization. To name just a few: Fortitude … agility … deftness … self-awareness … communication … empathy. But is there one skill, one art, one trait that supersedes and transcends the others by virtue of its capacity to bring permanence and change into harmony, that integrates faithfulness to mission and advancing prospects for vision achievement? I would say there is and posit that it is resilience.

Colloquial use of the term "resilience" tends to focus on rebounding from adversity. And while this is certainly important, there is an equally proactive dimension to the term. Bouncing back doesn't simply mean "fighting through." It means adapting, navigating, growing, discovering new ways, new paths, cultivating inner strengths, fortifying existing relationships, and developing new ones. Moreover, resilience is not an isolated experience, not merely a self-directed phenomenon. In a broader sense, resilience is a force of inspiration; it brings out the best in others, selflessness driven by a common good.

In crafting a leadership competency profile through several books, Dr. Alan T. Belasen has few peers in capturing the skills necessary to successfully oversee healthcare organizations. In this current outstanding work, *Resilience in Healthcare Leadership: Practical Strategies and Self-Assessment Tools for Identifying Strengths and Weaknesses*, Dr. Belasen draws on research as well as his lengthy examination of and involvement in healthcare to establish resilience as a central organizing leadership proficiency. The COVID-19 pandemic serves as the aptest point of departure for his analysis. Why have some organizations managed successfully while others experienced backbreaking stress? Why have some come out stronger and others emerge depleted of energy, motivation, and resources? Surely, there are countless factors and circumstances, including location and populations served. Notwithstanding, all organizations have leaders. And it is on the excursion through the province of resilient leadership that Dr. Belasen proves to be a most eloquent tour guide.

In the paradigm constructed by Dr. Belasen, the resilient leader is less the superhero who conquers insurmountable odds, and more the role model, mentor, facilitator, and primary spokesperson for giving the organization voice, stature, credibility, and direction. As he indicates, such leaders "balance logic and emotion, ego and humility." They understand not only what must be done to advance an organization's prospects, but what it takes to define that direction and mobilize the organization's collective energy to bring it to fruition. A resilient leader recognizes the importance of the megaphone and at the same time is humbled by the magnitude of responsibility it confers. Thus, rather than demanding attention and credit for success, the resilient leader pays tribute to those in the organization for its accomplishments.

But it takes more than building a case for the soundness of the resilient leadership theory for a book on the subject to be most helpful. It takes an author's ability to show what resiliency looks like and, even more, to provide the reader with the tools for assessing strengths and areas for development as well as guidance on how to leverage those strengths and convert weaker areas into assets. Accordingly, Dr. Belasen fills his text with examples from diverse corners of the healthcare universe—from the large hospital systems to small community hospitals and elsewhere—to demonstrate the broad applicability of the resilience leadership framework.

Additionally, the self-assessments throughout enable readers to ascertain their profiles across a spectrum of leadership skills derived from the resiliency paradigm. For example, "Assessment: Perceptual Gaps—Diversity and Inclusion" helps readers evaluate their aptitude for creating an environment in which staff see their work as meaningful as well as their capacity for breaking down cultural barriers which could impede its achievement. The book encourages each reader to engage in guided and constructive reflection, coming away with a plan for personal development intertwined with the development of the organization.

If there is a core message throughout *Resilience in Healthcare Leadership: Practical Strategies and Self-Assessment Tools for Identifying Strengths and Weaknesses*, it is that a leader cannot succeed alone. In instilling resilience in the organization, the resilient leader both embodies and reflects the duality of steadiness and dexterity of the organization. Consequently, it is not surprising that the resilient organization sees itself as a "team." Dr. Belasen acknowledges the complexity of fostering this organization-wide belief. It takes the right mix of self-confidence, transparency, accountability, and an understanding of the importance of building an environment of trust, perhaps the most essential of all cultural assets.

Healthcare organizations are complex environments. They are comprised of people with a great diversity of educational and training backgrounds, professions, incomes, traits, and demographic features. Such differences can easily come to dominate the institutional culture, making it seem like the organization is more a collection of small businesses than a highly, coordinated, interprofessional entity that is driven by a common set of patient-centered goals. Added to that is the challenge of helping all feel that the work is meaningful, that a commitment to ethnocultural inclusiveness is sincere, that employees believe their personal values align with those of the organization, and that their input counts in organizational decision-making. When leadership understands all this and takes on the hard work of bringing it to fruition, their organizations will be that much more efficient and effective. In fact, in such environments, efficiency and effectiveness are highly integrated pillars of institutional success. When we come across it, we will know firsthand the capability of resilient leadership to achieve organizational actualization. And we'll have Dr. Belasen to thank for giving us the language and tools to do so.

Barry Eisenberg, PhD

Acknowledgments

This book benefited from the advice and insights of many colleagues from numerous networks and affiliates including the *Management Education and Development, Gender and Diversity in Organizations*, and *Healthcare Management* Divisions of the Academy of Management.

Special thanks go to my research partners whose collaboration with me on many COVID-related research projects has sparked important insights into the qualities of resilient leadership that are now infused throughout the book. Ari Belasen and Marlon Tracey, both from the Department of Economics and Finance, Southern Illinois University Edwardsville; Attila Hertelendy, College of Business, Florida International University; and Jane Oppenlander, David D. Reh School of Business, Clarkson University, shaped my thoughts about the impact of COVID-19 on hospital strategic responses and stakeholder communication through lengthy discussions and exchanges.

Special thanks to Anat Belasen, David H. Smith Conservation Research Postdoctoral Fellow, Department of Ecology and Evolutionary Biology, Cornell University; and Abigail Belasen, Resident Physician, Department of Internal Medicine, Icahn School of Medicine at Mount Sinai whose ideas inspired me to focus sections of this book on collaborative forms of leadership, and diversity and inclusion at the top.

The anonymous reviewers of many journals helped stimulate my thinking about new directions for managing the complexity of healthcare environments, especially at times of crisis. These include reviewers from *Gender in Management: An International Journal*; *Journal of Healthcare Management*; *International Journal for Quality in Health Care*; *International Journal of Strategic Communication*; *Journal of Health Organization and Management*; as well as the reviewers of my previous book: *Dyad Leadership and Clinical Integration: Driving Change, Aligning Strategies.*

I am grateful to Barry Eisenberg, head of the MBA in Healthcare Leadership, SUNY Empire State College, for collaborating with me on curriculum development and dozens of conference papers and publications on topics such as healthcare innovation, executive education, organizational development in healthcare settings, and adaptive leadership in healthcare. His insights and terrific sense of humor inspired me to think deeply about the complexity of hospitals and integrated health services and why resilience in healthcare leadership is key to a sustainable future of health systems.

Special thanks go to Kristine Mednansky, Acquisitions Editor, Taylor & Francis Group, who believed in the importance and relevance of this book project and was instrumental in moving this book project through the various production phases.

My wife Susan provided the social and emotional support as well as the sounding board for many of the ideas in this book. Being surrounded by my five As has always been rewarding and intellectually stimulating. Ari, an accomplished scholar and professor of economics at SIUE; Amy, an accomplished author, founder of ABD Creative, podcast host, marketing expert, and travel blogger; Anat, David H. Smith Conservation Research Postdoctoral Fellow, Department of Ecology and Evolutionary Biology, Cornell University; Amanda, a client service specialist in a global organization; and Abigail, a hospitalist at Albany Medical Center.

I am indebted to everyone.

Alan T. Belasen

About the Author

Alan Belasen holds a PhD from Rockefeller College, SUNY. For over 25 years, Dr. Belasen has been involved in executive education and development programs in the U.S. and abroad in various organizations and industries. Dr. Belasen chaired the MBA Program at SUNY, Empire State College, from 2004 to 2015 where he co-designed the MBA in Management and the MBA in Healthcare Leadership, along with multiple advanced certificate programs.

Dr. Belasen has written over 150 journal articles, book chapters, and conference papers on topics such as executive education, self-managed teams, HR competencies, work motivation, women's leadership, communication innovation, corruption in business, trusted leadership, healthcare curriculum, healthcare management, and leadership development. He is the author of many books including *Dyad Leadership and Clinical Integration: Driving Change, Aligning Strategies* (Health Administration Press, 2019); and Mastering *Leadership: A Vital Resource for Healthcare Organizations* (Jones & Bartlett Learning, 2015).

Chapter 1

Introduction—Resilience in Healthcare Leadership

The COVID-19 pandemic has been an ultimate challenge for leadership resiliency. Resilient leaders are thoughtful and deliberate. They balance logic and emotion, ego, and humility. They lead through compassionate empathy by focusing on the "how," not only the "what." They use their influence to drive positive change, diversity, and inclusion, and create an equitable community.

Most books on resilient leadership appear to focus on spirituality and tools to grow an "unshakable core of calm, strength, and happiness" (Hanson, 2018) or "bounce back without getting stuck in the toxic emotions of guilt, false guilt, anger, and bitterness" (Dees, 2013). These books are very similar to handbooks focusing on mental toughness and providing guides for overcoming adversity and managing negative emotions (Greitens, 2016; Lisson, 2017; Reivich & Shatte, 2003; St. John & Haines, 2017; Zolli & Healy, 2013).

Resilience in Healthcare Leadership, on the other hand, defines resilience as a critical competency of high-performing leaders. Leaders must cultivate resilience in themselves and foster it throughout their organizations and multidisciplinary teams to adapt and succeed. The book is differentiated by offering practical strategies and self-assessment instruments for identifying strengths and weaknesses and for developing and sustaining the performance of resilient leaders. It also focuses on best practices to help build a talent pipeline and develop resilient care team leaders to effectively manage the challenges of disruptive environments.

The book draws on credible sources of academic research and compelling governmental and industry data to demonstrate how the transformations in healthcare can be met with the strengths of resilient leaders: Senior executives, middle managers, and care team leaders. Central themes in this book include:

DOI: 10.4324/9781003190929-1

Promoting a strong leadership pipeline—as the turnover rate of hospital CEOs—has remained relatively high in the last five years (about 17–18%), the need to build a strong talent pipeline with resilient leaders has become critical, especially during the challenges posed by the COVID pandemic. However, senior executives in healthcare organizations increasingly have shown a bias towards a closer handling of operational levels, often bypassing middle managers, de-emphasizing the need to cultivate the next cadre of leaders, and thus creating the potential for leadership discontinuity.

Leading from the middle out—with rising CEO turnover rates, health systems need to develop adequate succession programs to identify and train new leaders. Moreover, these programs must include a robust talent pipeline with appropriate selection and development strategies. The book addresses the strategic value of middle managers in healthcare organizations and reviews the benefits of including them in leadership development and succession planning programs that are linked with the strategic direction of the organization.

Building successful interprofessional care teams—the book explores the vital role of the interprofessional team leader in ensuring quality across the continuum of care. Knowing in advance what senior managers communicate and detecting the tone of the messages is empowering in helping team leaders avoid second guessing higher levels, and instead, turn their attention to articulating messages that are consistent with the expectations of senior executives and key stakeholders.

Leveraging strengths through competency assessment and development—many sections in the book include assessment instruments with examples and suggestions for self-improvement and with practical strategies that help maximize resilience. When traits, skills, and roles are aligned with business objectives and goals, transparency is improved throughout the organization and the value proposition of employees increases for the organization. This helps retain talent and mitigate risks associated with high turnover, especially at the top.

Resilience in Healthcare Leadership provides hands-on approaches for playing to personal strengths and for handling transitions in healthcare environments. It offers strategies for building a culture of trust, fostering teamwork, promoting interprofessional cooperation, and improving patient outcomes. The book features self-assessment instruments for identifying personal strengths and weaknesses, and for distinguishing leadership roles and traits that are associated with resilient leaders and adaptive cultures.

Additional assessment instruments cover emotional intelligence skills, message orientations, organizational culture, and teamwork. Practical suggestions and examples demonstrate how the instruments can be used, data analyzed, and results interpreted for self-development and for improving resilience in healthcare leadership.

Book Chapters

Chapter 2. Disruptive Innovation and Ambidextrous Leadership in Healthcare

This chapter focuses on how healthcare executives respond to crisis and use it as an impetus for meaningful change, innovation, and inspiration. The COVID-19 crisis has challenged health leaders to rethink their business model, and how patient outcomes can be achieved effectively. Disruptive innovations including robotic surgery, telemedicine, self-monitoring, and self-management of chronic conditions such as diabetes, the use of ultrasound by non-radiologists, reading glasses in retail stores, medical tourism, and retail medical clinics are changing how healthcare is accessed by the public and delivered by health systems. As continual redesign in healthcare settings becomes a core competency, proactive healthcare leaders are also engaged in building and sustaining resilient care teams to cope with the complexity of the rapidly changing healthcare landscape.

The rapid adoption of telehealth as an effective response to stay-at-home orders and self-quarantine measures due to the COVID-19 pandemic has also led to the transition of many patients to telemedicine solutions. Some of the new drugs to treat various cancers, and mitral valve repair instead of mitral valve replacement, are all examples of disruptive technologies. Many inpatient procedures are delivered in outpatient settings now, and the need for hospital care is decreasing while home care needs are increasing. Healthcare organizations must learn to live with these new innovations to survive the disruptions.

The key to effective management of these rapid and disruptive changes is building and sustaining agility and resilience through adaptive capacity—the ability to initiate and implement innovation from everywhere, including crowdsourcing.

Resilient leaders help inspire and energize people to think onward and outward (outside-in) in addition to directing and focusing organizational resources and capabilities inwardly (inside-out) to achieve organizational goals. They focus on the mission while also painting a compelling vision of success that inspires others to engage. They use analytics and sensitivity skills to energize employees and set higher performance targets. Resilient leaders ask "how," not just "why"—they guide rather than find fault. They convert the process of doing into an opportunity for learning by establishing ambidexterity as a shared vision across the organization's explorative and exploitative care units.

Chapter 3. Qualities of Resilient Leadership

The COVID-19 pandemic has been the ultimate test of leadership resiliency. Resilient leaders are thoughtful and deliberate. They balance logic and emotion, ego, and humility. They lead through compassionate empathy by focusing on the "how," not only the "what."

They use their influence to drive positive change, diversity, and inclusion, and create an equitable community. This chapter will focus on four important qualities that describe the mindsets and behaviors of resilient leaders:

Analytical—resilient leaders have the know-how to align goals, behaviors, and processes to sustain high reliability at all levels of the healthcare organization. They rely on evidence-based practices that integrate clinical expertise with critical reasoning to analyze and make smart choices that are also ethical and consider the broader needs of stakeholders.

Adaptive—resilient leaders are adaptable and adjust to their circumstances innovatively and proactively. Resilient leaders create adaptive cultures and promote supportive communication practices that serve as a viable strategy for aligning partners and communities.

Empathetic—resilient leaders are skilled at triage, able to build trusting relationships for attracting and retaining the right talent, inspire learning, and actively encourage interprofessional collaboration. They are compassionate and empathetic. With strong self-awareness and emotional intelligence (EI) skills, they build trust with followers and team members and foster quality relationships. Resilient leaders use influence to create a culture of collaboration by cultivating empathy and by inspiring and supporting individuals and teams to work together for the greater good.

Confident—resilient leaders relentlessly pursue impact by establishing performance targets and by ensuring accountability for results. They inspire employees and team members with symbolic value and empower care teams to stay focused on facts and data that inform long-term goals. They meet crisis conditions head-on, identifying opportunities as catalysts for long-term growth and success. They track costs and benefits of emerging risks ethically and responsibly and move forward with confidence and resilience.

Chapter 4. Learning from Resilient Leaders—The Role of Trust

The COVID-19 pandemic is one of the most difficult and challenging crises for leaders to manage in the 21st century. By the first week of March 2021, the coronavirus had sickened 117 million people around the world, and 2.5 million people had died due to the coronavirus. In the United States alone, as of this writing, over 537,000 have died because of COVID-19 complications, leading to a sharp drop in U.S. life expectancy. The virus is not yet contained with many countries sprinting to develop a coronavirus vaccine or treatment with unclear policies, shifting priorities, and contradictory strategies.

Handling COVID-19 and future pandemics at national and global levels requires effective mitigation strategies and organizational systems and processes but also leadership qualities and traits that help establish trust. Resilient leaders embody spiritual values such as integrity, honesty, and humility, creating the self as a role model of a leader who can be trusted, relied upon, and admired. Resilience in healthcare leadership is about making ethical choices transparent and the struggles to balance competing interests become publicly known.

National leaders such as Angela Merkel (Germany), Mette Fredriksen (Denmark), Erna Solberg (Norway), and Tsai Ing-Wen (Taiwan), all women, have demonstrated their resilience through honesty, accountability, credibility, and transparency. Angela Merkel's leadership is highlighted as directly responsible for a substantial decrease in the German public's sense of anxiety and depression and the heightening of their sense of well-being and trust in their leaders.

Lessons learned to date require investments in developing crisis leadership competencies for all genders with a specific focus on the special contributions of women to leading during the COVID-19 crisis. Therefore, this chapter explores the potential benefit of having female leaders at times of crises that disrupt organizational or social functioning and pose relational threats.

The chapter provides an overview of the crisis literature within the context of COVID-19, a rationale for using a theoretical framework for organizing executive responses to crisis situations, discusses characteristics of trusted leadership, and highlights the benefits of having trusted leaders at times of high-impact events that disrupt organizational or social functioning. Common characteristics associated with trusted leadership—honesty, accountability, credibility, and transparency—are explored, and assessment instruments are used for self-discovery with implications for practice and for leadership development.

Chapter 5. Enhancing Resilience through Inclusive Leadership

The sweeping changes in the complex healthcare environment and the need to embrace population health management, interprofessional cooperation, and accountable care are transforming the way healthcare is delivered, managed, and led.

Building a culture of diversity, inclusion, and collaboration, so essential for the success of integrated health networks, begins at the top. However, gender disparity is still prevalent in senior healthcare positions even though women continue to play a critical role in strengthening the integration of health services.

Women are significantly less likely to be promoted to senior healthcare management, and in most cases, even after controlling for individual and organizational level characteristics. When promoted, women more likely than men are pigeonholed into support functions such as HR, marketing, risk, legal, and nursing, that, while important, are not perceived as high-profile, strategic service lines.

Provider organizations with at least 40% of their C-suite positions held by women also had 1.5 times larger C-suites than those with only 20% women in the C-suite with the additional roles assumed by women designated primarily technical. The women can sit at the table, but not be the key players that have high-impact, strategic responsibilities.

How can we bridge the gap between mounting evidence of resilient women's leadership and the shortfall of women's representation in healthcare senior management? If women are better than or as good as men on most competency evaluation criteria and leadership qualities and if men excel primarily on traits associated with less formidable transactional, command and control attributes—how can we explain the gap between desired leadership qualities and the shunning of talented women?

This chapter focuses on gender within the context of management and leadership in healthcare systems. It describes an inclusive co-leadership model with distinct and overlapping roles, which inspires administrative and clinical leaders to collaborate and build resilience in healthcare leadership.

This is an untapped but promising option for win–win outcomes: Increasing healthcare system efficiency by promoting the inclusion of women in senior roles and tapping into the leadership skills and expertise that women bring to these roles. The chapter also includes success strategies for aspiring women leaders and implications for practice and leadership development.

Chapter 6. Resilience from the Middle Out

This chapter focuses on the vital role of middle managers in transitioning healthcare systems and on their unique contributions to building resilience in healthcare leadership.

In the healthcare industry, the 422,000 middle managers are an important part of the organizational resources, with most working in state, local, and private hospitals (39%); ambulatory healthcare services (26%); group medical services and outpatient healthcare centers (16%); nursing and residential care facilities (11%); and government (8%).

In hospitals, for example, middle managers convert strategic goals into actionable improvement plans at the department or work unit level, engage employees in safety and quality assurance efforts through CQI and Kaizen, and identify processes for continuous improvement. They may manage an entire facility, a specific clinical area or department, or a medical practice for a group of physicians, improve efficiency and quality in delivering healthcare services, develop departmental goals and objectives, represent the facility at investor meetings or on governing boards, and communicate with members of the medical staff and department heads.

Some scholars would liken the middle manager's responsibilities to those of a strategist or change architect who facilitates the communication about corporate thought, action, and results.

Middle managers with active involvement in the strategy process have been found to demonstrate higher levels of commitment to organizational goals and to contribute to the success of strategic initiatives. Furthermore, evidence suggests that middle managers' upward leadership and downward influence appear to affect the alignment of organizational activities within the strategic context.

Middle managers' duality of operating experience and proximity to decision makers makes their "clutch roles" during transitions critical for organizational success. They search for new opportunities, evaluate the merits of strategic initiatives, and propose new projects. This chapter will demonstrate the value of middle managers to leadership continuity in healthcare settings and the importance of including them in succession planning and leadership development.

Chapter 7. Building a Culture of Resilient Care Teams

Leadership is critical for the success of teamwork, which, in turn, helps establish a more positive and engaging culture of collaboration. Creating an adaptive culture of interprofessional collaboration and cross-functional synergies reinforces the implementation of strategic goals across the continuum of care. Studies demonstrate a positive association between empowered team leadership and cross-functional synergies (teamwork and interprofessional cooperation) and clinical patient outcomes including lower rates of errors and patient mortality.

Assessments of organizational culture are useful because they help managers and organizational leaders to target the trajectory of change and enhance organizational performance. A systematic cultural assessment such as the one described in this chapter is a necessary precursor to implementing effective change efforts. Adaptive cultures and supportive communication practices serve as a viable strategy for attracting and retaining talents in organizations and for strengthening teaming across boundaries.

The first part of this chapter will focus on identifying important functions of organizational culture, particularly with respect to the establishment of a culture of interprofessional collaboration. Assessment instruments and strategies for diagnosing organizational cultures including key techniques for managing cultural change will be offered with examples and key takeaways.

Organizational culture influences the operating conditions (e.g., norms, communication patterns, commitment, and accountability) that promote the effectiveness of teamwork. Therefore, the second part of this chapter focuses on teamwork and interprofessional cooperation.

Expertise in teams is often highly distributed, formal leadership (e.g., attending physicians) is rotated or shared, often with a different communication style, diverse team membership, and varied degree of informal communication across specialties or interdependent care units. When clinical and nonclinical staff collaborate effectively, healthcare teams can improve patient outcomes, prevent medical errors, improve efficiency, and increase patient satisfaction.

Teamwork expands the traditional roles of clinicians and staff members to share in the decision-making process. It involves shared responsibility, mutual trust, and enhanced communication. It can take place across units when members cooperate and coordinate with one another to provide the best care for patients over prolonged periods.

Teamwork can also take place within units where members coach and mentor each other professionally and with mutual respect. Teamwork may also involve interdisciplinary structures requiring adaptive coordination, listening skills, critical task execution, synthesizing information, shared team leadership, and effective conflict resolution with professionals from different disciplines, specialized language, norms, and training.

A competency-based assessment instrument will offer team leaders an opportunity to assess the value they place on teamwork across different dimensions of teamwork and compare it against what team members think. The gap between the ratings (i.e., current vs. desired) provides important clues about prioritizing teamwork training and development needs.

Chapter 8. Leveraging Strengths to Maximize Resilience in Leadership

This chapter showcases self-assessment instruments to demonstrate how to achieve a good alignment between leadership roles and organizational goals. When the alignment is effective, members have a clear and shared sense of purpose; energy and inspiration run high, and interprofessional cooperation is strong.

The chapter also includes instruments for identifying and evaluating message orientations and communication strategies for clarifying expectations during organizational transitions. Knowing in advance what senior managers communicate and detecting the tone of the messages is empowering in helping managers avoid second guessing higher levels and, instead, focus attention on messages that are consistent with the expectations of senior management and key stakeholders.

Keeping the organization's strategic objectives at the center of attention helps achieve the mission and goals of the integrated health system. Further, the leadership roles that C-level executives assume, and even current leadership development programs and skill-building initiatives need to align with the strategic objectives. For example, the strategy of providing health services across the continuum of care through partnerships and alliances at the accountable care organization (ACO) level is supported and aligned with teamwork and interprofessional collaboration at the local hospital level.

Members perform better when they fully understand and accept the mission and goals of their health settings, and they develop a better sense of ownership when they understand the impact they make in achieving those goals.

A "balanced leadership" framework is described to help C-level executives and managers identify personal strengths and weaknesses, develop improvement plans, and realign their leadership roles with organizational goals and strategies.

By aligning strengths with business objectives, top executives can ensure that the investment they make in their leadership development is focused and reflects the strategic direction of the organization.

Chapter 9. Conclusion—Sustaining Resilience in Healthcare Organizations

COVID-19 has disrupted how leaders interact with employees and how coworkers connect with each other. The need to adapt quickly and act resiliently during the pandemic has also revealed the importance of workplace flexibility, interfunctional collaboration, and the role of middle managers in innovation implementation. In a time of crisis, resilient leaders at all levels of the organization must resort to efficient communication to protect its most important asset, its employees.

Senior leaders are tasked with establishing a communication strategy that is aligned with an open, accessible sharing of information. Middle managers are responsible for operationalizing this strategy by establishing objectives, allocating resources, developing functional strategies, and devising implementation plans and policies. Strategic objectives serve as guidelines for action, tracking and coordinating efforts and activities of staff and clinical care units. Leaders need to communicate clearly and frequently to all stakeholders in a crisis. However, first and foremost, they must share information with their teams on how the organization will meet their needs.

This chapter focuses on flexible workplaces and the responsibilities of leaders and managers to align the qualities and attributes of resilient leadership with the complex context of healthcare environments. Profile awareness is a powerful medium which allows leaders to understand their strengths and weaknesses, what motivates them, and how they make decisions. Assessment tools that are designed to help increase self-awareness or understanding of one's strengths and weaknesses, behavioral patterns, and motivations are described and illustrated. Executives can use these instruments for self-development but also to evaluate whether gaps in the behavior of aspiring leaders have been addressed and make important decisions about their suitability to lead work units, teams, or organizations.

Audience

This book is for current and aspiring CEOs, senior-level executives in provider organizations, physicians sought for administrative positions, clinician professionals in practice, and board members interested in developing the core competencies of senior managers and executives and identifying physicians for leadership positions, as well as preparing themselves for their roles in the evolving value-based healthcare market.

It is also aimed at healthcare management consultants, educators and graduate students of healthcare administration, MD/MBA programs, clinicians or professionals in Master of Health Administration (MHA), hospital management, and health MBA programs with candidates who aspire to become hospital administrators.

Value Proposition

Whether senior or mid-level manager, you will learn to apply knowledge and skills to initiate cultural change, assess your strengths and weaknesses, align your leadership roles with organizational goals, and position yourself to become a resilient leader. Know how to identify message strategies consistent with stakeholders' needs, resolve conflicts, lead multidisciplinary teams, and realize the impact of resilient leadership in influencing outcomes. Takeaways and tools to guide your progressive learning and leadership development and build a strong succession pipeline will help you and your health system become more prepared to respond to challenges facing healthcare in the future. Learn ways to become a more resilient leader who can successfully navigate through competing tensions and challenges, inspire a shared vision, and guide others with courage and confidence.

References

Dees, R. F. (2013). *Resilient Leaders: The Resilience Trilogy*. San Diego: Creative Team Publishing.

Greitens, E. (2016). *Resilience: Hard-Won Wisdom for Living a Better Life*. Boston: HMH Books.

Hanson, R. (2018). *Resilient: How to Grow an Unshakable Core of Calm, Strength, and Happiness*. New York: Harmony.

Lisson, L. (2017). *Resilience: Navigating Life, Loss and the Road to Success*. Ontario, CA: ECW Press.

Reivich, K., & Shatté, A. (2003). *The Resilience Factor: 7 Essential Skills for Overcoming Life's Inevitable Obstacles*. New York: Broadway Books.

St. John, B., & Haines, A. P. (2017). *Micro-Resilience: Minor Shifts for Major Boosts in Focus, Drive, and Energy*. New York, NY: The Center Street.

Zolli, A., & Healy, A. M. (2013). *Resilience: Why Things Bounce Back*. New York: Simon & Schuster.

Chapter 2

Disruptive Innovation and Ambidextrous Leadership in Healthcare

In today's fast-changing and disruptive global business environment, continuous redesign of organizational systems, processes, and structures is critical for sustaining business success and competitive advantage. Adaptive organizations learn to develop creative and flexible design options to cope with the challenges of rapidly increasing global competition, shrinking product life cycles, and changing customer needs. The key to effective management of these rapid and disruptive changes is building and sustaining agility and resilience through adaptive capacity, the ability to initiate and implement innovation in response to changes in the marketplace. Adaptive capacity creates competitive advantages in times of instability and uncertainty (Belasen & Luber, 2017; Belasen & Rufer, 2013; Belasen & Lus, 2013).

This chapter focuses on examining how successful healthcare organizations leverage competitive advantages through the management of innovation. It points out the competing commitments associated with the challenge of combining high-volume operations with elements of complex systems. On the one hand, striving for a higher level of efficiency helps boost organizational reputation as a stable, high-reliability organization. On the other hand, maintaining a higher level of stability creates an organizational mindset that resists change or that limits the ability of the organization to adapt to customer needs or respond quickly to crises. Within this context, we explore the critical roles of resilient leaders in managing the tension between these competing commitments through redesign of the delivery system, improving care quality and outcomes, managing risk and reputation, and focusing on lowering costs.

DOI: 10.4324/9781003190929-2

Adaptive Organizations

Most organizations are variants or a mix of two archetypes: Volume operations and complex systems (Moore, 2005). Volume operations are based on standardization and scalability or mass production. Firms in this category tend to be more formalized and centralized and with a larger span of control and predicable workflow. Complex systems, on the other hand, are based on specialized operations and build-to-order production processes. Firms in this category tend to be more decentralized and with technical and managerial responsibilities delegated to lower levels.

Volume operations such as Procter and Gamble, Nike, eBay, and Amazon compete on cost leadership by building their operations around thousands of transactions with lower marginal costs. They source at the mean, employ control systems to lower inventory costs and run efficient deliveries, and have multiple bases of businesses and consumers which generate high revenue streams for the companies.

Complex systems such as IBM and Boeing, on the other hand, have higher than average cost per transaction; they target fewer dependable businesses with built-in brand differentiation and use niche market pricing and strategies to command premium prices for their customized products.

Competition between these two business models occurs when high-volume companies offer substitutes at a lower price, although they cannot compete well on variety and service quality. The supply chain in high-volume operations is fully connected and geared towards the result where end-users are expecting deliverables reliably and on time. Complex systems increase their competitive advantage by implementing lean manufacturing to reduce production costs and increase operating efficiencies.

Complex systems source at the margin and zealously monitor scheduling to avoid or reduce cost overruns. Branding and focusing on the supply chain are critical for the success of complex organizations. One example is Apple Inc., which remains at the forefront of the smartphone market by launching and tightening its control over the supply chain procurement of its iPhone.

Innovations create low-cost, high-value products in a new market or in a niche that industry leaders avoid because of small scale or difficulties to adapt. High-volume operations draw on the standardization of work processes to achieve consistency and scalability. The sequentially interdependent units generate end-to-end products that compete more on volume and price rather than quality and innovation.

The risk of setting the assembly line wrong or producing unwanted products or going through unnecessary rework loops is too costly. Disruptive change (e.g., regulation, technology, competition) creates inefficiencies as the highly interdependent workflow is not designed to adapt quickly. High-volume operations often get stuck and fail to introduce innovation. In *Escape Velocity: Free Your Company's Future from the Pull of the Past* (2011),

Geoffrey Moore includes Sperry Univac, Honeywell, Digital Equipment, Prime, Kodak, Polaroid, Lucent, Nortel, Compaq, Gateway, Lotus, Ashton Tate, Borland, Novell, Nokia, Tower Records, Borders, Barnes and Noble, and Blockbuster among companies that suffered due to lack of appropriate response to disruptive technology.

Adaptive organizations use ambidextrous platforms that mix operating efficiency and scale with innovation and agility to sustain their competitive advantage. The results are companies, like Honda and Canon, with dual structures and hybrid technologies and production lines that are geared simultaneously towards high-end and low-end markets. HP printing technology for the high-end office market in addition to its consumer products exemplifies the ambidextrous approach. AMD in the semiconductor industry and Pfizer in the pharmaceutical industry are examples of companies that combine the strengths of the two models to achieve the strategy of joint optimization. Others include Nestlé, Procter and Gamble, Nike, Dell, Apple, Sony, Hertz, Hilton, United Airlines, Microsoft, Adobe, Electronic Arts, Google, IBM, Cisco, SAP, Goldman Sachs, Boeing, Tektronix, Honeywell, Bechtel, Accenture, Apache, Halliburton, Burlington Northern, and Amazon.

These organizations are driven by a strong business-to-business branding and marketing research to meet the expectations of customers for highly differentiated products or services. They use tested experiments, investments in human capital, and business development groups that interact with externals (e.g., customers, researchers, competitors), and that collaborate across functions internally to implement innovation successfully.

Crowdsourcing Innovation

Crowdsourcing is the process of aggregating crowd knowledge to solve unique problems. Two new shows—*Diagnosis* on Netflix using wisdom of the crowd methods and *Chasing the Cure* on TNT/TBS to diagnose people suffering from unexplained illnesses by using crowdsourcing—demonstrate the power of crowdsourcing in improving medical treatments when conventional, expert-driven solutions to medical problems often fail. Open innovation and crowdsourcing technological tools create more access for patients, optimize their treatments, and improve the quality of healthcare (Belasen, 2019).

Accenture's HealthTech Innovation Challenge connected leading-edge digital health startups with large health and life sciences companies looking for innovative technology solutions. More than 700 companies from around the world entered the 2017 challenge. The winner, New York City-based Nanowear, developed a congestive heart failure (CHF) monitoring device worn by patients undergoing treatment in the hospital. The device captures and transmits CHF data to the cloud, providing medical professionals with continuous diagnostic data that streamlines the feedback process, improving health outcomes.

Pfizer teamed up with 23andMe to examine the DNA data of 140,000 individuals with a history of depression. A control group of an additional 337,000 23andMe customers reported no history of depression. Researchers were able to identify 15 genetic mutations linked to depression. Previous studies had detected, at best, two, and most detected none.

Crowdsourcing is optimal when it does not overwhelm the company or cause a diversion of the company's energy due to information overload that can lessen productivity. Crowdsourcing also tends to restrict the amount of managerial oversight and control over the company's direction as reporting becomes a key time allocation in this model. One example is Frito Lay and its "Do Us a Flavor" campaign for their Doritos brand. The four flavors in the final were chosen from over 14.4 million public submissions. Lay's new potato chip flavors for 2020 included the comeback of Fried Green Tomato and Crispy Taco after being introduced in 2017. During the competition, fans voted on the next big potato chip flavor.

These ideas do not come free as the company needed to pay a team of market researchers and personnel to sift through these submissions, conduct demand analysis for such flavor ideas, manufacture, and perform quality tests to eliminate unappealing and impractical proposals. The advantages, however, outweigh the costs as crowdsourcing significantly helped the company to increase sales, as customers try the new flavors, while also increasing Lay's social media presence.

Telework

The COVID-19 pandemic has shaken world economies and fundamentally shifted the way many companies and organizations operate. Businesses have rapidly adapted into new approaches to remain profitable and ensure long-term survivability. One of the most common methods employed by organizations is the increased utilization of teleworking, or having employees work remotely, to accommodate social distancing necessitated by the pandemic.

The U.S. Bureau of Labor Statistics (BLS, 2020) has developed new data on how U.S. businesses changed their operations and employment since the onset of the coronavirus pandemic through September 2020. During the COVID-19 pandemic, 31% of establishments (employing 68.6 million workers) increased telework offered to employees. The industries with the largest percentage of establishments that increased telework offered to employees were educational services (60%), finance and insurance (58%), and management of companies and enterprises (54%). Resistance is more evident in the healthcare, manufacturing, and retail industries.

An upside of COVID-19 is that businesses which resisted the shift to telework saw that their employees could still be productive when they had no choice. Siemens recently announced that mobile working will become "a core component of its 'new normal' and will make it a permanent standard, both during the global pandemic and beyond." The Labor Director there acknowledged the competitive advantage that can come from employees who are enabled to do their best work on their own terms:

> We trust our employees and empower them to shape their work themselves so that they can achieve the best possible results. With the new way of working, we are motivating our employees while improving the company's performance capabilities and sharpening Siemens' profile as a flexible and attractive employer.
>
> **(Siemens AG, 2020)**

Telework allows companies to cast wider nets for talent, reduce costs spent on office space, eliminate inefficiencies caused by social office distractions, enhance ADA compliance for disabled employees, and achieve higher worker productivity. Employee benefits include reduced or no commute time and the attendant cost savings, improved flexibility, and ability for dual-career households. Tradeoffs include the inability to monitor quality or time spent on non-work activities, risks to information security, and increased costs of technology and investment in training programs.

Indeed, in addition to some possible pitfalls like blurring the boundaries between work and life, social isolation, loss of visibility to management for promotional consideration, and data security concerns, managers' reluctance to give up control over their employees' activities inhibits the wider uptake of flexible working arrangements (Biron & van Veldhoven, 2016).

Managers who remain entrenched in a process-driven framework rather than a results-oriented one will find the concept of telework unpalatable, because they lose visibility of employees' actions and schedules, and the inability to witness work being done. For telework to thrive, managers must shift their mindset to focus on flexibility, results, and trust. They must also spend some time carefully creating metrics and objectives by which employees will be evaluated and cultivating a team culture which recognizes wins and prioritizes communication. This will help teleworkers remain motivated and confident that the manager trusts them.

Telemedicine

Telehealth is becoming a key weapon in the fight against the COVID-19 pandemic. Services via telehealth limit the unnecessary exposure of patients and health professionals to COVID-19, wherever treatment can be safely delivered by phone or videoconferencing. Expanding the consultation services available through telehealth is the next critical stage in the government's response to COVID-19. This takes pressure off hospitals and emergency departments. Telehealth allows people to access essential health services in their home and supports self-isolation and quarantine policies to reduce the risk of exposure to and spread of COVID-19. It also helps doctors to continue to deliver services safely to their patients. Telehealth services also reduce disease exposure for staff members and patients, preserve scarce supplies of personal protective equipment, and lower patient surge on facilities (Koonin, et al., 2020).

Primary care practices and specialists are using telehealth technology to diagnose and treat their patients, reducing the risk of people's exposure to the virus that causes COVID-19 for offices and patients. Benefits include patient convenience and increased access, which is significant for those who live in remote areas and especially during the pandemic, reduced costs, and faster care, both of which influence patient satisfaction and promote compliance.

A downfall of telehealth is that telemedicine risks "de-personalization" of the physician–patient relationship. This risk can be reduced by forming an in-person physician–patient relationship upfront with the option for follow-up virtual visits. Other resources such as patient portals allow for communications to continue after the patient's appointment as well as receiving test results and message providers. These are all essential during a pandemic when patients still need to see their doctors and be comfortable asking questions and voicing concerns, rather than rushing to a hospital.

The new AMA (2016) ethical guidance notes that while new technologies and new models of care will continue to emerge, physicians' fundamental ethical responsibilities do not change. According to the new policy, any physician engaging in telemedicine must:

- Disclose any financial or other interests in particular telemedicine applications or services
- Protect patient privacy and confidentiality

The policy outlines guidelines for physicians who either respond to individual health queries electronically or provide clinical services through telemedicine. Broadly, some of these guidelines include:

- Informing patients about the limitations of the relationship and services provided
- Encouraging telemedicine patients who have a primary care physician to inform them about their online health consultation and ensure the information from the encounter can be accessed for future episodes of care
- Recognizing the limitations of technology and taking appropriate steps to overcome them, such as by having another healthcare professional at the patient's location conduct an exam or obtaining vital information through remote technologies

- Ensuring patients have a basic understanding of how telemedicine technologies are used in their care, the limitations of the technologies, and ways the information will be used after the patient encounter

Doctor–patient communication must be considered a vital part of successful telehealth implementation and training as it lacks the in-person aspects of patient care. In thinking of the older patient population, involving family and/or caregivers in the communication and visits will be essential as well. For most elderly and disabled individuals, learning how to use patient portals and telehealth technologies is practically impossible. Just as in face-to-face visits, providers must embrace these individuals to ensure that the patient is able to get the needed care and be able to stay safe at home. This is just one example of individualizing telehealth to the patient.

Other examples involve "Millennials" and "Generation Z" patients, as these segments of the population tend to be dissatisfied with traditional treatment solutions such as check-ups and in-clinic care. Younger consumers are more receptive and communicate their needs and expectations of medical treatment better and more explicitly (Siwicki, 2020). Healthcare providers must not be reluctant to change but focus on using the technology efficiently as well as tailoring their communications to each patient. The success of doctor/nurse–patient communication has also been identified as a critical driver for patient satisfaction and overall hospital ratings (Belasen, et al., 2020).

Because CMS has adopted regulatory waivers and added new rules, radiation oncologists, for example, can now provide more services to beneficiaries via telehealth so that clinicians can take care of their patients while mitigating the risk of the spread of the virus. Under the public health emergency, all beneficiaries across the country can receive Medicare telehealth and other communications technology-based services wherever they are located. Clinicians can provide these services to new or established patients. In addition, providers can waive Medicare co-payments for these telehealth services for beneficiaries in Original Medicare. Some of the procedure's codes such as follow-ups, outpatient subsequent visits, and consults are now covered for patients. For immune-compromised and other vulnerable patients, it is desirable to continue with continuum of care for a positive outcome.

> We are ensuring there are no unintended barriers to services for vulnerable patients. At the same time, we need to support general practitioners (GPs) to keep their doors open during these extremely difficult times. These initiatives will support both them and their patients.
>
> **(Hunt, 2020)**

> OCR will exercise its enforcement discretion and will not impose penalties for noncompliance with the regulatory requirements under the HIPAA Rules against covered health care providers in connection with the good faith provision of telehealth during the COVID-19 nationwide public health emergency.
>
> **(Notification of Enforcement Discretion, 2020)**

> In any model for care, patients need to be able to trust that physicians will place patient welfare above other interests, provide competent care, provide the information patients need to make well-considered decisions about care, respect patient privacy and confidentiality, and take steps needed to ensure continuity of care.
>
> **(AMA Adopts New Guidance, 2016)**

Teledentistry

Teledentistry allows dental professionals to remotely review records and diagnose patients over video more efficiently and to practice more safely during pandemic situations. However, widespread adoption is limited due to the unwillingness of insurance companies to reimburse for teledentistry procedures. While Medicaid and the Children's Health Insurance Program pay for many dental procedures for participating members, only 38% of U.S. dentists participate in Medicaid or CHIP for child dental services (ADA, 2015) primarily due to insufficient payments.

Teledentistry is not reimbursable under Medicare, and Medicaid typically reimburses at a significantly lower rate than those of private insurance plans. This is problematic also because 43% of rural Americans lack access to dental care. To increase access for rural residents to oral health services, not only are more dentists needed in rural communities, but more dentists who are willing to accept one of rural America's major sources of healthcare payment, Medicaid (NRHA, 2013).

Procompetitive Collaboration in Biopharma to Fight COVID-19

Advances in technology and broadband wireless access have made incremental innovations easily imitated by competitors and consequently put pressure on many large-scale companies to revert to short-term planning. With knowledge so widely distributed and easily accessible, companies move to acquire inventions or intellectual property from other companies to offset R&D costs, reduce risk, accelerate time to market, and increase their visibility in the marketplace.

Others, especially in high-technology industries, have adopted the strategy of open innovation. For example, Magneti Marelli is a subsidiary of the Fiat Group that maintains 12 R&D centers with most ideas coming from users around the world.

For open innovation to be successful, it must be distributed both internally and externally through collaborative networks. AstraZeneca, the global, science-led biopharmaceutical company that focuses on the discovery, development, and commercialization of prescription medicines, has spent the past few years forging partnerships with groups including health charities, academic researchers, and even its industry rivals, such as GlaxoSmithKline.

The collaborations work by openly sharing early-stage research and allowing all the parties to use the shared knowledge to develop solutions. Often, they involve AstraZeneca scientists that share the lab with researchers from other organizations. The company noted:

> It enables us to get more out of our research dollars than by just doing things on our own. You're creating an ecosystem where you can collaborate and get more out of it than if you were just doing something on your own.
>
> **(Roland, 2014)**

As costs rise and concerns grow about the quality and pace of pharmaceutical innovation, both federal agencies and industry competitors are turning to new forms of collaboration and shared R&D projects. The prevailing understanding is that these "procompetitive" initiatives are not only permissible but needed. When it comes to the sourcing and production of COVID-19-related treatments, in March 2020, the U.S. Justice Department and Federal Trade Commission issued a joint statement stating, "there are many ways firms, including competitors, can engage in procompetitive collaboration that does not violate the antitrust laws" (DOJ, 2020). The DOJ statement reaffirmed the Antitrust Division's support of joint public health initiatives between potential competitors to facilitate pandemic-related solutions so long as the parties implement appropriate safeguards to mitigate the risks of anticompetitive behavior. The DOJ finds that exchanging this information in this context is unlikely to harm competition "because the likely result is that the information exchange will expand output of these critical treatments," rather than restrict them.

In September 2020, the CEOs of AstraZeneca, BioNTech, GlaxoSmithKline, Johnson & Johnson, Merck, Moderna, Inc., Novavax, Inc., Pfizer Inc., and Sanofi co-signed a letter of commitment to uphold the integrity of the scientific process as they work towards potential global regulatory filings and approvals of the first COVID-19 vaccines (CNBC, 2020). Together, these 9 companies have developed more than 70 novel vaccines that have helped eradicate some of the world's deadliest health threats, underscoring their collective experience in clinical development and regulatory rigor, as well as their longstanding commitments to patient safety and public health.

We, the undersigned biopharmaceutical companies, want to make clear our ongoing commitment to developing and testing potential vaccines for COVID-19 in accordance with high ethical standards and sound scientific principles.

The safety and efficacy of vaccines, including any potential vaccine for COVID-19, is reviewed, and determined by expert regulatory agencies around the world, such as the United States Food and Drug Administration (FDA). FDA has established clear guidance for the development of COVID-19 vaccines and clear criteria for their potential authorization or approval in the United States. FDA's guidance and criteria are based on the scientific and medical principles necessary to clearly demonstrate the safety and efficacy of potential COVID-19 vaccines. More specifically, the agency requires that scientific evidence for regulatory approval must come from large, high-quality clinical trials that are randomized and observer-blinded, with an expectation of appropriately designed studies with significant numbers of participants across diverse populations.

Following guidance from expert regulatory authorities such as FDA regarding the development of COVID-19 vaccines, consistent with existing standards and practices, and in the interest of public health, we pledge to:

- *Always make the safety and well-being of vaccinated individuals our top priority.*
- *Continue to adhere to high scientific and ethical standards regarding the conduct of clinical trials and the rigor of manufacturing processes.*
- *Only submit for approval or emergency use authorization after demonstrating safety and efficacy through a Phase 3 clinical study that is designed and conducted to meet requirements of expert regulatory authorities such as FDA.*
- *Work to ensure a sufficient supply and range of vaccine options, including those suitable for global access.*

We believe this pledge will help ensure public confidence in the rigorous scientific and regulatory process by which COVID-19 vaccines are evaluated and may ultimately be approved.

The sharing of information will benefit the public by allowing the procompetitive collaboration to advance planning that could significantly reduce the lead time necessary to identify and test vaccines with greater efficacy. The goal is to ensure equitable global access, the protection of diverse subjects, and immunity against viral variants by producing large quantities of the vaccine at an extremely low cost.

Ambidextrous Leadership

Complex adaptive systems display high levels of member engagement, co-evolution, balanced exploration and exploitation, disruptive innovation, and the reintegration and disintegration of structures and processes. These systems rely on non-linear dynamics of punctuated equilibrium (switching between temporary structures of stability and change) to transform and self-organize into structures more compatible with handling disruptions in the marketplace. The results are organizations with hybrid technologies and processes that could function effectively in high-end and low-end markets.

Adaptive systems and disruptive innovation require leaders with the capacity to simultaneously optimize the current business model through exploitation and inspire new ventures and outcomes through exploration. The ability to be ambidextrous is essential.

Ambidextrous leadership focuses on a dual logic: (a) a humanistic or collaborative approach to developing ideas and initiating innovation; and (b) managerial or rationalistic, which is concerned with the efficient use of resources to implement innovation. In healthcare, this dual focus matches the conditions for a successful adaptive organization, with clinical and administrative champions that facilitate the transformation to value-based care and population health.

> A first element emerging from different hospitals is that—focusing on producing, finding, analyzing, and sharing information through digital media—EMR manifests its ambidextrous potential in triggering and enabling augmented capabilities in knowledge exploration and knowledge exploitation by increasing the coordination among hospital processes. The CEO of one of the hospitals stated:
>
> > I've always thought of ICT as a lever to cut costs. As a matter of fact, there are tremendous benefits in terms of quality improvement as well: once you connect the different departments, you discover new and better ways to provide healthcare services and have an impact on patients' outcome.
>
> **(Gastaldi, et al., 2012)**

Ambidextrous leadership and innovation competencies enhance the effectiveness of healthcare leadership (Akenroye & Kuenne, 2015; Baker, 2015; Gutberg & Berta, 2017) and contribute to the efficient delivery of safe, effective, and high-quality care.

One of the challenges is how to resolve the innovator's dilemma or the binary choice between catering to current customers' needs ("strategic fit") or adopting new innovations and technologies to accommodate future needs ("strategic stretch"). O'Reilly and Tushman (2016) provide guidance about how the concept of ambidexterity can become an organizational capability. Structurally, they call for a clear strategic intent that identifies and embraces both exploitation and exploration opportunities; the funding and nurturing of new ventures by senior management; a separation between existing and new businesses; and the vision, values, and culture that support a common identity between the explore-and-exploit units.

Pursuing innovative new ventures while simultaneously seeking to maximize efficiency often puts the ambidextrous executive in the middle of the tensions associated with executing on both fronts. But how can CEOs cultivate ambidexterity both in themselves and in their organizations? The key is to master paradoxical skills. Ambidextrous leaders embrace change, ambiguity, ambivalence, and tension, and have the execution skills to guide innovation implementation.

> The effective ambidextrous CEO not only holds a paradoxical mindset, but also articulates and continually reinforces it to establish ambidexterity as a common vision and value across the organization's explorative and exploitative units. Within this vision must be a compelling strategic intent that clearly justifies the story that *both* exploration and exploitation are central to the business's goals. When successfully communicated, this vision helps to create a shared organizational culture that knits together the business's various subcultures, enhances information and resource-sharing, and builds trust ... [Further,] the CEO should consider putting structures in place to maintain the creative tension between exploitation and exploration. One possibility is to have the innovation units report directly to the CEO, while another is to make clear the expectation that the businesses into which the innovation units report give them the appropriate leeway and resources to pursue the top team's vision.
>
> **(Finzi, Firth, & Lipton, 2018)**

Health Innovator: Assessment

Increasing safety through interprofessional collaboration, breaking down silos, identifying innovative ways of care delivery, and leveraging resources and capabilities across the organization are important areas of focus for innovation leadership. The 15 questions in the assessment survey (Table 2.1) reflect typical expectations associated with the role of leaders in the capacity of health innovators. Respond to the questions twice—first, as you are performing these roles, and second, as you wish to perform these roles.

A simple Excel spreadsheet that lists the responses (or ratings) helps to produce charts that display respondents' relative strengths and weaknesses. For example, the chart in Figure 2.1 shows a desire to collaborate more with industry partners and initiate greater investments in safety and population health. The gap between the "actual" and "desired" ratings can help health leaders brainstorm ideas for improvement and prioritize plans and resources for further development.

Creating a culture of safety requires the mindset of a high-reliability organization (HRO) that transcends specialized areas and that empowers staff members to collaborate in identifying possible failures and tackling them innovatively and responsibly. Leadership is about making employees feel safe, creating an atmosphere that supports innovation and that integrates safety messages into daily activities and meetings. Good leaders model the way by walking the talk and by giving employees access to the right tools and resources to be successful.

Building a Culture of Collaborative Innovation

Resilient leaders initiate ambidexterity by creating a compelling vision of success that draws on existing resources and capabilities and promotes learning and forward thinking. They use a style that encourages the coexistence of competing agendas and that requires members to adopt non-binary behaviors—exploratory and exploitative behaviors. They model the way by encouraging top executives to adopt a similar style of leadership, recognize competing tensions, articulate explicit goals and metrics for exploitation and exploration initiatives, boost the collective intelligence of the organization, and build a culture of collaborative innovation.

Isaacs and Ancona (2019) suggest three strategies for initiating and sustaining a culture of collaborative innovation: Communicating strategically, cultivating new ideas collectively, and removing barriers to innovation implementation.

Communicating strategically. Resilient leaders brainstorm ideas from all levels of the organization for a strategic vision and mobilize support for that vision. The Defense Advanced Research Projects Agency (DARPA), for example, the innovative government agency which focuses on transformational breakthroughs in national security, uses a set of simple questions following the Heilmeier Catechism principles, to think through and evaluate proposed research programs. These questions are well suited to deliberating about startup efforts. The answers to these questions map well into innovative thinking

Table 2.1 Health Innovator Leadership Role

Frequency level—Likert 7 point—Next to each statement indicate the response that best matches your situation.

1—Never
2—Rarely, in less than 10% of the chances when I could have
3—Occasionally, in about 30% of the chances when I could have
4—Sometimes, in about 50% of the chances when I could have
5—Frequently, in about 70% of the chances when I could have
6—Usually, in about 90% of the chances I could have
7—Every time

		Actual	Desired
1	I pursue an ACO contract or revamp existing partnerships for an ACO contract		
2	I consider an investment in population health analytics to be a high priority		
3	I use analytics to help measure performance across cost and quality measures		
4	I promote the use of EHR and health information technology to improve safety across the continuum of care		
5	I initiate data sharing with ancillary providers		
6	I initiate improvement in safety and sharing of best practices among ACOs		
7	I track the attainment of the "Triple Aim" goals		
8	I view problems through the patient's perspective rather than the provider		
9	I collaborate with industry partners, technology developers, healthcare leaders, clinicians, and patients to increase safety and reliability		
10	I use needs assessment to identify potential innovations		
11	I secure sustainable funding to implement innovations		
12	I find ways to reduce the cost of care through innovation implementation		
13	I work with hospital partners to leverage resources to improve community health		
14	I spur interprofessional collaboration across the entire continuum of care		
15	I promote a culture of safety and reliability in my health system		

Adapted from: Belasen, A. (2019). Dyad Leadership.

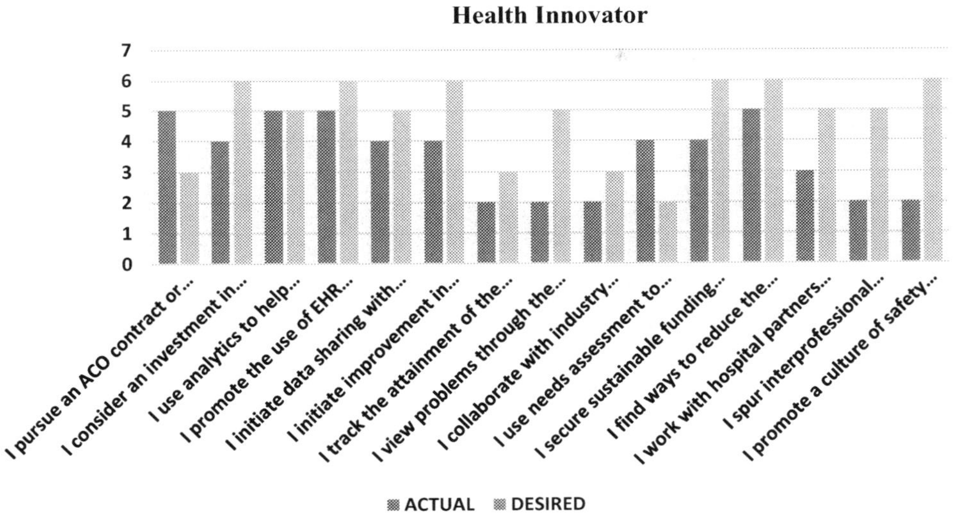

Figure 2.1 Actual and desired expectations.

that centers on what, how, industry conditions, competition, risks, costs and benefits, why you, why now, and milestones.

- What are you trying to do? Articulate your objectives using absolutely no jargon.
- How is it done today, and what are the limits of current practice?
- What is new in your approach and why do you think it will be successful?
- Who cares? If you are successful, what difference will it make?
- What are the risks?
- How much will it cost?
- How long will it take?
- What are the mid-term and final "exams" [that will allow you to measure] success?

Cultivating new ideas collectively. In adaptive organizations, innovation comes from everywhere and continuously with the objective to keep the momentum around good ideas going with diverse stakeholders joining in early and often to help evaluate and refine the ideas. At W. L. Gore, if the idea gains support, the champion schedules regular peer review sessions with people from manufacturing, R&D, sales and marketing, and other relevant areas of expertise to evaluate the usefulness of the idea. Senior leaders review the ideas and use their knowledge of organizational capabilities and market/technology trends to create organizational strategy.

To rejuvenate its innovation pipeline, Corning created a set of simple rules, derived from successful past innovations:

- Address new markets with more than $500 million in potential revenue.
- Leverage the company's expertise in materials science.
- Represent a critical component in a complex system.
- Be protected from competition by patents and proprietary process expertise.

Removing barriers to innovation implementation. Resilient leaders in adaptive organizations support members closer to "points of impact," removing major barriers to innovation by clearing the way for promising new projects and getting innovation teams the resources they need. NASA's leaders solicit their employees for new ideas by giving people more time, money, recognition, and dedicated physical space for innovation. Others focus on reducing process requirements for innovations, for instance, fast-tracking low-cost missions and giving special treatment to high-potential technologies. Proposals may include an element of innovation to encourage informed, appropriate R&D risk, to counter the agency's risk-averse culture.

These three strategies allow resilient leaders to harness the insights and energy of employees at all levels of the organization. In so doing, adaptive organizations make full use of and derive benefits from the collective intelligence of their employees to improve exploration efforts and outcomes.

References

ADA (2015). Dentist Participation in Medicaid or CHIP, Retrieved from https://www.ada.org/~/media/ADA/Science%20and%20Research/HPI/Files/HPIGraphic_0217_1.pdf?la=en

Akenroye, T. O., & Kuenne, C. W. (2015). Key competencies for promoting service innovation: What are implications for the health sector? *The Innovation Journal*, 20(1), 2–21, Retrieved from https://www.innovation.cc/

AMA (2016). AMA Adopts New Guidance for Ethical Practice in Telemedicine, Retrieved from https://www.ama-assn.org/press-center/press-releases/ama-adopts-new-guidance-ethical-practice-telemedicine

Baker, J. D. (2015). Getting buzzed on innovative leadership. *Association of Operating Room Nurses Journal*, 101(4), 401–403. doi:10.1016/j.aorn.2015.01.020

Belasen, A. T. (2019). *Dyad Leadership and Clinical Integration, Driving Change and Aligning Strategies*, Chicago, IL: Health Administration Press.

Belasen, A., & Luber, E. (2017). Innovation implementation: Leading from the middle out. In Nicole Pfeffermann & Julie Gould (Eds.), *Strategy and Communication for Innovation: Integrative Perspectives on Innovation in the Digital Economy* (pp. 229–243). Germany: Springer.

Belasen, A. & Lus, B. (2013). Adaptive Capacity and Managing Relationships in the Supply Chain. In Michele Paludi (Ed.), *Implementing Best Practices in Human Resources* (pp. 141–152). Santa Barbara, CA: Praeger.

Belasen, A. & Rufer, R. (2013). Innovation Communication for Effective Interprofessional Collaboration: A Stakeholder Perspective. In Nicole Pfeffermann, Tim Minshall, & Letizia Mortara (Eds.), *Strategy and Communication for Innovation*, 2nd edition (pp. 227–240). Germany: Springer.

Belasen, A. T., Oppenlander, J., Belasen, A. R., & Hertelendy, A. (2020). Provider-patient communication and hospital ratings: Perceived gaps and forward thinking about the effects of COVID-19, *International Journal for Quality in Health Care*. doi:10.1093/intqhc/mzaa140.

Biron, M., & van Veldhoven, M. (2016). When control becomes a liability rather than an asset: comparing home and office days among part-time teleworkers: Within-individual study on part-time telework. *Journal of Organizational Behavior*, 37(8), 1317–1337. doi:10.1002/job.2106

BLS (2020). Business Response Survey to the Coronavirus Pandemic, Retrieved from https://www.bls.gov/brs/2020-results.htm

CNBC (2020). U.S., European Drugmakers Pledge to Make Safety the main Focus in Coronavirus Vaccine Development, September 9, Retrieved from https://www.cnbc.com/2020/09/08/nine-biopharma-ceos-pledge-to-make-safety-the-main-focus-in-coronavirus-vaccine-development.html

DOJ (2020). Joint Antitrust Statement Regarding Covid-19, Retrieved from https://www.justice.gov/atr/joint-antitrust-statement-regarding-covid-19

Finzi, B., Firth, V., & Lipton, M. (2018). Ambidextrous leadership: Keystone of the undisruptable CEO. *Deloitte*, Retrieved from https://www2.deloitte.com/us/en/insights/topics/leadership/ambidextrous-leadership-ceo-traits-in-digital-era.html

Gastaldi, L., Lettieri, E., Corso, M., & Masella, C. (2012). Performance improvement in hospitals: Leveraging on knowledge asset dynamics through the introduction of an electronic medical record. *Measuring Business Excellence*, 16(4), 14–30.

Gutberg, J., & Berta, W. (2017). Understanding middle managers influence in implementing patient safety culture. *BioMed Central (BMC) Health Services Research*, 17(1), 582–592.

Hunt, M. P. (2020). *COVID-19: Whole of Population Telehealth for Patients, General Practice, Primary Care, and Other Medical Services*. Ministers Department of Health, Retrieved from https://www.health.gov.au/ministers/the-hon-greg-hunt-mp/media/covid-19-whole-of-population-telehealth-for-patients-general-practice-primary-care-and-other-medical-services

Isaacs, K. & Ancona, D. (2019). 3 Ways to Build a Culture of Collaborative Innovation. *HBR*, Retrieved from https://hbr.org/2019/08/3-ways-to-build-a-culture-of-collaborative-innovation

Koonin, L.M., et al. 2020. *Trends in the Use of Telehealth During the Emergence of the COVID-19 Pandemic — United States*, January–March 2020. Centers for Disease and Control Prevention, Retrieved from https://www.cdc.gov/mmwr/volumes/69/wr/mm6943a3.htm

Moore, G. A. (2011). *Escape Velocity: Free Your Company's Future from the Pull of the Past*, New York: HarperCollins Publishers

Moore, G. A. (2005). Strategy and your stronger hand. *Harvard Business Review*, December, 62–75.

NRHA (2013). Rural America's Oral Health Care Needs, Retrieved from https://www.ruralhealthweb.org/getattachment/Advocate/PolicyDocuments/RuralAmericasOralHealthCareNeeds-(1).pdf.aspx?lang=en-US

Notification of Enforcement Discretion for Telehealth Remote Communications During the COVID-19 Nationwide Public Health Emergency (2020, March 30). U.S. Department of Health & Human Services, Retrieved from https://www.hhs.gov/hipaa/for-professionals/special-topics/emergency-preparedness/notification-enforcement-discretion-telehealth/index.html

O'Reilly, C., & Tushman, M. (2016). *Lead and Disrupt*, Redwood City CA: Stanford University Press.

Roland, D. (2014). AstraZeneca Reinforces Pipeline with 'open innovation' (April, 28), Retrieved from http://www.telegraph.co.uk/finance/newsbysector/pharmaceuticalsandchemicals/10775160/AstraZeneca-reinforces-pipeline-with-open-innovation.html

Siemens, A. G. (2020). Siemens to Establish Mobile Working as Core Component of the "new normal" [Press release], Retrieved from https://press.siemens.com/global/en/pressrelease/siemens-establish-mobile-working-core-component-new-normal

Siwicki, B. (2020). Survey: Americans' Perceptions of Telehealth in the COVID-19 Era. *Healthcare IT News*, Retrieved from https://www.healthcareitnews.com/news/survey-americans-perceptions-telehealth-covid-19-era

Chapter 3

Qualities of Resilient Leadership

The COVID-19 pandemic pushed industries and organizations to the limits of their resources and capabilities with organizations driving *investment* and *digitalization* innovations to outlast the pandemic (McKinsey, 2020). As consumers have moved dramatically towards online channels, companies and industries *have been* seeking to *develop* the *digital capabilities* critical for sustaining their customer and supply-chain interactions.

Healthcare systems throughout the world were hard hit as hospitals were pushed to their limits in attempting to contain the virus. Most commonly, problems with resource management (for ventilators, beds, personal protective equipment, and especially clinicians) brought emergency planning shortfalls to light. Health systems need to ensure their business strategy incorporates crisis management, disaster recovery, and risk management to adapt and ensure business continuity. Health leaders have been challenged to accelerate the integration of cloud-based business functions and artificial intelligence to provide digitally efficient products that improve telehealth capabilities and increase their flexibility through a more robust public healthcare system and more efficient ways to monitor public health.

As the outbreak has intensified across the country infecting more than 100,000 people per day, hospitals have ramped up testing efforts, treating hundreds of thousands of Americans to save lives and reduce the virus's spread. By spring 2020, the American Hospital Association estimated a financial impact of $202.6 billion in lost revenue for America's hospitals and healthcare systems, or an average of $50.7 billion per month (AHA, 2020). This included establishing testing sites, adding general and intensive care unit (ICU) bed capacity, canceling elective and forgone surgeries and services, and developing COVID-19 units to isolate and treat patients with the disease while safeguarding the health of other patients and hospital staff.

Treatment for COVID-19 has also created extensive demand for certain medical equipment and supplies and additional costs associated with purchasing needed personal

DOI: 10.4324/9781003190929-3

protective equipment (PPE). As the coronavirus continues to disrupt supply chains, increasing the costs that hospitals face to treat COVID-19 patients, *physician assistants* and *nurse practitioners* have been called in to fill the gap for hospitals, taking on expanded responsibilities for COVID-19 with states initiating temporary suspension of licensure requirements for healthcare professionals, including registered nurses, licensed practical nurses, and APRNs.

In solving issues such as ventilator shortages, triage techniques, and supporting hospital staff, the COVID-19 pandemic demonstrated how crisis situations require specific kinds of leaders and how unique leadership qualities can promote more successful outcomes.

Attributes of Resilient Leaders

The COVID-19 pandemic has been the ultimate test for leadership resiliency. Resilient leaders can sustain their energy level under pressure and have the confidence to take calculated risks to cope with disruptive changes and realign people with evolving operating models. They bounce back from setbacks by being thoughtful and deliberate. They balance logic and emotion, ego, and humility. They lead through compassionate empathy by setting the right example and by focusing on the "how," not only the "what." Resilient leaders can recover from adversity and manage disruptions with personal confidence and courage. They use their influence to drive positive change, promote diversity and inclusion, and create an equitable community (Renjen, 2020).

Figure 3.1 displays four important attributes that describe the mindsets and behaviors of resilient leaders—adaptive, empathetic, analytical, and confident. These attributes invoke apparent contradictions that need to be balanced and reconciled to improve performance. How can one possibly be adaptive and flexible in realizing growth goals and strategies and yet pursue operational effectiveness with tightly aligned structures and systems? Is it

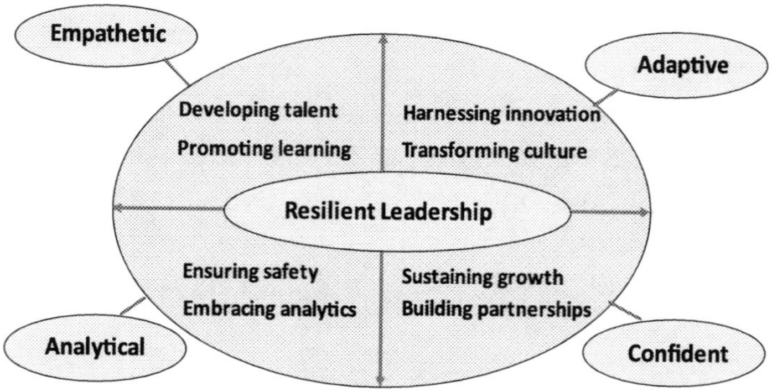

Figure 3.1 Resilient leadership.

possible to cut operational expenses to increase profit margins, expand while pursuing more efficient ways to conserve resources, reduce costs without impacting care quality or not losing sight of clinical competencies?

Adaptive—resilient leaders are adaptable and adjust to their circumstances innovatively and proactively. Resilient leaders create the capabilities that match the vision and promote supportive communication practices that serve as a viable strategy for aligning partners and communities.

Empathetic—resilient leaders are skilled at triage, able to build trusting relationships for attracting and retaining the right talent, inspire learning, and actively encourage inter-professional collaboration. They are compassionate and empathetic. They promote action by asking the right questions and actively listening to followers, and responsibly guide, acknowledge, and support team members to pursue common goals. Resilient leaders use influence to create a culture of collaboration by cultivating empathy and by inspiring and supporting individuals and teams to work together for the greater good. With strong self-awareness and EI skills, they build trust with others and foster quality relationships, making the transformation meaningful.

Analytical—resilient leaders have the know-how to align goals, behaviors, and processes to sustain the reliability and efficiency of specialized units and care teams. They rely on evidence-based practices that integrate clinical expertise with critical reasoning to analyze and make rational choices and consider the broader needs of stakeholders.

Confident—resilient leaders relentlessly pursue impact by establishing performance targets and by ensuring accountability for results. They inspire employees and team members with symbolic value and empower care teams to stay focused on facts and data that inform long-term goals. Resilient leaders take bold decisive actions with confidence and with added responsibility—based on imperfect information, knowing that expediency is essential. They meet crisis conditions head-on, identifying opportunities as catalysts for long-term growth and success. They track costs and benefits of emerging risks ethically and responsibly and move forward with confidence.

Within the framework of these broad characteristics, resilient leaders can take tactical steps to integrate these expectations, mitigate their negative impact on performance, and help their organizations emerge stronger. We elaborate on each characteristic in the next sections.

Adaptive

The COVID-19 pandemic is constantly evolving, with leaders challenged to adapt to a fast-changing and disruptive business environment that requires continuous realignment of capabilities with *incomplete* data and information. The key to success is building and sustaining agility and resilience. Effective response to the pandemic begins with anticipation of trends and needs, articulation of possibilities, recalibration, sharing of information, and accountability. Both Moderna's and Pfizer's COVID vaccines use innovative messenger RNA, or mRNA technology similar to DNA, genetic material that contains instructions to cells for making proteins.

While Pfizer, a pharmaceutical giant and one of the leading vaccine makers in the world, has the experience and infrastructure to scale up more quickly, both it and Moderna have had to retrofit their plants to ramp up production in the short term to produce the necessary doses and set up their own supply chain for distribution. Yet pharma companies now suddenly face the unanticipated challenge of fast-spreading and potentially dangerous mutations of the virus (e.g., the Delta variant) with the need to tweak the vaccines to adapt to new variants more easily than with conventional vaccines. So even as they ramp up production in the early stages of a massive rollout, both Moderna and Pfizer must accountably retool their vaccine strategies.

According to Ramalingam, et al. (2020), the COVID-19 response increasingly should be viewed as a marathon and not a sprint, reinforcing the need for resilience strategies and policies to contain the pandemic. Operationally, it is critical to strengthen evidence-based adaptive management practices, to adjust the mix and type of interventions being implemented and learn to achieve shared goals. This requires adaptive leadership capacities, being open and transparent about learning, using collective decision-making processes and building trust with communities and individuals. These authors identified five common principles to guide adaptive leaders during crisis situations.

1. *Ensure evidence-based learning and adaptation* including defining a set of key measures for determining success or failure; ensuring an ongoing collection of operationally relevant data; and setting out a clear process for how changes in data and trends trigger new actions.
2. *Stress-test underlying theories, assumptions, and beliefs* to ensure a robust and rigorous reflection and examination through scenario planning and strategic foresight that helps underpin business decision-making. This involves exploring and preparing for different scenarios, identifying opportunities and challenges, and developing innovative ways of improving health and safety. The first step in scenario planning is to identify plausible situations and evaluate the likelihood of occurrence.

   In general, the "right" action plan to take will depend on the type of industry, capital structure, and organizational characteristics and factors. However, the updated information from the uncertainty cube also permits business leaders to evaluate gaps in resources and capabilities. Leaders can explore options and probable consequences free of biases or prevailing mindsets that can interfere with their ability to question prior assumptions or develop different perspectives.

McKinsey's risk management team (Koller, et al., 2020) developed a more focused uncertainty cube that enables leaders to explore different scenarios with different outcomes. They proposed three potential scenarios on the coronavirus for businesses:

- Quick recovery (least likely) with rapid and effective control of the virus spread and partially effective interventions with the outbreak growing slowly and with statewide reopening plans and mitigation measures.
- Moderate shock (base case) typified by effective public health responses, but regional virus resurgence and partially effective interventions. Impact on sectors varies based upon the magnitude of transmission, death rate, seasonality effects, and consumer reaction. Hardest-hit areas include aviation, tourism, hospitality, and consumer goods.
- Severe shock (conservative case) with high levels of health impact and prolonged downturn. Global pandemic and recession with widespread interruptions in supply chains, and continued community outbreaks.

3. *Streamline deliberative decision-making to explicate what is being done and why,* and how decisions are made so that if errors are identified, trust can still be maintained in the process.

   In the most successful countries that tackled the COVID pandemic head-on—South Korea, Taiwan, Germany—COVID responses were used as catalysts for recalibrating policies, making the process more transparent and dynamic. These responses also improved coordination across the supply chain—from healthcare to transportation to energy—which has resulted in unprecedented levels of planning, information sharing, and integration.

4. *Strengthen transparency, inclusion, and accountability* by recognizing that mistakes are likely to be made and proactively identify shared learning opportunities. Adaptive leaders need to commit to sharing their thinking in an open and transparent way, and create an environment of candor, psychological safety, and mutual trust, vital for effective crisis response. They make health-related data openly available and consult experts as widely as possible to reduce the impact of disinformation and to help affected parties to make ethical decisions informed by evidence. Participation makes decision-making more explicit and sustainable, and public institutions more effective, accountable, and transparent. This in turn enhances the legitimacy of national decisions and creates high commitment by all stakeholders (Norheim, et al., 2021).

   For example, the UK's National Health Service has held an open, honest, and challenging dialogue about how institutionalized biases in dealing with COVID-19 have led to greater levels of pain and suffering among black and ethnic minority patients and staff alike. Findings reveal that minority groups are disproportionately affected by chronic medical conditions and lower access to healthcare that may signify worse

COVID-19 outcomes, with higher death rates in African American, Native American, and Latinx communities (Belasen, et al., 2021).

The UK's Intensive Care National Audit and Research Centre reported that while ethnic minorities make up 13% of the UK population, by the end of April 2020, 16.2% of patients in hospitals in England who tested positive were from black, Asian, and minority ethnic (BAME) communities (Massey & Makoni, 2020). In the United States, 22% of the counties are in this category, and 90% of those are in the South. By April 2020, 97% of disproportionately black counties (counties with more than the national average of black residents) reported at least one case of COVID-19, compared to 80% of all other counties (Tai, et al., 2021).

5. *Mobilize collective action to tackle COVID-19* not just as a public health crisis but also as an economic, social, and political crisis. It is a complex problem that requires changes in behaviors and incentives and in the relationships between different groups, organizations, and countries. Effective responses therefore need to build on collaboration across different sectors, industries, and professionals and between international, national, and local levels—an ambitious challenge that has often proved difficult to achieve.

Adaptive leadership has a crucial role to play in helping to identify common goals for collective action across different players and levels of the response. Collective action in this regard might be in the form of coordination among businesses, partnerships among different interest groups (e.g., businesses and communities), or dialogue across a range of stakeholders.

In the UK, shared awareness of the existing healthcare capacity has led to an accelerated scaling up of available beds and equipment by the National Health Service. Civil society and citizen groups have also played a central role in mobilizing inclusive approaches to the pandemic, especially in resource-constrained settings. Such interactions enrich debate, are inclusive, and improve ownership of decisions. Importantly, they require behavioral flexibility, proactive demeanor, and openness—the practices of adaptive leadership.

Heifetz, Grashow, and Linsky (2009) define an adaptive challenge as one that cannot be met by the existing technical fixes or repertoire of management responses. Instead, they require unique mindsets and behaviors:

Get on the balcony. Take a broader perspective by moving back and forth between the "action" and the "balcony." This high-level perspective helps you spot trends and prevents you from unwittingly becoming a prisoner of the system. Ask yourself, what is changing? What inhibits change from happening? Who is going to be affected by the change?

Identify the adaptive challenge. Routine challenges are made up of technical work that is clear, predictable, and consistent. Adaptive challenges require responses to nonroutine problems and involve collaboration of individuals with complementary skills.

Regulate distress. Leaders must strike a balance between having people feel the need to change and having them feel overwhelmed by change. An adaptive leader must keep attuned to the collective distress and support the adaptive work at a pace that is tolerable. Acclimate and guide people to new roles and responsibilities by clarifying business goals and key values. Raise tough questions without exhibiting signs of anxiety. Communicate with confidence and poise.

Maintain disciplined attention. Build momentum by inspiring people to contribute to and confront issues by deepening the debate to get to the bottom of problems. As momentum decreases over time, adaptive leaders bring focus back to the organization both proactively and collaboratively.

Give the work back to employees. Instill confidence and promote trusting relationships with people. Encourage risk-taking and responsibility. Empower people to recognize problems and offer ideas for solving these problems.

Protect leadership voices from below. Do not promote groupthink or conformity. People need a collective effort to understand, recognize, and own the problems and solutions. Diverse perspectives can provoke fresh thinking. Ask: What are members really talking about? Have we missed something? Shifts in values, beliefs, and practices cannot be identified and implemented by a single person, even if that person has the sole authority.

Empathetic

Having strong empathy while carrying out critical leadership responsibilities is a plus. Empathy helps leaders build trust, stay focused, and adopt a rational and intuitive decision style despite facing highly stressful situations. Empathetic leaders must also be adept at receiving and evaluating feedback on the effectiveness of their decisions.

Experience shows that shifting decisions to those closest to handling COVID-19 challenges helps improve organizational agility and enhance innovation. The Seattle-based Swedish Health Services' senior executives demonstrated that by delegating decision-making, empowered caregiver teams were able to craft creative responses to the unique challenges that COVID-19 poses.

Jacinda Ardern, the prime minister of New Zealand, is a great example. During the crisis, she held regular briefings, both formal and informal (the latter using Facebook Live). Her Facebook Live chats became popular among New Zealanders because they show that she is human, just like us. She talked about her own concerns for her family, the science behind the government's decisions, and the difficulties lockdown brings. Ardern keeps her updates positive and inspiring and urges people to unite. And, most importantly, she listens to what people have to say (Pope, 2020).

Leaders gain credibility when they project compassion and demonstrate that they understand the risks and probable impact of unanticipated consequences. They are aware of their weaknesses and have the humility to defer to experts and delegate responsibilities to competent team members (Petriglieri, 2020). Singapore, South Korean, and Taiwan carried out systematic and exhaustive monitoring to reduce the risk of COVID-19 spread and keep the public well-informed. This helps the public to maintain its confidence and trust in the political leadership as well as isolate and contain the COVID-19 outbreak.

Leaders need to be sensitive, attuned, and listen nonjudgmentally and optimistically to moments of differences, and feel responsible for working with those differences. Leaders who are sensitive to the needs of their employees also provide them with the emotional support to press ahead, to deal with the stressful challenges that might be holding them back from pursuing their goals.

Good leaders make sure that their socioemotional messages generate unity and hope and reinforce the collective identity of togetherness. This is the reason why many women governors and mayors have been able to deal successfully with the effects of the pandemic (Lee, 2020). To enhance the effectiveness of crisis responses, they use their relational and emotional skills to build or restore trust among those affected by the crisis. They focus on the common purpose, are inspirational, and project trustworthiness to ensure people stay calm and engaged. And employees respond well. Survey shows 92% of employees and 98% of HR professionals say an empathetic employer drives retention, and 75% of all respondents would leave their organization if it became less empathetic (Businessolver, 2017).

Businessolver survey shows that 87% of CEOs—as do nearly eight in ten HR professionals—agree that the financial performance of a company is tied to empathy (and 43% strongly agree). However, even with this acknowledgment from leadership and years of progress, the study reports an "empathy gap"—the difference between CEO and employee perception of empathy in the workplace—still exists. For example, more than half of employees (51%) struggle to demonstrate empathy at work daily, significantly more than HR professionals (34%) and CEOs (45%). Furthermore, only 33% of women believe today's organizations are showing empathy, compared to 71% of men (Businessolver, 2018).

By understanding and empathizing with employees, leaders build a sense of trust, which allows employees to feel safe and bond with their leaders. Empathy increases employee loyalty to the organization and strengthens their commitment to achieving common goals, leading to greater collaboration and improved productivity. Employees who view their employers as empathetic are more likely to be productive, work longer hours, and remain loyal. The 2020 State of Workplace Empathy study (Businessolver, 2020) showed that 76% of employees believe empathy drives higher levels of productivity.

The leader-follower empathetic relationship also has parallel paths in the medical field. Patients may rely more on nonverbal cues in medical encounters when verbal and nonverbal messages are inconsistent and during direct consultation when emotional or relational communication is taking place. Being empathetic with patients helps clinicians to validate that the communication is meaningful and well understood. Meaningful provider-patient communication can enhance patient satisfaction and increase adherence as well as contribute to patients' understanding of illness and the risks and benefits of treatment.

When patient satisfaction is high, compliance with medical directives increases; predisposition to follow up with the provider is strengthened; the inclination to initiate litigation against providers tends to decrease; and 30-day readmission rates are lower. Physicians who understand and who respond appropriately to the emotional needs of their patients are less likely to be sued (Belasen & Belasen, 2018). Further, optimizing physician-patient communication can lead to better patient health and outcomes for patients and hospitals (Belasen, et al., 2021). Thus, organizational efforts that are aimed at improving physician alignment should also take physicians' emotional intelligence, interpersonal communication, and relational skills into consideration (Hammerly, et al., 2014).

On the personal side, emotional intelligence (EI) skills enhance leaders' understanding of their own mood, emotions, drives, and the ability to control impulses and re-channel negative attitudes towards more positive outcomes. Resilient leaders cannot be self-absorbed or focus solely on themselves. They still have a commitment to their organization. They need to ask the right questions and act in harmony. They balance "what needs to be done" with "what is right for the health system." They devise plans in consultation with others and use EI skills to generate the moral commitment of individuals and groups to implement the plans (Belasen, 2019).

Uncertain times call for resilient hospital CEOs that lead by example. Empathy will not only intrinsically motivate and inspire healthcare teams, but it will also help guide leaders through the financial and organizational challenges triggered by the COVID-19 pandemic. CEOs need to embrace a dual role: *Chief Executive Officer* and *Chief Empathy Officer.*

> Yet despite empathy's value to employees—each year our data shows over 90% of employees believe it is important for organizations to demonstrate—there are persistent disconnects between what leaders think about empathy and the way that employees experience it. To support a resilient workforce and overcome the challenges we are currently facing, leaders must take on a dual role and that starts at the top as the Chief Executive Officer must also be the Chief Empathy Officer (Shanahan, J., Businessolver President and CEO, 2020).

Analytical

The success of health settings hinges on proactive strategies by resilient leaders who assume greater responsibility not only for providing medical services or pharmaceuticals, but also for sustaining community care. Many of the challenges they face in transforming their health systems are interrelated and weigh equally in consideration and impact. Resilient leaders in integrated health systems unify the mission, clarify the strategic vision for their organizations, employ evidence-based best practices to improve patient quality and safety, and enhance the overall efficiency and effectiveness of the organization.

Health systems must increase their analytical capacity and develop a strong foundation of informatics and systems analysis when they are tested by disruptive events such as COVID-19. However, many years of investing in implementing electronic health records (EHR) have not really reaped the full benefits of using data analytics or increased productivity. To deal effectively with disruptions, health systems require greater analytical agility by improving the quality and integration of data, enhancing system capacity, and leveraging talent capable of bridging hospital needs with analytics to find opportunity in the data.

Analytical leaders strategically combine openness, communication, and collaboration to effectively engage others and leverage existing human and financial resources and technological capabilities for achieving broader organizational goals. In a survey by McKinsey (2016), direct involvement of senior leaders, coupled with the right organizational structure, was singled out as the key to successful implementation of a company's analytics efforts.

The presence of leaders with expertise in data analytics facilitates the design and implementation of analytical strategies and improved business strategies. Their engagement also helps bridge the planning-doing gap between analytics teams and senior leaders. High-performing organizations that reported successful outcomes with analytics also had significantly more buy-in and support from top executives.

In addition to aligning quality goals and incentives, harnessing innovation technology, and embracing evidence-based medicine, resilient leaders maintain a long-term perspective by pursuing value-driven strategies that may not have immediate payoffs. They recognize that capital investments in health information technology, hiring, training and development, and cultural transformation often come with the risk of investing in programs that are not reimbursable under fee-for service. They believe that the programs are morally right to pursue and that in the end they will yield savings in the value-based payment.

Healthcare leaders, IT experts, and clinical leaders collaborate in the design and implementation of analytics to help cut down unnecessary inefficiencies and administrative costs, upgrade care coordination, and improve interoperability and patient wellness. Interoperability involves the ability of IT systems and software applications to communicate and share data across clinicians, labs, hospitals, pharmacies, and patients. A primary goal is to invest in an effective EHR platform that supports the goal of clinical integration, evidence-based care through data collection, analysis and sharing to reduce clinical variance, supports the needs of health populations, and ensures the most effective outcomes. Taken together, the ability to effectively influence people, processes, and plans within the context of this data-rich environment is the hallmark of an analytical leader.

High volumes of sensitive data, information overload, complexity in medical informatics, and shifting health systems' innovation priorities due to the pandemic prevent healthcare leaders from acting quickly. Information overload may also create difficulties in understanding critical issues, properly contextualizing them, and effectively making smart choices.

Health settings may run into common source errors by doing the wrong thing (errors of commission) or by failing to do the right thing (errors of omission) at either the planning or execution phase created by gaps in the knowledge and skills of health professionals. Examples may include inaccurate or incomplete patient medical records and lapses in patient confidentiality related to the administration of patient records. Notably, the COVID-19 crisis with its demand for data management, electronic medical records, computerized coding, and streamlined communications can overwhelm health leaders.

The uncertainty around COVID-19 has led to difficulty for many epidemiologists and executives to decide who to include in any data set, how much relative weight to assign to different factors when investigating causal chains or how to interpret the data, and when to report the results. Procuring data and information that only align with existing beliefs and ignoring that which runs counter to common arguments may trigger a "confirmation trap" (i.e., obtaining information that confirms what one knows) or even selection bias in sampling (i.e., choosing non-random data for statistical analysis). For example, once the number of COVID-19 cases is adjusted per capita, the numbers may look very different across countries with different populations.

Widening the scope of their strategic vision by using a broader perspective help resilient leaders to further explore and open themselves up to the full range of possibilities across the health setting. Building on ideas and insights of trustees, physician executives, nurses, and IT professionals, and integrating adaptive feedback loops into the ongoing operational and strategy development is crucial for executing effective digital transformation strategy. Engaging others typically should occur before tapering off the number of options for solving problems. This also helps inform the decision-making process.

O'Donovan, et al. (2018) suggested the concept of "adaptive strategy" by building activities into a strategy process such as an in-depth scan of trends in an organization's area of focus, a review of how new concepts from related fields like behavioral economics or crowdsourced data analysis might influence current operating models, or a landscaping effort to anticipate changes in target beneficiary populations. This helps to bridge the strategy-to-execution gap by avoiding getting trapped in a growth treadmill and, instead, focusing on creating strategic plans with a sound grounding of the business vision in the current operational reality. Infusing the formal planning and strategic decision-making with a thorough understanding of existing organizational resources and capabilities can result in a more execution-ready strategy, with clearer roles and responsibilities for health leaders, trustees, and interprofessional care teams.

Effective execution is about empowering and building care teams' capacity to focus on key objectives by having a clear strategy that is also agile and that guides choices and attainment of patient outcomes. This strategy is aimed at a shared purpose, not just implementing a static plan imposed from above. Bridging the strategy-to-execution gap requires honest conversations about the vision and involves consistent, ongoing communication about strategy rather than a single grand reveal, and a commitment from the leaders of the organization to work with their staff to ground the strategy in changes to the teams' existing roles and responsibilities.

Crucial to the success of effective execution of strategy is ensuring that interfunctional collaboration is continuous, interactive, and inclusive, with both health leaders and care teams present so that the data is accurately interpreted, and all stakeholders understand the process for properly implementing the plans.

Confident

Coping with crises is daunting. The coronavirus pandemic has been an epic test of character and determination for health leaders requiring them to be assertive and empathetic, analytical, and adaptive, lead with confidence and emerge stronger (Hatami, Sjatil, & Sneader, 2020). They are expected to balance short-term needs with courage and calm and develop long-term goals with vision and imagination. The COVID-19 outbreak is a life-altering catastrophic event, and no preparation or previous experience can prepare leaders to deal with its unpredictability.

Leaders are expected to be mentally and physically fit. Mental toughness and physical fitness help to boost personal strength and stamina and increase focus and confidence in identifying creative solutions to complex problems and in building trust with stakeholders. They use persuasion and thoughtfulness in their communications and can influence others with tact and diplomacy. They have the moral courage and integrity to speak frankly and give constructive feedback even when the implications might be negative.

Resilient leaders are aware of their personal strengths and weaknesses, prioritize tasks, and delegate with confidence and competence. Effective delegation helps remove unnecessary bottlenecks and frees up the time they need to focus on the big picture and solve higher-level problems. They gain the trust of followers by asking the right questions and by avoiding the "availability trap" or the tendency to look for recent evidence that confirms what they already know.

Pursuing self-worth or self-validation forces less confident leaders to ignore contrary information, inspire fear and insecurity, and expose their dark side. Confident leaders, however, adapt their operating model to become future-ready by using behaviors that match aspirations of stakeholders for a better future in the post-COVID era. Since confidence builds on logic and evidence, health system leaders find ways to communicate directly with clinicians and care teams to reduce their anxiety level, provide emotional support, and engage and strengthen their overall relationships with employees.

Unlike less effective leaders, confident leaders know how to manage the competing tensions between short and long time periods, stability and change, control and flexibility—binary challenges with potential paradoxes, contradictions, and opposing forces that pull the organization in different directions. Confident leaders know how to navigate these "either-or" challenges by creating linkages and synergies that induce "both-and" opportunities and cooperative behaviors within the system and across partners engaged in simultaneously managing the direct consequences of the COVID-19 outbreak.

> The pandemic broke down the walls of competition between hospitals. Healthcare is a business, and like any other business, organizations strive to outdo competitors. But during catastrophic situations, topping each other is no longer important. What's more important is doing the right thing for the greater good. In the case of these three hospitals (one in Manhattan, one on Long Island, and one in upstate New York) it meant moving the sickest patients to where the greatest resources were and moving other patients where there was more capacity. There also was more willingness to share supplies. The healthcare "system" truly worked as a system. Together, as colleagues not competitors, they continued working to solve various challenges at each location, including preserving supplies of personal protective equipment (PPE). Even more impressive was how they were sharing ideas on how to generate revenue because so many elective surgeries were canceled. The collective creativity and moral support have been remarkable (Collins, 2020).

Understanding how to craft and frame effective social media messaging is vital for capturing the attention of the public and curtailing the impact of misinformation. Top executives and experts may use storytelling and symbols along with powerful media to counteract dangerous narratives in a rich, colorful way that connects with the audience on impact. Confident leaders help reduce linguistic ambiguity in strategic communications and the potential for miscommunication especially at times of crisis.

Developing effective communication and community engagement strategies using social media is critical to fighting the pandemic and informing populations about the health risks posed by COVID-19. Social media outlets Facebook with 2.26 billion users, YouTube with 1.9 billion, WeChat with nearly 1 billion, Instagram with 1 billion users, and TikTok with half a billion users enable health organizations to disseminate information quickly and update the public in real time. They also provide an opportunity for health organizations to counteract medical misinformation such as that the Pfizer-BioNTech coronavirus vaccine could cause infertility in women and respond to misconceptions about COVID-19 with reliable information that the public wants. How healthcare organizations communicate about the COVID-19 crisis can be profoundly influential in creating clarity, building a resilient workforce, and triggering the trust and confidence of the public.

Against this frenzied backdrop, it would be easy for leaders to reflexively plunge into the maelstrom of social-media misinformation, copy what others are doing, or seek big, one-off, bold gestures. It is also true that crises can produce great leaders and communicators whose words and actions comfort in the present, restore faith in the long term, and are remembered long after the crisis has been quelled.

So we counsel this: Pause, take a breath. The good news is that the fundamental tools of effective communication still work. Define and point to long-term goals, listen to and understand your stakeholders, and create openings for dialogue. Be proactive. But don't stop there. In this crisis leaders can draw on a wealth of research, precedent, and experience to build organizational resilience through an extended period of uncertainty, and even turn a crisis into a catalyst for positive change. Great communicators tend to do five things well:

Give people what they need when they need it. People's need for pertinent information grows in a crisis. So should a good communicator's messaging. Different forms of information can help listeners to stay safe, cope mentally, and connect to a deeper sense of purpose and stability.

Communicate clearly, simply, frequently. A crisis tends to limit people's capacity to absorb information in the early days. Focus on keeping listeners safe and healthy. Then repeat, repeat, repeat.

Choose candor over charisma. Trust is never more important than in a crisis. Be honest about where things stand, do not be afraid to show vulnerability, and maintain transparency to build loyalty and lead more effectively.

Revitalize resilience. As the health crisis metastasizes into an economic crisis, accentuate the positive and strengthen communal bonds to restore confidence.

Distill meaning from chaos. The crisis will end. Help people make sense of all that has happened. Establish a clear vision, or mantra, for how the organization and its people will emerge (Mendy, Lass, & VanAkin, 2020).

Confident leaders in integrated health systems unify the mission, clarify the strategic vision for their organizations, employ evidence-based best practices to improve patient quality and safety, and enhance the overall efficiency and effectiveness of the organization. They visibly and consistently support the narratives of interprofessional collaboration and engage in ongoing dialogue with staff members and clinicians.

When faced with an overwhelming volume of critical decisions, leaders may feel the urge to centralize and tighten control. But resilience depends on soliciting more insights and perspectives across the continuum of care with communication with staff, patients, and members of the interdisciplinary healthcare team. Empowering team members helps to build trust and demonstrate that leaders have good listening skills, are curious and flexible, and are willing to make tough, even unpopular decisions (Hilton, 2020).

The *Leadership Confidence Pulse* is a set of seven questions that have been tracked annually since 2003. We also have used these items to assess confidence in numerous client organizations. Leadership confidence, in many ways, parallels consumer confidence. When consumers are confident, they buy more. When employees are confident, they are more willing to go "above and beyond." Employees spend time focusing not only on the key aspects of their core job but also on four other non-job roles that we have defined and studied. Those are a team member role (doing things to help out your team, even when not part of the core job), an innovator/entrepreneurial role (engaging in the support of and development of new ideas and products/services), a career role (spending time doing things that will help build new skills and enhance an individual's career), and lastly the organization member role (doing activities that help the company overall, even though it is not part of the core job).

These non-core job roles are important when we find ourselves in high-change situations; thus, higher levels of confidence bode well for organizations and leaders. While we might expect confidence to go down during high-stress times, the data shows that for most of the confidence items, the change from last year is positive.

The two items that had negative or no change are confidence in economic climate and ability to execute on vision. However, all other items (e.g., having right people and skills, ability to change, leadership, and strategy) show positive changes from last year. Thus, under conditions of high fear, general instability, and lots of unknowns, respondents are expressing higher confidence in items that have been difficult to change in prior years.

We also track employee energy when we do each Leadership Pulse, and we asked respondents to tell us how their overall confidence levels are affecting their personal energy. Below are some answers to this question:

I definitely think that when I have a high level of confidence, I am more energized by what I am doing.

When I am less confident that I have the knowledge and abilities to do a certain task, it takes a lot of energy from me to do it.

Lack of confidence (as a whole) lowers my energy. I need to trust my skilled colleagues to have higher energy.

Right now, I am executing, so I am riding the confidence bull.

Lack of confidence zaps energy.

Major impact. The higher our confidence, the more energy and momentum we have.

(Welbourne, 2020)

Conclusions

Resilient leaders project positive attitudes and maintain their composure despite the stress. They play the role of devil's advocate, testing the validity of arguments by asking "why" and "how" questions and by swapping dominant alternatives with ideas that organizational and team members can consider. The devil's advocate facilitates members' thinking about cause-and-effect relationships and improves the depth and breadth of their communication processes and the quality of performance outcomes. When accepted solutions to problems are adopted, the leader uses an empowering mindset with a sense of purpose to explore plans and underscore action paths for implementation.

In times of crisis, employees, consumers, and partners alike tend to gravitate towards health systems whose purpose aligns with their values and beliefs. Identifying their needs and taking steps to actively foster and promote a strong culture of safety is an important goal of resilient leadership. This helps to inspire employees to change their way of thinking about patient care and the culture of the organization, avoid confusion during transitions, and facilitate collaborative behaviors. According to the *Joint Commission Center for Transforming Healthcare*, these measures include:

- Sufficient support of patient safety event reporting
- Meaningful feedback and positive support to staff who report safety vulnerabilities
- Prioritizing and implementing safety provisions
- Addressing staff and clinician burnout
- Establishing teamwork and building relationships (Sentinel Event Alert, 2017)

Resilient leaders build trust by demonstrating high levels of personal integrity and accountability. They have a high tolerance for ambiguity, steer away from blaming others for failure and, instead, encourage peers and followers to become systems thinkers, and cast the net wide. They are aware of their strengths and limitations, have an optimistic mindset, enjoy a high level of self-discipline, learn from errors, and recognize contributions by others.

COVID-19 is an adaptive challenge that needs adaptive leadership. This challenge requires new approaches and innovation, and importantly, changes in the values, beliefs, and assumptions of people and organizations. Complex problems cannot be solved with a set of prescribed solutions. They require situational awareness and behavioral flexibility that effective leaders use to identify problems and then mobilize employees to come up with possible answers.

You need resilient leaders, not transactional managers, to identify long-term solutions to complex problems, especially at times of crisis.

References

AHA (2020). Hospitals and Health Systems Face Unprecedented Financial Pressures Due to COVID-19, Retrieved from https://www.aha.org/guidesreports/2020-05-05-hospitals-and-health-systems-face-unprecedented-financial-pressures-due#:~:text=The%20AHA%20estimates%20that%2C%20as,from%20March%20to%20June%202020.

Belasen, A. R., Tracey, M., & Belasen, A. T. (2021). Demographics matter! The potentially disproportionate effect of COVID-19 on hospital ratings. *International Journal for Quality in Health Care*, 33(1). https://doi.org/10.1093/intqhc/mzab036

Belasen, A. T., Oppenlander, J., Belasen, A. R., & Hertelendy, A. (2021). Provider-patient communication and hospital ratings: Perceived gaps and forward thinking about the effects of COVID-19. *International Journal for Quality in Health Care*, 33(1). https://doi.org/10.1093/intqhc/mzaa140

Belasen, A. (2019). *Dyad Leadership and Clinical Integration: Driving Change, Aligning Strategies*, Chicago, IL: Health Administration Press.

Belasen, A. R., & Belasen, A. T. (2018). Doctor-patient communication: A review and a rationale for using an assessment framework. *Journal of Health Organization and Management*, 32(7), 891–907.

Businessolver (2020). 2020 State of Workplace Empathy, Retrieved from https://www.businessolver.com/workplace-empathy-executive-summary

Businessolver (2018). Businessolver Quantifies Empathy in the Workplace: 87 Percent of CEOs Agree That a Company's Financial Performance is Tied to Empathy, April 12, Retrieved from https://www.businessolver.com/who-we-are/news/businessolver-quantifies-empathy-in-the-workplace-

Businessolver (2017). Empathy: The Solution to Employees' Engagement Crisis, Retrieved from https://hrdailyadvisor.blr.com/2017/06/27/empathy-solution-employees-engagement-crisis/

Collins, R. (2020). Healthcare Leaders Choose Collaboration Over Competing During Covid-19, *HealthLeaders*, Retrieved from https://www.healthleadersmedia.com/covid-19/healthcare-leaders-choose-collaboration-over-competing-during-covid-19, June 8.

Hammerly, M. E., Harmon, L., & Schwaitzberg, S. D. (2014). Good to great: Using 360-degree feedback to improve physician emotional intelligence. *Journal of Healthcare Management*, 59(5), 354–365.

Hatami, H., Sjatil, P. E., & Sneader, K. (2020). The Toughest Leadership Test, *McKinsey & Company*, May 26, Retrieved from https://www.mckinsey.com/featured-insights/leadership/the-toughest-leadership-test

Heifetz, R. A., Grashow, A., & Linsky, M. (2009). *The Practice of Adaptive Leadership: Tools and Tactics for Changing Your Organization and the World*, Boston, MA: Harvard Business Press.

Hilton, S. (2020). Positive Leadership in Uncertain Times, *McKinsey & Company*, April 23, Retrieved from https://www.mckinsey.com/business-functions/organization/our-insights/positive-leadership-in-uncertain-times

Koller, T., Petrov, A., Polyakov, Y., & Ishaan, S. (2020). Are Scenarios Limiting Your Pandemic Recovery Strategy? *Mckinsey*, Retrieved from https://www.mckinsey.com/business-functions/strategy-and-corporate-finance/our-insights/are-scenarios-limiting-your-pandemic-recovery-strategy

Lee, B. (2020). The Coronavirus Crisis is Proving We Need More Women Governors and Mayors, *Newsweek*. April 21, Retrieved from https://www.newsweek.com/coronavirus-crisis-proving-weneed-more-women-governors-mayors-opinion-1496897.

Massey, N., & Makoni, A. (2020). Coronavirus Disproportionately Affecting BAME Communities in UK, New Figures Show, *Independent*, April 21, Retrieved from https://www.independent.co.uk/news/uk/home-news/coronavirus-bame-communities-deaths-infections-uk-statistics-a9475406.html

McKinsey Survey (2016). The Need to Lead in Data and Analytics, Retrieved from https://www.mckinsey.com/business-functions/mckinsey-digital/our-insights/the-need-to-lead-in-data-and-analytics

McKinsey & Company (2020). How COVID-19 has Pushed Companies Over the Technology Tipping Point. October 5, Retrieved from https://www.mckinsey.com/business-functions/strategy-and-corporate-finance/our-insights/how-covid-19-has-pushed-companies-over-the-technology-tipping-point-and-transformed-business-forever

Mendy, A., Lass, M., & VanAkin, K. (2020). A Leader's Guide: Communicating with Teams, Stakeholders, and Communities during COVID-19, April 17, *McKinsey & Company*, Retrieved from https://www.mckinsey.com/business-functions/organization/our-insights/a-leaders-guide-communicating-with-teams-stakeholders-and-communities-during-covid-19

Norheim, O. F., Abi-Rached, J. M., & Bright, L. K. et al. (2021). Difficult tradeoffs in response to COVID-19: The case for open and inclusive decision making. *Nature Medicine*, 27, 10–13. doi:10.1038/s41591-020-01204-6

O'Donovan, D., Kasper, G., & Dubbs, N. L. (2018). How Adaptive Strategy is Adapting, Retrieved from https://ssir.org/articles/entry/how:adaptive_strategy_is_adapting#

Petriglieri, G. (2020). The Psychology Behind Effective Crisis Leadership, April 22, *Harvard Business Review*, Retrieved from https://hbr.org/2020/04/the-psychology-behind-effective-crisis-leadership

Pope, K. (2020). Why Empathy is Vital for Effective Leadership, Especially in Times of Crisis, *Forbes*, June 19, (forbes.com)

Ramalingam, B., Nabarro, D., Oqubay, A., Carnall, D. R., & Wild L. (2020). Five Principles to Guide Adaptive Leadership, Retrieved from hbr.org/2020/09/5-principles-to-guide-adaptive-leadership

Renjen, P. (2020). The Heart of Resilient Leadership: Responding to COVID-19, Retrieved from https://www2.deloitte.com/us/en/insights/economy/covid-19/heart-of-resilient-leadership-responding-to-covid-19.html

Sentinel Event Alert (2017). The Essential Role of Leadership in Developing a Safety Culture, issue 57, March 1, Retrieved from https://www.jointcommission.org/

Shanahan, J. (2020). Chief Empathy Officer: What the 2020 State of Workplace Empathy Study Reveals for Leaders, June 16, Retrieved from https://blog.businessolver.com/chief-empathy-officer-what-the-2020-state-of-workplace-empathy-study-reveals-for-leaders

Tai, D. B. G., Shah, A., & Doubeni, C. A., et al. (2021). The disproportionate impact of COVID-19 on racial and ethnic minorities in the United States. *Clinical Infectious Diseases*, 72(4), 703–706. https://doi.org/10.1093/cid/ciaa815

Welbourne, T. M. (2020). Leadership Confidence Strong During 2020 Pandemic, May 28, Retrieved from https://www.tlnt.com/leadership-confidence-strong-during-2020-pandemic/

Chapter 4

Learning from Resilient Leaders—The Role of Trust

The COVID-19 pandemic is one of the most difficult and challenging crises for leaders to manage in the 21st century. By the first week of June 2021, the coronavirus has sickened 173 million people around the world. By that time 3.73 million people have died due to the coronavirus. In the United States alone, over 597,000 have died because of COVID-19 complications. American life expectancy fell by one year, to 77.8 years, in the first half of 2020. The virus is not yet contained with many countries sprinting to develop a coronavirus vaccine or treatment with unclear policies, shifting priorities, and contradictory strategies.

Handling COVID-19 and future pandemics at national and global levels requires mitigation strategies, updated systems, and well-synchronized supply chain but also leadership qualities and traits that help establish trust among key stakeholders. Trusted leadership exemplifies spiritual values such as integrity, honesty, and humility manifested in leadership-centric behaviors. Building trust helps resilient leaders to focus their attention on recovery by reviewing relevant information, rapidly determining priorities, and making smart choices with confidence and conviction. Recovery efforts require a shift in mindset from crisis management to program management, and from backup plans to scenario planning, reinvention, and adaptation to new realities (Deloitte, 2020).

National leaders such as Angela Merkel (Germany), Mette Fredriksen (Denmark), Erna Solberg (Norway), and Tsai Ing-Wen (Taiwan), have demonstrated empathy, honesty, and transparency (Nimbs-Nyce, 2020). Angela Merkel's decisive efforts were highlighted as directly responsible for a substantial decrease in the German public's sense of anxiety and depression and the heightening of their sense of well-being and trust in their leader (Ocklenburg, 2020).

DOI: 10.4324/9781003190929-4

A good model to emulate, which succeeded in conveying clear and trustworthy advice to the public consistent with the best available medical knowledge, is Singapore's political leadership where health officials and even the prime minister have delivered a series of informative and medically accurate communications to the public. While Singapore had early cases of infection, it has been broadly successful in limiting the spread of COVID-19 despite the high level of socio-economic connectivity with China. The wise and trusted advice from the government has played an important role in building trust and showing unity (Wei, 2020).

Having strong EI skills can be a game changer when it comes to managing crises such as COVID-19. Scholars found that emotional intelligence helps leaders stay focused and adopt effective decision styles despite facing highly stressful situations (Dilawar, Durrani, & Anjum, 2021). Empathy and EI skills have also been noted as the defining leadership style of Jacinda Ardern the prime minister of New Zealand. She communicates in a clear, consistent, and soothing manner. There is a high level of trust and confidence in her leadership skills and ability to manage the COVID-19 pandemic (Friedman, 2020). At the time when the global coronavirus cases and deaths were surging in June 2020, New Zealand reported no new cases of the coronavirus and lifted social distancing restrictions.

Managing the COVID-19 crisis also requires confidence in technical competence and scientific expertise. Many of the leaders that handled the COVID-19 contagion successfully have also been women leaders. A standout is Taiwan's President Tsai who is regarded as a competent and trusted leader who uses science at the fore of decision-making (Hass, 2020). Remarkably, Taiwan did not shut down its economy to prevent the coronavirus from spreading. Instead, when the first infected patient was discovered in Taiwan on January 21, 2020, she led swift, decisive, and rigorous investigative efforts to trace potentially infected contacts. This helped to isolate and contain the COVID-19 outbreak. By the end of June 29, 2020, Taiwan registered as few as 447 cases with 435 recovered and 7 deaths (Bremmer, 2020).

Leading through Crisis

Crisis is an incident with undesirable outcomes or a threat to the reputation, financial stability, or even survival of organizations. How a leader manages a crisis can have profound implications for the organization's relationships with stakeholders, especially consumers.

With open access to multiple channels of communication, consumers are becoming major players in the mass consumption, creation, and distribution of information. Faster, immediate, and multi-directional communications spread messages beyond their targeted audiences, making it more difficult to trace attitudes or changes or monitor their direction and potential impact. An indication of this is the increase in firms' multi-pronged efforts and investments in social media channels that help build brand recognition and loyalty and increase ROI.

It is therefore vital for communication strategists to create dialogic loops with useful information to all publics, use conversational forms of communication, and generate return visits to a company's website with regular updates. A good example is Paul Polman, Unilever's CEO, who engaged the media in February 2017 to spurn a takeover bid by food industry giant Kraft Heinz, strongly arguing that it had no merit for any of Unilever's internal and external stakeholders.

Once Polman rebuffed the offer, he published a statement explaining to the public—and particularly the company's shareholders—the rationale for rejecting the $143 billion offer. He deputized executives to call the media and spread the rumor that a deal would destroy the company's strong financial standing. Since the takeover fiasco, he has used appearances on television, print media, conferences, and tweets to continue to support his objection. "Do we choose to serve a few billionaires, or do we choose to serve the billions?", he tweeted on September 10, 2017. Polman's discourse underscores the important responsibility of focused leadership—influencing the public's perception and sustaining the positive image of the corporation.

Another example, however, with less successful results involved Uber. In January 2017, an executive order that banned refugees and immigrants from traveling to the United States caused a one-hour protest organized by the taxi union in NYC in which they refused to drive people from JFK Airport. Uber, trying to capitalize on the opportunity, responded with a tweet: "Surge pricing has been turned off at #JFK Airport. This may result in longer wait times. Please be patient." The tweet stirred negative press for Uber with a Twitter user initiating #DeleteUber to urge riders to delete their app (Isaac, 2017a). Celebrities and influencers retweeting the original message started a trend with over 200,000 users deleting the app with Uber trying to salvage their reputation through corporate apology. Lyft, which had been rapidly expanding its coverage, seized on the opportunity to brand itself as a more socially conscious alternative.

To restore its corporate reputation Uber replaced Travis Kalanick as CEO with Dara Khorosrowshasi who tried immediately to rebrand Uber's corporate identity by articulating new corporate values: "We are customer obsessed," "We celebrate differences," and "We do the right thing." The efforts to regain its reputation were heroic but insufficient as the social media-driven movement had a significant impact on the company's U.S. operations following stories about bizarre behaviors of Uber's executives and staff and aggressive cultural identity (Isaac, 2017b). Uber's market share dropped 5% following the week of the incident and it suffered a 10% decrease in riders. In 2018, Lyft experienced a 41% increase in riders narrowing the gap with its rival (Graham, 2018).

When crises strike, they tend to overwhelm the communication systems of organizations, often causing miscalculations or tendencies to fall back on inadequate or misguided responses. Communication failures may include rushing to judgment, overreacting, failing to act quickly, misreading facts, lacking empathy, deflecting responsibilities, developing tunnel vision, reluctance to involve others in decision-making, withholding information, and failing to plan. Often highly empathic CEOs recognize warning signs more quickly, communicate with stakeholders, and initiate steps to restore the communication systems. On the other hand, they also may be more predisposed to false alarms, more biased in processing crisis-related information, and less committed to repairing the organization's communication system (König, et al., 2020). Chipotle is a case in point.

In winter 2016, the FDA and the Centers for Disease Control and Prevention (CDC) along with state and local officials were investigating 2 separate outbreaks of *E. coli* O26 infections in a total of 55 people linked to food served at Chipotle restaurants in several states. There were 21 reported hospitalizations. Most of these cases occurred in Oregon and Washington during October 2015. In response, Chipotle decided to close 43 restaurants in Washington and Oregon in early November 2015 and then reopened them quickly in consultation with health officials.

The initial response to the outbreak transpired through press releases and articulation of newly adopted safety protocols and programs on the company's websites. Social media and dialogic engagement with the public was quite limited and selective. By winter 2015/16, no major social media outlets were utilized except for a few tweets that addressed stakeholders and customers. While Chipotle responded to individual tweets from customers who had gotten sick, it ignored the general conversation and focused almost entirely on marketing. The company also averted attention to recycling efforts, safety standards, and initiatives to support local growers. By February 2016, Chipotle offered no further responses or information regarding the outbreaks or new procedures. However, in a regulatory disclosure filed by the company, Chipotle acknowledged that safety and health-related food problems were inevitable at its restaurants. Meanwhile, investors sued Chipotle for making "materially false and misleading statements," and not disclosing that "quality controls were not in compliance with applicable consumer and workplace safety regulations." Notably, the company's damage control was limited and reactive, reframing the issue as isolated and well under control.

As food poisoning had become a part of the company's evolving identity, Chipotle held mandatory food safety training meetings for employees and implemented new sanitary policies that all employees must follow to minimize the risk of human-spread illnesses. In September 2016, the company launched a renewed effort to restore its tarnished reputation by using corporate advertising that displayed its new internal programs and tracking systems aimed at improving safety and quality standards.

Aside from free food and discounts, Chipotle also tried to salvage its reputation as an innovative and socially responsible company by highlighting some of its other programs and promotions like a student essay contest, a sustainability program, and drone deliveries. However, Chipotle's reputation appeared to be significantly damaged and not so easily repaired. News coverage of Chipotle's financial standing and reputation in 2016 became increasingly negative and critical. By the first two quarters of 2016, Chipotle reported net losses.

While Chipotle did manage to earn $7.8 million in its third quarter, it continued to report significant declines in revenue and comparable restaurant sales and transactions as compared to the same quarter in 2015. Analysts attributed much of Chipotle's first ever quarterly loss (Jan–Apr 2016) of approximately $30 million to giveaways of free food items to segments of the markets, e.g., students and teachers.

Chipotle not only failed to understand its stakeholders, but it also failed to tailor responses to specific segments such as loyal/regular customers, those sickened by the food, those affected by closures, shareholders, and regulators. The messages were not transformational (idea-centered, insightful, visionary, emphatic) or relational (honest, receiver-centered) with the purpose to establish integrity and restore trust and confidence. Instead, the company blanketed the general community with promotional coupons. Such a generalized and impersonal approach towards its own customers did not seem to prove very effective (Belasen & Belasen, 2019).

Disagreements between Chipotle and its regulatory agency, the CDC, over the severity of the situation quickly amounted to challenging communications.

Chipotle: "The Centers for Disease Control and Prevention's Dec. 4, 2015, update misinformed the public and made no effort to advise the public that some sick people had no known connection to Chipotle."

CDC response:

> The Dec. 4, 2015, web posting provided the public as well as public health and regulatory partners in federal, state, and local agencies with updated information regarding an ongoing investigation. This included information on the seven-ill people which had been newly identified since the preceding web posting on Nov. 20, 2015.

(CDC, 2016)

As of December 2016, a full year after the outbreak, Chipotle co-CEO Steve Ells admitted that he was "nervous" about the company's ability to reach its 2017 sales forecast following the 2015 outbreak. However, only limited executive communications (rules, standards, policy statements) and promotional communications (selling products, press releases) were used to address stakeholders with relevant and timely narratives and without much attention to transformational (change and innovation) or relational (interpersonal, interactive) communications with internal and external stakeholders. Chipotle's tone on social media ranged from serious and apologetic, to humorous and inappropriate. Its initial response was defensive with its top executives adopting a bunker mentality with narratives addressing safety measures and often cracking inappropriate jokes.

The *E. coli* crisis has drastically affected Chipotle's brand image and financial credibility as investors, regulators, customers, and even employees received ambiguous signals and messages from Chipotle's executives.

In July 2017, Chipotle faced a norovirus breakout in Sterling, Virginia, triggering a downgrade of its stock that dipped 2% on the reports. While shares traded around $730 in 2015, by the end of 2017, Chipotle shares have since shed 60% and the investment banking firm BTIG, projecting that Chipotle would miss its 2017 targets, lowered its 2017 earnings per share estimates to $7.48, down from $8.38, and below Chipotle's goal of $10 (Fortune, 2017).

One way to organize the communication system during a major crisis at the organizational level is provided in Figure 4.1 (Belasen, 2008, 2019). Leaders can implement a well-synchronized plan that includes responses to early warning signals of a threatening crisis. Proactive measures include disclosure through the sharing of information with the public (INFORM); preparation and prevention by mobilizing employees internally, developing crisis teams and conducting training and exercises to strengthen open communication, honesty, and engagement (REFORM); containing the damage through the creation of operating rules, procedures, and codes of ethics to guide future actions (CONFORM); and recovery and evaluation by re-establishing organizational routines and feedback systems to prevent future reoccurrences (PERFORM).

Trusted leaders are accountable. These leaders do not hide bad news or provide false impressions. The role of leadership in diffusing the negative effects of crises and in

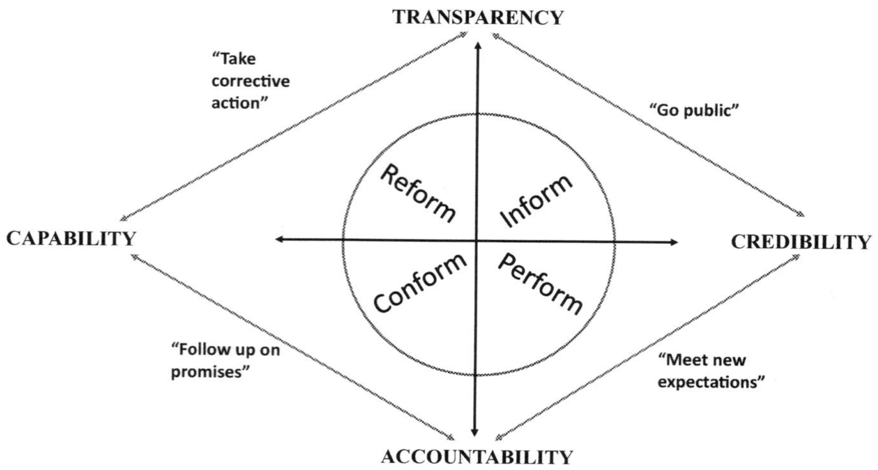

Figure 4.1 Organizing the corporate response to crises.

restoring the public trust is critical. It is also important for leaders to maintain a sense of continuity, to be relevant and consistent in the dissemination of information, to remain calm, and to be visible, truthful, trustworthy, and responsive. Accurate and timely communication is vital during times of uncertainty. Great crisis leaders earn the public's trust with clarity, focus, transparency, and compassion. Without transparency, the public may sense deception, which can reduce the credibility of any leader.

Trusted leaders acknowledge uncertainty, communicate with compassion, show understanding, and are empathetic. They embrace paradoxical skills to navigate the seemingly competing tensions and demands in crisis situations. They use mixed strategies of messaging to achieve organizational goals: communication lines and persuasion to promote cooperation; authority lines for marshaling capabilities for achieving results and business continuity. Messaging that appeals to the collective values and history plays a key role in enhancing public trust and stakeholders' acceptance.

Leadership during any crisis is not an enviable position to be in. One small decision can change the outcome for better or worse. A wrong move could erode trust and trigger unrest that exacerbates the existing conditions. The true test of executive leadership does not occur when everything is running smoothly; it occurs amid unexpected situations when it is crucial to act quickly and communicate sensibly and effectively. When organizations and their leaders are naïve, they fail to realize the importance of preparation or use defense mechanisms, treat the crisis with less rigor, and open themselves up to social media activism and public criticism.

Trusted Leadership

During uncertain and chaotic times such as the global COVID-19 pandemic, the need for strong, credible, transparent, and trustworthy leadership is critical as insecurity can creep in on even the most successful executive. Trust will surely be tested by companies' commitment to their employees during the COVID-19 crisis. And the Edelman *Trust Barometer* with responses of more than 34,000 respondents across 28 countries confirm this. The survey is based on a combined measurement of two distinct attributes: Competence (delivering on promises) and ethical behavior (doing the right thing and working to improve society).

In 2013, the report noted a "crisis in leadership" and then in 2017 it was trust itself that was in crisis. This was followed in 2018 by "the battle for truth." The 2019 *Edelman Trust Barometer* reveals that trust has changed profoundly in the past year with "my employer" emerging as the most sought-after institution.

A striking 90% of the survey respondents preferred that companies and brands act to protect the well-being and financial security of their employees and suppliers, even if it meant suffering big financial losses during the COVID-19 pandemic. The disincentive for companies that put profit ahead of people is severe, with 71% of people saying that this will erode their trust in a business forever. Fittingly, 55% of the survey respondents said that business is more competent and trustworthy than government in responding more credibly to the pandemic (Aziz, 2020).

Credibility and trustworthiness are a combination of character, expertise, and dependability. Leaders gain credibility when they project compassion and demonstrate that they understand the risks and probable impact of unanticipated consequences. They are aware of their weaknesses and have the humility to defer to experts and delegate responsibilities to competent team members (Petriglieri, 2020). The Singaporean political leadership's cohesive messaging and understanding that detailed knowledge matters and that the health and economic risks were asymmetrically distributed also helped the process of confidence-building.

South Korea also carried out systematic and exhaustive monitoring to reduce the risk of spread, enhancing leadership credibility and boosting public trust. In Singapore, the messaging was consistently clear and evidence-based, and the public has remained well-informed. This has continued to reassure the population about the measures to counteract COVID-19 and maintain confidence and trust in the political leadership (Quah, 2020).

Events such as the COVID-19 pandemic require authentic leaders who are aware of their vulnerabilities and can empower and trust others to carry out critical tasks. Integrating weaknesses into the scope of responses to crisis situations is also the essence of dependability that not only enhances authentic leadership attributes of self-awareness and relational transparency but also benefits followers. Authentic leaders have the capacity to unleash followers' full potential. They are effective in creating positive work environments and in achieving positive and enduring outcomes in organizations.

Leaders must also be adept at receiving and evaluating feedback on the effectiveness of their decisions. Experience shows that shifting decisions to those closest to handling COVID-19 challenges helps improve organizational agility and enhance innovation. The Seattle-based Swedish Health Services' senior executives showed that delegating decision-making not only flattened the hierarchy but also empowered caregiver teams to develop creative responses to the unique challenges posed by COVID-19 (Dale, Welling, & Clearfield, 2020).

The Advantage of Diversity at the Top

Trusted leaders make sure that their socioemotional messages generate unity and hope and reinforce the collective identity of togetherness. To enhance the effectiveness of crisis responses, they require a great deal of relational and emotional skills to build or restore trust among those affected by the crisis (Kahn, Barton, & Fellows, 2013). Leaders need to be sensitive, attuned, and responsive to moments of differences, and feel responsible for working with those differences. They focus on the common purpose, are inspirational, and project trustworthiness to ensure people stay calm and engaged.

Leadership traits like emotional intelligence, empathy, and compassion have been found to be more prevalent in women (Rueckert, 2011). A study of 55,000 professionals across 90 countries and all levels of management by the Korn Ferry Hay Group (2016) revealed that women outperformed men in 11 of 12 key EI competencies. The greatest difference was in EI self-awareness, where women were 86% more likely than men to use the competency consistently. Other competencies in the study of Korn Ferry with women outperforming men included empathy, coaching and mentoring, influence, inspirational leadership, conflict management, organizational awareness, adaptability, teamwork, and achievement orientation.

These qualities are also marked by the special contribution of women and their superior relational skills for leadership. Rather than being perceived as a weakness to be mitigated, the female leadership advantage is seen as an asset and as a strength. The special contribution indicates that "femininity" is a newly recognized asset and a potential advantage in organizations (Simpson, Ross-Smith, & Lewis, 2010). Female leaders were found to have greater transformational leadership qualities, espouse ethics and integrity, and manifest better transactional and organizational skills than men (Belasen & Frank, 2008; Belasen & Frank, 2012). Women can be go-getters in management and at the same time inspire others and model the way as trusted leaders (Ibarra & Obodaru, 2008).

Women leaders have the capacity to be more balanced in decision-making situations and seek out win–win solutions in decision-making situations. They examine causes and consequences of decisions and the potential impact of decisions and outcomes on affected employees, customers, and shareholders. This big-picture thinking may help women to deal more successfully with ambiguity in complex business settings. In situations of acute stress, women enable accurate social responses and are more empathic and open to others as a means of coping while men tend to become more self-centered and respond with increased egocentricity and less adaptive regulation (Tomova, et al., 2014).

Having more women on boards and management teams may give companies unique perspectives in promoting better relationships between consumers and employees. Studies have shown that greater diversity at the business unit level (Badal & Harter, 2014) and in executive leadership (Arioglu, 2020; Moreno-Gómez, et al., 2018) positively affects financial performance and is linked to companies' competitive advantage. Because women have a strong influence on what people buy, companies would be able to access the full range of resources available to a company. Gender-diverse boards are also associated with less aggressive investment policies, better acquisition decisions, reduced negative impact of crises on firm performance, and improved financial outcomes for firms operating in industries with a high prevalence of executive overconfidence (Chen, et al., 2019).

Given their strong EI skills, women leaders manifest important characteristics of trusted leadership: Honesty, transparency, credibility, and accountability. Women can act selflessly when the time comes, be safe and make others feel safe, perform quality services, and make decisions for the benefit of the collective (Dame, 2014).

The "glass cliff" which describes situations where women are assigned to positions associated with high risk of failure and criticism (Ryan, Haslam, & Postmes, 2007) is relevant to this discussion. Findings suggest that while stereotypically male attributes were most predictive of leader selection in a successful organization, stereotypically female attributes were most predictive in times of crisis. During the COVID-19 pandemic, however, women leaders who handled the high-risk fight against the coronavirus pandemic were more successful than their male counterparts in implementing social distancing and compliance protocols of quarantine and stay-at-home orders (Lee, 2020; Taub, 2020). Thus, events leading up to a selection or evaluation of leaders are just as important as their traits.

Diagnosing and Tracking Trusted Leadership Behavior

The trusted leadership questionnaire in Table 4.1 is designed to measure the dimensions that comprise the model in Figure 4.1. Since the level of analysis is individual (micro) rather than organizational (macro), honesty as a psychological capital, a straightforward and theoretically well-explained value through traditional principal-agent theory (Kaasa & Parts, 2013), is used to replace capability. The model configuration depicted in Figures 4.2 and 4.3 is an adaptation of the Competing Values Framework (Cameron, et al., 2014) with a construct validity well established in the literature (Belasen, 2008; Belasen & Frank, 2010). Research applications involving the use of the trusted leadership survey were also reported elsewhere (Belasen, 2016, 2017).

The survey questions in Table 4.1 address the extent to which managers focus on using inclusive leadership, are sensitive to stakeholders, whether they encourage feedback and joint decision-making, and how well they hold themselves to high ethical standards. The 40-item research instrument reflects the values associated with transparency, credibility, accountability, and honesty and consists of Likert-style response options with answers on a scale of 1 (I do not demonstrate this behavior) to 5 (I demonstrate this behavior to a great degree). Respondents are asked to answer the questions twice, first as a manifestation of their "actual" behavior, and second, as a reflection of their "desired" behavior. Examples of current and desired profiles are provided in Figures 4.2 and 4.3 consecutively.

Trusted Leadership Questionnaire

Rate each item on a scale from 1 to 5 where:

1 I do not demonstrate this behavior
2 I demonstrate this behavior to a small degree
3 I demonstrate this behavior to a moderate degree
4 I demonstrate this behavior frequently
5 I demonstrate this behavior to a great degree

Next, rate yourself again, this time by considering expectations from others that you specifically interact with (e.g., direct reports, people you coach or mentor, your supervisor, and so on) or by reflecting on how you would like to be perceived by others. Consider the gaps: Where do you need to change to become a trusted leader?

Figures 4.2 and 4.3 depict the ratings involving the actual behavior and the desired behavior. Understandably, the ratings in Figure 4.2, which denote current behaviors, are lower than the ratings in Figure 4.3, which represent future, expected, or desired behaviors. The gap between the two sets of ratings (see Figure 4.4) signifies opportunities for improvement.

Developing improvement strategies should also include several milestones and checkpoints when the survey may be taken again to see whether the gap has been eliminated. Another option is to obtain feedback from others and even allow board members to assess the attributes of the leader using the same survey. The differences between the self-assessment and assessment from others could be very revealing and should lead to a more valid and reliable understanding of the distance between behaviors and expectations. Subsequently, ideas and actions for improvement could be prioritized to reflect inputs from others and eventually lead to a better alignment between the leader's profile on the four dimensions and the ratings by others. Figure 4.4 transposes the two profiles to provide a single view of the gaps across the four domains of trusted leadership.

A leader's inability or incapacity to acknowledge the gap and initiate a shift from the current mindset or behavior to the acceptable level (one that is appreciated or recognized publicly) might potentially lead to failure. Trusted leadership is sustained through honesty and trustworthiness. When a top executive employs self-regulation and shows genuine concern for diversity or makes a personal sacrifice for others—a true form of trusted leadership emerges. Acting authentically, ensuring employees' safety, treating them with respect, and making sacrifices that benefit them generate a high level of commitment to the leader and organizational goals.

Table 4.1 Assessment: Trusted Leadership

	Actual	*Desired*
Transparency		
I feel my diversity goals are accepted by others		
I strive to achieve successful outcomes through inclusive leadership		
I pay close attention to how well I work with people		
I use a plan that is shared publicly and that guides the evaluation criteria		
I make sure that we understand each other's concerns		
I seek to understand the needs of my followers		
I revise my vision and goals based on inputs from diverse stakeholders		
Avg		
Credibility		
I am candid, honest, and openly express my thoughts and concerns		
I articulate shared goals and interests consistently		
I tell the truth with high conviction		
When I withhold information, I let people know the reason		
I consistently share personal commitments in the open		
I admit to personal mistakes and do not blame others for my failure		
I listen to my followers and peers attentively		
I welcome constructive criticism		
At times of change I remain open to new ideas		
I value feedback from others even if it negates my thinking		
I ask stakeholders for ideas to improve organizational performance		
Avg		
Accountability		
I clarify my actions to various stakeholders		
I encourage employees to explain our behavior to stakeholders		
I emphasize the importance of complying with regulations fairly and objectively		

(*Continued*)

Table 4.1 (Continued) Assessment: Trusted Leadership

	Actual	*Desired*
I strive to ensure that we openly and honestly share practices and outcomes		
I emphasize the obligation of carrying out government policies properly		
I ensure that we follow rules and procedures consistently and equitably		
I adhere to ethical codes of conduct		
I communicate and reinforce integrity guidelines		
I clarify the personal and collective consequences of misconduct		
I take responsibility for the outcomes of my decisions or behaviors		
I support diversity, equity, and inclusion goals		
Avg		
Honesty		
I am approachable when others need me		
I support giving back to the community		
I encourage everyone to participate in decision-making		
I act with respect for others		
I seek to meet others' expectation of me		
I hold myself and others to high ethical standards		
I put others' best interests above my own		
I have a thorough understanding of social values		
I would not compromise ethical principles to gain personal benefits		
I make sincere efforts to know about others' career goals		
I value honesty and equal opportunity		
Avg		

Adapted from: Belasen A. (2017). *Women in Management*.

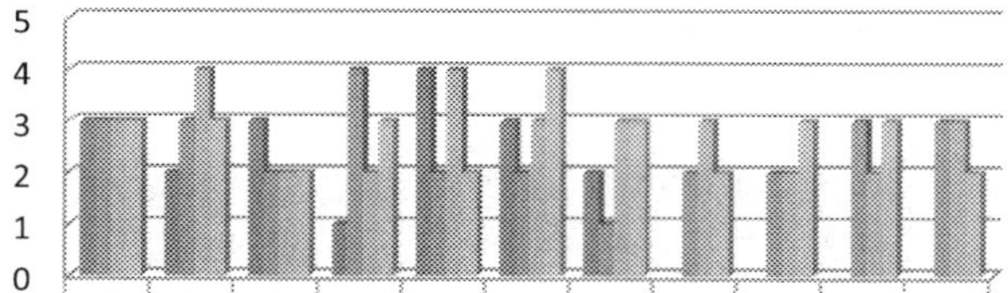

	1	2	3	4	5	6	7	8	9	10	11
TRANSPARENCY	3	2	3	1	4	3	2				
CREDIBILITY	3	3	2	4	2	2	1	2	2	3	3
ACCOUNTABILITY	3	4	2	2	4	3	3	3	2	2	3
HONESTY	3	3	2	3	2	4	3	2	3	3	2

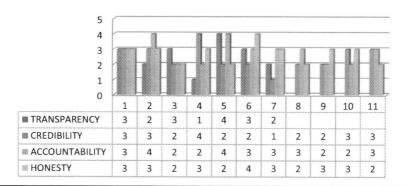

Figure 4.2 Current profile.

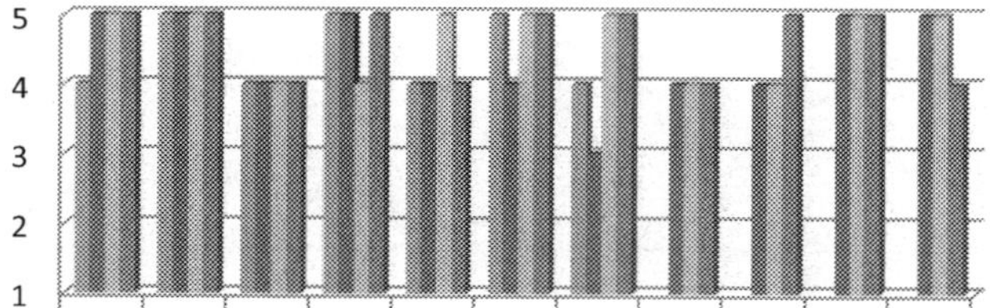

	1	2	3	4	5	6	7	8	9	10	11
TRANSPARENCY	4	5	4	5	4	5	4				
CREDIBILITY	5	5	4	5	4	4	3	4	4	5	5
ACCOUNTABILITY	5	5	4	4	5	5	5	4	4	5	5
HONESTY	5	5	4	5	4	5	5	4	5	5	4

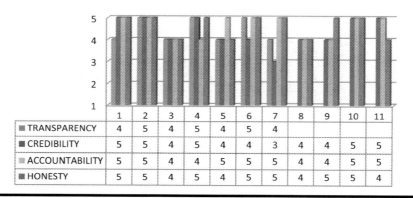

Figure 4.3 Desired profile.

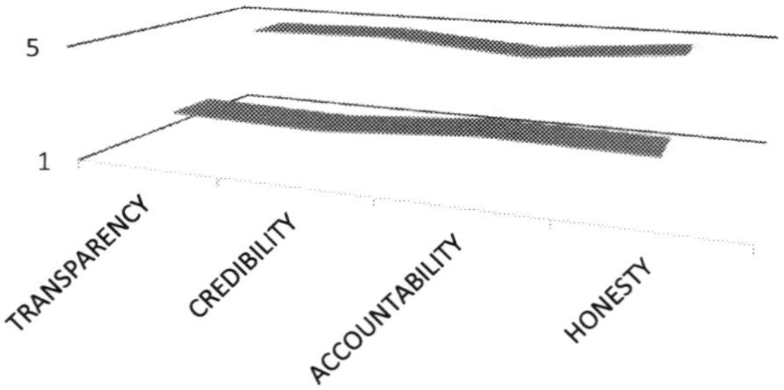

	TRANSPARENCY	CREDIBILITY	ACCOUNTABILITY	HONESTY
Current	2.57	2.45	2.81	2.72
Desired	4.65	4.75	4.35	4.8

Figure 4.4 Current and desired profiles.

Profile Awareness: Resisting Excess

The four dimensions that interlink these values and outcomes—transparency, credibility, accountability, and honesty—must be present simultaneously to increase the prospects for greater diversity and inclusiveness. A deficiency in **transparency** occurs when a leader is too inwardly focused, paying attention to operational and financial objectives, as well as to managing internal dynamics. While these are important matters and they cannot be ignored, the temptation among many leaders is to act with a sense of urgency rather than strategy. This is where excess (i.e., overemphasizing behaviors at the expense of other, equally important behaviors) can transform strengths into weaknesses. Refocusing behaviors on purposeful ideas as the basis for strengthening equity and fairness within the organization and for a good alignment of organizational values and stakeholders' views is at the core of trusted leadership.

Other leaders may experience a deficiency in **accountability**. This deficiency is usually marked by a tendency to shoot from the hip, resulting in making authoritative decisions without the benefit of input from affected stakeholders or all the available information. Executives who demonstrate lower levels of accountability need to resist the temptation to make decisions quickly, even though the urgent pressures of the moment may push them into deciding too quickly.

Unless the matter is extremely urgent and a decision absolutely must be made on the spot, leaders should pause and ask a few questions: Is there information or data to support the decision? What do we know? What don't we know? How long do we have to decide this? How long will it take to get the data? Who has it? Who is working on it? What is the risk and cost of making the wrong decision?

Deficiency in **honesty** may prove to be the most difficult to remedy, since it relies on the individual's emotional intelligence and the socio-psychological ability to empathize with others, especially followers. Bosses have tremendous impact on those who work in an organization. Recent surveys of employees have found extremely high levels of dissatisfaction with workplace environments. A poll by Gallup (2015) of more than 80,000 full- and part-time workers found that only 31.5% of employees are engaged and inspired at work. The vast majority—68.5%—are not engaged with their employers with severe consequences to organizational performance. Gallup (2018) shows that 53% of employees are in the "not engaged" category. They may be generally satisfied but are not cognitively and emotionally connected to their work and workplace.

Two years later, the percentage of "engaged" workers in the U.S.—those who are highly involved in, enthusiastic about, and committed to their work and workplace—reached 38% (Gallup, 2020). This is the highest it has been since Gallup began tracking the metric in 2000, and it has significant potential performance implications. But it also means that more can and should be done to improve employee engagement. Openness, honesty, authenticity, and mutual respect are great ways for building relationship in organizations.

The 2014 *Deloitte Global Human Capital Trends* report shows that 79% of business and HR leaders worldwide believe they have significant retention and engagement issues (Deloitte, 2014). Five years later, another report (Deloitte, 2019) showed that 80% of business and HR leaders worldwide indicated they need to develop leadership capabilities that can help to motivate and re-engage employees. Openness, honesty, authenticity, and mutual respect are great mitigations for building social capital in organizations.

Finally, leaders deficient in **credibility** often lose their reputation and ability to marshal resources for the common good. They are perceived as political and manipulative and unable to mobilize support for their vision and resort to making solo decisions. These leaders tend to withhold information and resort to secrecy and closed-door decisions. Credible leaders who lead by example in fostering healthy ethical climates characterized by transparency, trust, integrity, and high moral standards are not only true to themselves but also help others to become more ethical and trusted. To be recognized as authentic leaders, leaders must first evaluate their strengths and weaknesses, values and behavioral patterns, and the predominant ways they exercise influence. Authenticity is associated with heightened levels of self-awareness, self-clarity, and self-confidence.

Leaders practicing self-regulation must be mindful that the purpose of the analysis is to separate one's core values from modeled values that can result in skewing authentic acuteness.

> Self-regulation involves the exertion of self-control through (a) the setting of internal standards, which can be existing standards or newly formulated ones, (b) the evaluation of discrepancies between these standards and actual or potential outcomes, and (c) the identification of intended actions for resolving these discrepancies.
>
> **(Gardner, et al., 2005: 354)**

Trusted leaders understand that true leadership is a balancing act that requires strong sensitivity and communication skills. When leaders and followers alike are engaged in transparent, honest, accountable, and credible behaviors they also give more attention to self-reflection which can result in effective behavioral change. Leaders who consistently share information about themselves and the organization and who tie ethics and diversity to the long-term success of the organization build a culture of trust with followers and enhance organizational credibility with stakeholders. When people are entrusted with all the necessary information to make wise choices, they are likely to act responsibly and sustain a culture of higher purpose.

Mindfulness

Trusted leadership begins and ends as an important leadership responsibility. Responsible leaders are mindful of instilling the values of honesty, transparency, credibility, and accountability in the social fabric of the organization. In the end, we need leaders who draw heavily on self-regulation and ethical mindfulness. Mindfulness is a state of active awareness, a continual creation and refinement of these four values, an openness to new information, and a willingness to view contexts and respond to situations using multiple lenses of inquiry (Levinthal & Rerup, 2006).

Organizational leaders that pursue ethical mindfulness move from a leader-centric to leadership-centric approach focusing on excellence, ethics, role modeling, and endurance. Mindful leaders do not think of a binary "either-or," attaching mutually exclusive categories to people and values. Mutually exclusive categories often are the cause for leadership failure. Instead, trusted leaders spark mindful learning in others as an essential part of overcoming crises. Organizational members will be more likely to see the warning signals and failures in time to prevent, or at least reduce the damages of crises.

Mindfulness allows leaders to reframe the situation. Reframing brings into view the elements of the process and the ability to correct any deviations that may be out of place. When organizational members interact with trusted leaders who display self-regulatory behaviors, they also learn and subsequently follow such behaviors. Ethical mindfulness becomes a form of self-regulation that causes one to behave with an ethical consciousness from one decision or behavioral event to another. Self-regulation is associated with persistence in accomplishing goals and resistance against attempts that inhibit or hinder the achievement of goals.

Conclusions

The COVID-19 pandemic provides an opportunity for introspective analysis of leadership characteristics and traits that have been viewed by many as successful in combating the pandemic and restoring society and businesses to some degree of normalcy. Trusted leaders in the COVID-19 response have been caring, calm, empathetic, honest, and transparent in their communications and behavior with the media, public, and the employees they lead.

Trusted leadership is characterized by the absence of arrogance, pride, and deception. It is acting with honesty, transparency, credibility, and accountability and why so many women leaders were among the most successful leaders during the fight against COVID-19. It is acting unselfishly during crises and global pandemics (Kristof, 2020). Acknowledging women's leadership qualities in fighting crises and global pandemics enables countries and institutions to serve the people that rely on them, listen to their needs, give praise and recognition, show kindness, display true honesty, and be authentic.

There is a paucity of crisis leadership scholarship in general and few empirical studies that examine the role of women in leading businesses during a global crisis. From a population health perspective, promoting women to senior leadership positions during the

COVID-19 pandemic may help reduce deaths due to the infection and hasten economic recovery (Coscieme, et al., 2020). Utilizing the strengths of women and men in a collaborative and co-leadership strategy may also prove to be effective for healthcare management, the theme of the next chapter.

References

Arioglu, E. (2020). Female board members: The effect of director affiliation. *Gender in Management*, 35(2), 225–254. doi:10.1108/GM-05-2019-0080

Aziz, A. (2020). Edelman Trust Barometer Shows How Consumers Expect Brands to Step Up and Help Society During COVID-19. *Forbes*, April 14, Retrieved from https://www.forbes.com/sites/afdhelaziz/2020/04/14/edelman-trust-barometer-shows-how-consumers-expect-brands-to-step-up-and-help-society-during-covid19/#c2e86ca5e222

Badal, S., & Harter, J. K. (2014). Gender diversity, business-unit engagement, and performance. *Journal of Leadership and Organizational Studies*, 21(4), 354–365. doi:10.1177/1548051813504460

Belasen, A., & Frank, N. M. (2008). Competing values leadership: Quadrant roles and personality traits. *Leadership and Organizational Development Journal*, 29(2), 127–143.

Belasen, A. (2008). *The Theory and Practice of Corporate Communication*, Thousand Oaks, CA: Sage Publications.

Belasen, A., & Frank, N. M. (2010). A peek through the lens of the competing values framework: What managers communicate and how. *The Atlantic Journal of Communication*, 18, 280–296.

Belasen, A., & Frank, N. M. (2012). Using the competing values framework to evaluate the interactive effects of gender and personality traits on leadership roles. *The International Journal of Leadership Studies*, 7(2), 192–215.

Belasen, A. (2016). Deception and failure: Mitigating leader-centric behaviors. In A. Belasen & R. Toma (Eds.), *Confronting Corruption in Business: Trusted Leadership, Civic Engagement* (pp. 183–216), New York: Routledge.

Belasen, A. (2017). *Women in Management: A Framework for Sustainable Work-life Integration*, New York, NY: Routledge.

Belasen, A.T., & Belasen, A. R. (2019). The strategic value of integrated corporate Communication: Functions, social media, stakeholders. *International Journal of Strategic Communication*, 13, 4. doi:10.1080/1553118X.2019.1661842

Bremmer, I. (2020). The Best Global Responses to COVID-19 Pandemic. *Time*. June 12, Retrieved from https://time.com/5851633/best-global-responses-covid-19/

Cameron, K. S., Quinn, R. E., Degraff, J., & Thakor, A. V. (2014). *Competing Values* Leadership (2nd ed.). Northampton, MA: Edward Elgar Publishing.

Chen, J., Leung, W. S., Song, W., & Goergen M. (2019). Why female board representation matters: The role of female directors in reducing male CEO overconfidence. *Journal of Empirical Finance*, 53(C), 70–90.

CDC. (2016). Letter to Mr. Messner, April 15, 2016, Retrieved from https://www.marlerblog.com/files/2016/05/Blank-CDC-Letterhead-for-Outgoing-Correspondence.pdf

Coscieme, L., Fioramonti, L., & Trebeck, K. (2020). Women in Power: Countries with Female 10 Leaders Suffer Six Times Fewer COVID Deaths and Will Recover Sooner from Recession, Retrieved from https://www.opendemocracy.net/en/caneurope-make-it/women-power-countries-female-leaders-suffer-six-times-fewer-coviddeaths-and-will-recover-sooner-recession/

Dale, C. R., Welling, L., & Clearfield, C. (2020). How One Seattle Health System Is Managing the COVID-19 Crisis. *Harvard Business Review*, Retrieved from https://hbr.org/2020/04/how-one-seattle-health-system-is-managing-the-covid-19-crisis

Dame, J. (2014). The Four Keys to Being a Trusted Leader. *Harvard Business Review*, Retrieved from https://hbr.org/2014/03/the-four-keys-to-being-a-trusted-leader/

Deloitte. (2014). Global Human Capital Trends 2014, Retrieved from http://dupress.com/periodical/trends/global-human-capital-trends-2014

Deloitte. (2019). Leading the social enterprise: Reinvent with a human focus. *Deloitte Global Human Capital Trends*, Retrieved from https://www2.deloitte.com/content/dam/Deloitte/cz/Documents/human-capital/cz-hc-trends-reinvent-with-human-focus.pdf

Deloitte. (2020). Workforce Strategies for Post COVID Recovery, Retrieved from https://www2.deloitte.com/content/dam/Deloitte/us/Documents/about-deloitte/workforce-strategies-for-post-covid-19-recovery.pdf

Dilawar, S. M., Durrani, D. K., Li, X., & Anjum, M. A. (2021). Decision-making in highly stressful emergencies: The interactive effects of trait emotional intelligence. *Current Psychology*, 40, 2988–3005. https://doi.org/10.1007/s12144-019-00231-y

FORTUNE. (2017). Wall Street Sees Darks Days Ahead for Chipotle After Norovirus Outbreak in Virginia, by Lucinda Shen, July 19, Retrieved from https://fortune.com/2017/07/19/chipotle-stock-norovirus-outbreak/

Friedman, U. (2020 April). New Zealand's Prime Minister May Be the Most Effective Leader on the Planet. *The Atlantic*, Retrieved from https://www.theatlantic.com/politics/archive/2020/04/jacinda-ardern-new-zealand-leadership-coronavirus/610237/

Gallup. (2015). Majority of U.S. Employees Not Engaged Despite Gains in 2014, Retrieved from https://news.gallup.com/poll/181289/majority-employees-not-engaged-despite-gains-2014.aspx

Gallup (2018). Employee Engagement on the Rise in the U.S. by Jim Marter, August 26, Retrieved from https://news.gallup.com/poll/241649/employee-engagement-rise.aspx

Gallup. (2020). Historic Drop in Employee Engagement Follows Record Rise, Retrieved from https://www.gallup.com/workplace/313313/historic-drop-employee-engagement-follows-record-rise.aspx

Gardner, W., Avolio, B., Luthans, F., May, D., & Walumbwa, F. (2005). Can you see the real me? A self-based model of authentic leader and follower development. *The Leadership Quarterly*, 16(3), 343–372.

Graham, J. (2018). Vows to 'delete Uber' Weren't Just Talk: Uber Loses Market Share to Lyft After Year of Scandal, *USA Today*, USA TODAY, May 15, Retrieved from https://www.usatoday.com/story/tech/talkingtech/2018/05/15/uber-lost-market-share-lyft-after-year-scandals-emarketer-says/612348002/

Hass, R. (2020). The COVID-19 Crisis has Revealed Taiwan's Resilience. June 15. Retrieved from https://www.brookings.edu/blog/order-from-chaos/2020/06/15/the-covid-19-crisis-has-revealed-taiwans-resilience/

Ibarra, H., & Obodaru, O. (2008). Women and the Vision Thing. *Harvard Business Review*, 85(1), 40–47.

Isaac, M. (2017a). What You Need to Know About #DeleteUber, *The New York Times*, Retrieved from https://www.nytimes.com/2017/01/31/business/delete-uber.html.

Isaac, M. (2017b). Inside Uber's Aggressive, Unrestrained Workplace Culture, *The New York Times*, Retrieved from https://www.nytimes.com/2017/02/22/technology/uber-workplace-culture.html.

Kahn, W. A., Barton, M. A., & Fellows, S. (2013). Organizational crises and the disturbance of relational systems. *The Academy of Management Review*, 38(3), 377–396. doi:10.5465/amr.2011.0363

Kaasa, A., & Parts, E. (2013). Honesty and trust: Integrating the values of individuals, organizations, and the society. In T. Vissak & M. Vadi (Ed.), *(Dis)Honesty in Management* (Advanced Series in Management, Vol. 10, pp. 37–58), Bingley: Emerald Group Publishing Limited.

König, A., Graf-Vlachy, L., Bundy, J., & Little, L. M. (2020). A blessing and a curse: How CEOs' trait empathy affects their management of organizational crises. *Academy of Management Review*, 45(1), 130–153.

Korn Ferry Hay Group. (2016). New Research Shows Women are Better at Using Soft Skills Crucial for Effective Leadership and Superior Business Performance. March 07, Retrieved from https://www.businesswire.com/news/home/20160307005205/en/ (accessed on 15 February 2020).

Kristof, N. (2020). What the Pandemic Reveals About The Male Ego, *The New York Times*, Retrieved from https://www.nytimes.com/2020/06/13/opinion/sunday/women-leaders-coronavirus.html

Lee, B. (2020). The Coronavirus Crisis is Proving We Need More Women Governors and Mayors, *Newsweek*. April 21, Retrieved from https://www.newsweek.com/coronavirus-crisis-proving-weneed-more-women-governors-mayors-opinion-1496897.

Levinthal, D., & Rerup, C. (2006). Crossing an apparent chasm: Bridging mindful and less-mindful perspectives on organizational learning. *Organization Science*, 17(4), 502–513.

Moreno-Gómez, J., Lafuente, E., & Vaillant, Y. (2018). Gender diversity in the board, women's leadership and business performance. *Gender in Management*, 33(2), 104–122. doi:10.1108/GM-05-2017-0058

Nimbs-Nyce, C. (2020). Four Leaders Who Acted Swiftly. *The Atlantic Daily*, April 21, Retrieved from https://www.theatlantic.com/newsletters/archive/2020/04/ardern-merkel-breed-newsom/610351/

Ocklenburg, S. (2020). The Merkel Effect: How Leadership Reduces COVID-19 Anxiety, *Psychology Today*. June 3, Retrieved from https://www.psychologytoday.com/us/blog/the-asymmetric-brain/202006/the-merkel-effect-how-leadership-reduces-covid-19-anxiety

Petriglieri, G. (2020). The Psychology Behind Effective Crisis Leadership, April 22, *Harvard Business Review*, Retrieved from https://hbr.org/2020/04/the-psychology-behind-effective-crisis-leadership

Quah, D. (2020). Singapore's policy response to COVID-19, in Richard Baldwin & Beatrice. In Weder di Mauro (Ed.), *Mitigating the COVID Economic Crisis: Act Fast and Do Whatever It Takes* (pp. 103–111), London: CEPR Press.

Rueckert, L. (2011). Gender differences in empathy. *Psychology of Empathy*, 2, 221–234.

Ryan, M. K., Haslam, S. A., & Postmes, T. (2007). Reactions to the glass cliff; Gender differences in the explanations for the precariousness of women's leadership positions. *Journal of Organizational Change Management*, 20(2), 182–197.

Simpson, R., Ross-Smith, A., & Lewis, P. (2010). Merit, special contribution and choice: How women negotiate between sameness and difference in their organizational lives. *Gender in Management: An International Journal*, 25(3), 198–207.

Taub, A. (May 15, 2020). Why are Women-Led Nations Doing Better with COVID-19? *New York Times*, Retrived from https://www.nytimes.com/2020/05/15/world/coronavirus-women-leaders.html (Accessed on June 22, 2020).

Tomova, L., von Dawans, B., Heinrichs, M., Silani, G., & Lamm C. (2014). Is stress affecting our ability to tune into others? Evidence for gender differences in the effects of stress on self-other distinction. *Psychoneuroendocrinology*, 43, 95–104.

Wei, S. L. (2020). Ten keys to beating back COVID-19 and the associated economic pandemic. In R. Baldwin & B. Weder di Mauro (Eds.), *Mitigating the COVID Economic Crisis: Act Fast and Do Whatever It Takes* (pp. 71–76), London: CEPR Press.

Chapter 5

Enhancing Resilience through Inclusive Leadership

The sweeping changes in the complex healthcare environment and the need to embrace population health management, interprofessional cooperation, and accountable care are transforming the way healthcare is delivered, managed, and led.

Building a culture of diversity, inclusion, and collaboration, so essential for the success of integrated health networks, begins at the top. However, gender disparity is still prevalent in senior healthcare positions even though women continue to play a critical role in strengthening the integration of health services.

Women are significantly less likely to be promoted to senior healthcare management, and in most cases, even after controlling for individual- and organizational-level characteristics. When promoted, however, women more often than men are assigned to HR, marketing, risk, legal, and nursing that, while vital for the success of healthcare, are not perceived as high-profile, strategic service lines. Women leaders can sit at the table, but without the high-impact, strategic responsibilities.

The evidence is mind boggling. Women comprise 77% of all hospital employees, make up 92% of nursing students, and 50.7% of med students in American medical schools (Boyle, 2019). Yet, women are markedly underrepresented in healthcare executive suites and boardrooms (Hauser, 2014), comprising 13% of CEOs, 23% of CFOs, 29% of COOS, 24% of CIOs, and 22% of BOD members (Wyman, 2019).

A study of 55,000 professionals across 90 countries and all levels of management by the Korn Ferry Hay Group (2016) revealed that women outperformed men in 11 of 12 key emotional intelligence competencies. The greatest difference was in emotional self-awareness, where women were 86% more likely than men to use the competency consistently. Other competencies in which women outperformed men included empathy, coaching and

DOI: 10.4324/9781003190929-5

mentoring, influence, inspirational leadership, conflict management, organizational awareness, adaptability, teamwork, and achievement orientation.

How can the gap between mounting evidence of resilient women's leadership, discussed in Chapter 4, and the shortfall of women's representation in healthcare senior management be bridged? If women are better than or as good as men on most competency evaluation criteria (Belasen, 2017) and leadership qualities and if men excel primarily on traits associated with agentic behaviors—how can we explain the discrepancy between desired leadership qualities and the shunning of talented women?

This chapter focuses on gender diversity within the context of management and leadership in health systems. It describes an inclusive co-leadership model with distinct and overlapping roles, which inspires administrative and clinical leaders to collaborate and build resilience in healthcare leadership. This is an untapped but promising option for win–win outcomes: Increasing healthcare system efficiency by promoting the inclusion of women in senior roles and tapping into the leadership skills and expertise that women bring to these roles.

Stereotypical Barriers and Unconscious Biases

Behavioral scientists observed that longstanding unconscious gender bias has made it quite difficult to judge facts and evaluate attributes of effective leadership objectively. Often women may be judged unfairly (e.g., less competent, less experienced) or penalized for direct, explicit forms of assertiveness, such as negotiating for a promotion or higher salary or even if their behavior is identical to their male colleagues. When women display assertive and competitive behaviors, they are often judged as being too tough, abrasive, or not supportive of others. Women are judged against predominantly male norms, often eliciting negative evaluations about their behaviors and performance. When gendered organizations value the disembodied employee, the expectations are for women to fit this male-normed mold regardless of the perceived incongruity between stereotyping and women's roles in leadership positions.

The perceived incongruity could lead to two forms of prejudice: A less favorable evaluation of women's fitness for leadership roles, and a less favorable evaluation of the actual leadership behavior displayed by women because agentic behavior is perceived as less desirable in women than men. When women perform leadership roles they are often perceived as having violated their stereotypically prescribed feminine roles.

Existing structures of pay and reward systems tend to reinforce this incongruity—women are judged less favorably than men despite exhibiting similar role behaviors and accomplishments. Male contributions are measured in terms of bottom-line results and numeric values such as ROI and ROE. Binary measures of success, aggressive behavior, and competitiveness are overvalued and overemphasized. Traditional women's strengths such as maintaining relationships, resolving conflicts, sharing power, caring for employees, and reaching a consensus, especially in times of crisis, tend to be overlooked and undervalued.

Good communication skills, collaboration, mentoring, and developing others are important but less significant than quantitative measures of success—bottom-line factors that are used to reward male managers. Women are particularly vulnerable to these evaluative biases when they work in male-dominated settings. Female managers reportedly need to work harder to persuade senior managers to see their side of arguments, while male managers can negotiate, bargain, and obtain concessions. Feminine traits such as concern for others (relatedness), a consensual approach to decision-making, and consideration of feelings for others (empathy) prior to initiating action are less important in performance appraisal. This is problematic for several reasons.

In the healthcare field, interpersonal skills are key to better outcomes (Swensen & Mohta, 2017), and female CEOs were found to improve the interpersonal care experience faster than male CEOs, particularly in large urban environments and high-volume hospital facilities (Silvera & Clark, 2019). Diversity that starts at the top and trickles down to all levels of management was also found to improve healthcare financial performance and ensure stakeholder alignment (Fontenot, 2012).

Organizations, particularly those that are male-dominated, are not gender-neutral—they reflect settings in which women's behavior and accomplishments are scrutinized, measured, and evaluated differently from men. Success becomes increasingly challenging in organizations with bosses that see loyalty and "fit effects" as determinants in performance evaluation and promotion decisions. Humans tend to lean towards the axiom of "birds of a feather flock together."

Neuro-physiology research has shown that the lower portion of a brain region called the "medial prefrontal cortex" (MPFC) is active when people are focusing on themselves or when they are liked by others (Highfield, 2008). The upper portion of the MPFC indicates judgments about different people, especially when they are not "look alike." Because the MPFC plays a role in when we think about ourselves, research suggests that we empathize more easily with what is going through the minds of those of the same socio-cultural or political orientation, and see them as we see ourselves, rather than build up a judgment on a range of objective knowledge about a person.

The powerful impact of unconscious biases against women was also found among both male and female senior scientists, who noted that the bias was so deeply entrenched that they were unable to maintain complete objectivity when a study proved that each of them was more inclined to hire, mentor, and propose higher pay, when the same candidate for a vacancy was identified as John rather than Jennifer (Moss-Racusin, et al., 2012). This also reaffirms the agreement among researchers that gender bias is often an outcome of an implicit cognitive process in which pervasive gender stereotypes shape personal judgment, regardless of intention. Moss-Racusin confirmed that the participants in her study were likely unaware they were discriminating against Jennifer.

Social relationships are heavily influenced and constrained by homogeneity and prototypical attributes, which notably include gender. Many studies cite roadblocks to women's career advancement including lack of experience in line management which makes them ideal candidates for broader general management roles, exclusion from informal networks, stereotypes about women's roles and abilities, failure of senior executives to sponsor high-potential women, and inflexible work schedules that restrict women's commitment to personal/family responsibilities.

Gender diversity at the top is a necessity for businesses today. With the persistence of gender disparity on companies' boardrooms and executive suites, innovation and creativity might be stifled or suppressed in favor of alternative males' views. Having more women on boards and management teams may give companies unique and fresh ideas and promote better connections between consumers and employees. Firms with more women in the C-suite were also found to be more profitable.

According to the index provider MSCI (2016), companies with strong women leadership, three or more women on governing boards, or a female CEO and at least one other female board member, enjoy a 10.1% return on equity per year as compared to 7.4% for those without women in senior leadership. Gender-diverse boards are also associated with less aggressive investment policies, better acquisition decisions, reduced negative impact of crises on firm performance, and improved financial outcomes for firms operating in industries with a high prevalence of executive overconfidence (Chen, et al., 2019).

Because women have a strong influence on consumers' decision-making behavior, companies would benefit from having more women at the top as knowledge about needs and preferences of consumers can be translated into successful marketing messages and imagery. The healthcare field is a case in point—women drive 80% of consumer purchasing choices and usage decisions through a combination of their buying power and influence. Yet women continue to be underrepresented in senior healthcare management positions (LaPierre & Zimmerman, 2012; Wyman, 2019).

Inclusive Leadership

It is not enough to understand the impediments to the representation of women in senior management and agree that something needs to be done. If the goal is an effective and profitable healthcare organization, we clearly must ameliorate gender disparity in senior positions with women's representation in key strategic roles. There must also be the motivation to act and the appropriate structures in place to drive change.

An important pathway for shifting the gender pendulum is adopting an inclusive leadership model. The common, command-and-control style, the single authority line at the top or from the middle out, typically led by a non-clinical administrator, is inadequate for handling intricate tasks in health systems that are increasingly becoming more complex and matrixed (Health Research and Educational Trust, 2014). Contrast the traditional leadership approach with the more diverse and inclusive leadership model that makes better decisions up to 87% of the time, is faster 50% of the time, and delivers 60% better results (Larson, 2017).

The entrenched administrative leadership, which drives healthcare strategic planning, creates unclear reporting lines and misalignments between system-level physician leaders and settings such as medical groups and clinically integrated networks. Would it be beneficial to use a co-leadership structure which pairs physicians and nurses with administrators in a way that also responds to the dual needs of equality and efficiency?

Co-leadership could operate in multiple locations in health systems including upper echelon (e.g., CMO, CQO), divisions of care providers (e.g., RPCN, health centers), and service lines (e.g., cardiovascular, orthopedics, cancer care). In acute care hospitals, individuals in potentially transforming leadership roles are board chairpersons and directors, CEOs, operating, nursing, and medical officers as well as unit managers. In nursing homes, such leadership can come from facility owners, administrators, directors of nursing, and managers.

CHRISTUS Santa Rosa Health System announced it is adopting the dyad leadership model at CHRISTUS Santa Rosa Hospital–Medical Center (CSRH–MC), with two key leaders taking a focused approach to maximize the greatest opportunity for operational efficiency and to cement greater physician alignment and leadership for quality patient outcomes. The partners to the dyad are Dr. Ian Thompson, Jr.President, CSRH–MC, and Vice President Market Oncology Service Line; and Asha Rodriguez, Administrator, CSRH–MC. Ms. Rodriguez has worked in both healthcare and education for the last 16 years. Rodriguez has served as the Interim President at CSRH–MC since July 2016. Under her leadership, she managed ancillary operations, special projects, and facility planning.

(Definitive Healthcare, 2016)

Two variants of co-leadership structures in healthcare are *dyads* and *triads*, and both have the potential to transform hospitals and healthcare organizations. A survey of 868 Insights Council members by the *New England Journal of Medicine* (Swensen & Mohta, 2017) found that 72% use a dyad leadership model in their organizations and 85% believe that the dyad works effectively. The triad has also been found to be a highly functioning leadership structure with improved outcomes (Batcheller, 2016).

In the *dyad*, the co-equal partners, an administrator and a physician, bring diverse perspectives to create win–win outcomes. Administrators bring business skills essential for managing productivity and cost-effective delivery of care to health populations. Physicians bring clinical expertise for determining health initiatives, providing high-value patient care, assuring quality and patient safety, and assessing clinical outcomes.

In the *triad*, the value of nurse management to patient care and in improving hospital quality and efficiency is promoted via shared leadership in a physician-nurse-administrator partnership. Through a relational approach to leading, dyads and triads leverage the partners' synergy to achieve common strategic goals and advance the mission of the organization.

The partners in the co-leadership structure are advocates and supporters of each other and rely on open and honest interpersonal communication. After all, the exercise of leadership is about having strong interaction skills and a high degree of emotional intelligence, potential pathways for an increased understanding of social influence.

Synergistic Effects

The most effective dyads assume roles that are complementary and synergistic. Common leadership roles in health systems include the *Health Innovator Value Strategist*, *Clinical Integration Champion*, and *Patient Advocate*. The roles span target areas such as *Population Health*, *Financial Management*, *Clinical Integration*, and *Patient Engagement* (Belasen, 2019). While physicians' relative strengths are reflected through the *Patient Advocate* and *CI Champion roles*, administrators' strengths carry relatively more weight with the *Value Strategist* and *Health Innovator* roles.

When the co-leaders collaborate through the formal mechanism of the dyad, their combined roles and skills help mitigate personal shortcomings, adding strategic value to their overall strength. Together, these roles and responsibilities incorporate important facets of hospital performance management and provide co-leaders with additional opportunities to develop competencies and move up the career ladder as well as receive increased recognition for their competence.

As one examines the individual and shared roles of co-leaders (Table 5.1), the relevance of co-leadership for responding effectively to diverse stakeholders and for improving quality and patient safety across the continuum of care becomes clear. Physician leaders promote teamwork, self-direction, interfunctional collaboration, and joint accountability. They encourage care teams to meet broad population health and emerging goals.

At the same time, administrative control is needed to achieve tighter integration and higher operating efficiencies across allied partners and affiliates. Administrators are tasked

Table 5.1 Roles and Selected Responsibilities

Target: ***Population Health*** **Role:** ***Health Innovator***		
Administrator	**Shared**	**Physician**
Establishing collaborative partnerships, joint ventures, and affiliations that add expertise and scope	Creating partnerships and initiating post-acute integration strategies to improve care continuum	Improving care quality and patient safety through interfunctional collaboration and innovative solutions
Delivering services across the continuum of care at an affordable cost and appropriate quality to the community	Transforming care from episodic to value-focused, and provide meaningful coordination across the continuum of care	Improving care coordination and communication among clinicians, patients, and patients' families; engaging patients in shared decision-making
Target: ***Financial Performance*** **Role:** ***Value Strategist***		
Administrator	**Shared**	**Physician**
Scaling clinically integrated provider networks and care systems	Expanding market share for ambulatory surgery centers (ASCs) and outpatient procedure	Engaging in the revenue cycle process
Evaluating accounting and information systems and methods; monitoring KPIs	Creating new service lines and revenue streams to increase profitability	Reducing risk and ensuring high-value care is delivered promoting higher rates of utilization
Conducting competitor strategic analysis; evaluating market share performance	Developing and implementing strategic plans	Recruiting physicians to support growth and patient loyalty
Target: ***Clinical Integration*** **Role:** ***Clinical Integration Champion***		
Administrator	**Shared**	**Physician**
Integrating IT systems and managing health informatics	Optimizing clinical informatics and data analytics systems including design, transparency, patient care and quality, and compliance	Promoting teamwork and improving interprofessional collaboration

(Continued)

Table 5.1 (Continued) Roles and Selected Responsibilities

Improving cost containment and efficiency	Increasing rate of interoperability to improve quality and reduce cost	Providing high-value care by incorporating evidence-based information into patient diagnosis and treatment
Ensuring compliance with medical and legal regulations and internal policies	Using analytics to improve coordination of care optimizing	Keeping physicians informed about EHR implementation and securing physician buy-in to ongoing improvement projects involving clinical and operational integration
Target: *Patient Engagement*	**Role: *Patient Advocate***	
Administrator	**Shared**	**Physician**
Providing resources for training and development	Improving teamwork training and interpersonal skill building	Engaging physicians and patients in lowering clinical variation
Enhancing hospital ratings and reputation	Increasing patient satisfaction and quality outcomes; reducing readmissions	Tracking physician adherence with evidence-based practices
		Improving provider–patient communications

Adapted from Belasen A. (2019). *Dyad Leadership.*

with aligning structures and processes, achieving internal consistency, applying proven solutions to problems, setting performance targets, monitoring implementation, and tracking results.

The co-leadership roles converge at the need to align socio-technical systems (e.g., care teams, IT capabilities, minimizing clinical variation) to increase quality and reduce the per capita cost of care for populations. Externally, the partners focus on stakeholders (e.g., regulators, communities, affiliates) to ensure a healthy revenue cycle and strategic growth by improving ambulatory access, strengthening primary care alignment, and streamlining services for population health. Internally, the partners strive to align clinical practices and services to ensure that the system operates reliably and complies effectively with laws and regulations, and that resources are allocated based on community health needs.

Thomas Deering, MD, chief of Clinical Centers of Excellence and the Arrhythmia Center of Excellence at Piedmont Heart Institute, and his partner, Katie Lund, say:

> We work together as a team to create a better product that looks at everything from the whole perspective ... We learn from each other so that I become more administrative and my dyad partner becomes more clinical and understands the subtleties a little more.

A productive partnership can help quell another concern sometimes voiced over dyad rule: Who is really in charge? Jennifer Zelensky, executive director at Providence Heart and Vascular Institute in Oregon and a dyad co-leader, maintains that she and her physician partner are "reasonably interchangeable," adding:

> He can go to certain meetings, and I can go to others and people know that we're in sync. If an issue arises over medical quality, he's much more the lead, whereas if it is about budget or long-range financial plans, it is clear I am on-point.

(Young, 2017)

Women and Men in Co-Leadership Roles

The co-leadership model raises the level of engagement throughout the organization and supports the inclusion of women, the expertise, and valuable skills they bring to executive dyads, triads, and other leadership roles. Women administrators have the necessary business skills for providing cost-effective, sustainable delivery of care to broad populations. Women physicians have clinical expertise for ascertaining population health initiatives, caring for patients, and evaluating health outcomes and patient experiences by measuring clinical outcomes.

After a nationwide search, CHRISTUS Health selected Cris Daskevich, FACHE, as Chief Executive Officer at the Children's Hospital of San Antonio. As part of the strategy to elevate the status of the Children's Hospital of San Antonio along with pediatric and maternal services within CHRISTUS Health, Daskevich also served as Senior Vice President of Maternal Services for the CHRISTUS Health system in the U.S. and Latin America. She is joined by Charles Hankins, MD, President and Chief Medical Officer at the Children's Hospital of San Antonio. Together, they are part of a dyad leadership model which has proven to be effective in ensuring strategy and decision-making are done jointly by taking advantage of both physician and administrative leadership expertise with insight into clinical, administrative, and support operations. In their roles with the Children's Hospital of San Antonio, Daskevich and Hankins provide experience and leadership as CHRISTUS continues its strategic growth and development of maternal and pediatric services. They also oversee facility and ambulatory expansion throughout the community, including the recruitment of pediatric and maternal fetal medicine specialists through partnership with Baylor College of Medicine. Of great importance, they spend significant time and effort working with physicians and clinicians to accelerate clinical program development and maximize access to the communities they serve.

> *Cris Daskevich*: It has been really a wonderful relationship for us in that we bring similar skill sets to the table, but we also have very different skill sets with Dr. Hankins having clinical experience as a physician and neonatologist and my background in operations in pediatrics and women's health. We worked together previously for 15 years so we know each other well; we trust one another. Our relationship here allows us to divide and conquer and it brings different perspectives to complex problems. We also are providing a model for throughout the hospital so every physician who is in a leadership role is comfortable with having an administrative partner.

(Petty, 2019)

When diverse strengths are combined, men and women dyad partners can rely on their complementary skills to respond well to their task environment. Furthermore, involving physician leaders in operational and strategic decision-making increases their commitment to the organization's mission and aligns them well with the shared vision. Trust between physician leaders and administrative leaders is based on transparent communication and reciprocal exchanges of information—the key for a successful collaboration (Oostra, 2016).

Co-leadership promotes robust management structures by providing broader competence, continuous learning, and joint responsibility for clinical services. Co-leaders create synergistic work environments that promote trust and interprofessional collaboration with the mutual understanding of when to lead and when to step back and let others do so. Co-leadership enables the promotion of women to leadership positions, accelerates gender parity at the top, and improves the recruitment and retention of women leaders. The model is workable when

- Women are included on all search and promotion committees for senior leadership positions. Of course, recruitment and selection processes for medical leadership positions must be transparent to avoid the impression that they are subversive or

politicized, selecting for those who are most visible rather than those who are most qualified (Roth, et al., 2016).
  - However, be aware of the relative burden on women in the workforce: If only a small proportion of the workforce is women, these women will need to serve on many or all search committees while men only serve on a small fraction.
- The roles, qualifications, expectations, and evaluation criteria of formal leadership positions are equitable and transparent, and unconscious biases that affect performance reviews and promotions and that contribute to gender imbalance are carefully monitored and managed. As noted by the Korn Ferry consulting group (2019), 55% of the healthcare executives in their sample indicated that women in their organizations have been passed over for an opportunity or promotion based on their gender.
  - Remember, however, that women also exhibit bias towards other women like men do (Hoffmann & Musch, 2018).
- The partners in the dyad or triad build trusting relationships and mutual respect.
- Focus is on coaching rather than resolving disagreements or poor accountability.
- Operational and strategic decisions are shared by both sides.
- Mentorship and sponsorship programs are available to help navigate relationships and clarify issues.
- Flexible work arrangements are available to facilitate improvements in women's representation in leadership.
- Team building and leadership development programs exist to overcome potential conflicts and mitigate subtle and informal differences of power between the two leaders.
- A culture of collaboration is cultivated where the co-equal partners are in lockstep with each other, identify the best way to synergize, and build on each other's strength to bring about a transformative experience (Belasen, et al., 2021).

By adopting an inclusive co-leadership structure, health systems align themselves strategically to accomplish the *Quadruple Aim* of enhancing the patient experience of care, reducing the per capita cost of healthcare, improving the health of populations, and fostering work satisfaction, member engagement, and retention of talent.

Roadmap for Development

The reality for most women and men in organizations is that they must find ways to collaborate and share key strategic and operational responsibilities—and they may do so in ways that could bring multiple benefits (e.g., less socio-economic costs, more equitable rewards, greater mutual respect). Why not pursue that goal as a win–win solution through co-leadership structures? Celebrating the success stories of women and men who share co-leadership roles and manage to balance multiple responsibilities in ways that are fulfilling and challenging amplifies their achievements, facilitates peer learning, and champions similar experiences across industries.

While the co-leadership can help accelerate the development of women leaders in healthcare settings, it might also help reverse the trend of what is holding women back from assuming leadership roles and how to further accelerate gender parity in medicine (Mangurian, et al., 2018).

The survey in Table 5.2 can help organizational members evaluate perceived gaps in their behaviors and organizational diversity practices. Reflecting on institutional and organizational constraints, and cultural and personal biases, the survey gives respondents a chance to assess equity and gender equality gaps through self-understanding (Figure 5.1) and taking back control (Figure 5.2). . Respondents can also look at Figure 5.2 as the desired situation and employ development strategies to close the gender diversity gap and improve quality of work-life.

To sustain gender parity, successful strategies for women leaders include sponsorship, mentoring, learning, coaching, visibility, confidence, and development. These strategies are discussed below (Belasen, et al., 2021).

Identify an active sponsor within or outside the organization. Active advocacy by willing sponsors can help women to navigate their career paths, overcome bureaucratic hurdles, gain social support, and follow through on development of networking and human capital skills. Seeking out sponsors is not a sign of weakness but a way to level the playing field. Men often have access to networks and sponsors in spaces from which women are excluded. Active sponsors that guide and coach the development of physician leaders, for example, can help accelerate the progressive learning of dyad or triad physician leaders.

Get a transformational mentor. A transformational mentor can help facilitate the attainment of women's self-development and self-clarity. Mentoring can go beyond a one-on-one relationship. Mentoring can take shape in a group setting with peer mentoring and with reciprocal relationships in which everyone in the group is a mentor and a mentee. Mentoring can also help raise women's visibility and exposure to key people and projects with limited access.

Pursue peer learning. Working side-by-side with business managers or experienced physicians, who often serve as transformational mentors or role models for aspiring women leaders could become a valuable learning experience.

Seek out professional coaching. Effective coaching can help boost personal efficacy and self-confidence. Coaching has the potential to improve individual and team performance, retain leadership talent, support succession planning, and help healthcare leaders meet professional and personal goals.

Enhance your visibility. Proactively pursue high-profile, high-visibility projects of strategic value. Since the system of promotion puts additional weight on those that are more

Table 5.2 Assessment: Perceptual Gaps—Diversity and Inclusion

Rate each item from 1 to 5:
5—Strongly agree
4—Agree
3—Uncertain
2—Disagree
1—Strongly disagree

Personal (Self-Identity, Self-Confidence)

1. I feel confident when performing my job
2. I feel quite secure about my relationships with others
3. I feel that my work allows me to succeed
4. People can speak up and voice their opinions frankly without fear of being punished
5. I feel empowered and supported by peers and supervisors
6. I identify my values with the values of the organization
7. I feel affiliated with my organization
8. Overall, I would say my morale on the job is high
9. I plan to stay with this organization for the foreseeable future

Institutional (Flexible Schedule, Meaningful Work)

10. My organization allows a flextime option
11. I can do my job from home
12. I am involved in making decisions that affect work
13. Conditions on my job allow me to be as productive as I could be
14. My work environment is good and highly motivating
15. Taking time off during work to take care of personal or family matters is tolerated
16. I feel empowered in fulfilling my managerial duties
17. I get personal satisfaction from my work
18. The organization offers me opportunities to grow and apply my skills

Cultural (Removing Barriers, Achieving Parity)

19. I have open channels to executives
20. The wage policies adopted by my organization are fair
21. The exchange of communication within the organization is transparent
22. I feel safe around people in my organization
23. I am treated fairly and respectfully
24. The culture and values in my organization are based on honesty and integrity
25. I feel that I am given an adequate and fair compensation for the work I do
26. People have an equal chance to get ahead in this organization regardless of gender
27. I am not discriminated in my job because of my gender

Organizational (Promoting Role Congruence, Retaining Key Positions)

28. My organization does a good job of linking rewards to job performance
29. My supervisor handles performance problems constructively and objectively
30. Promotions in my organization are handled fairly
31. My supervisor shows appreciation for the contribution I make
32. My performance is evaluated objectively and positively
33. I am not judged or discredited when performing my leadership role
34. I have equal opportunity to climb up the hierarchy in my organization
35. Coaching by female mentors is available in my organization
36. My contributions are highly appreciated by men and women in my organization

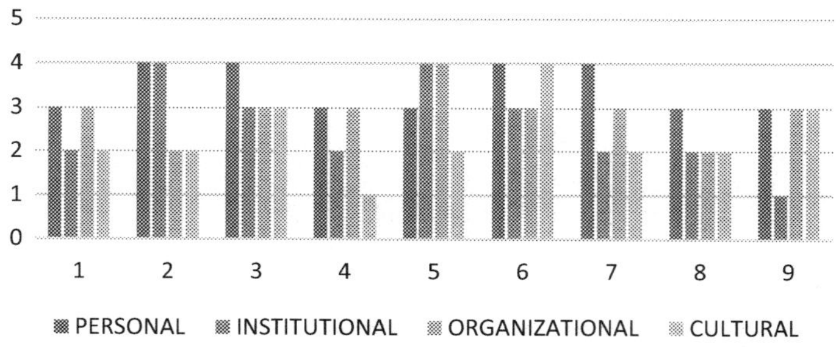

Figure 5.1 Assessment 1 Actual.

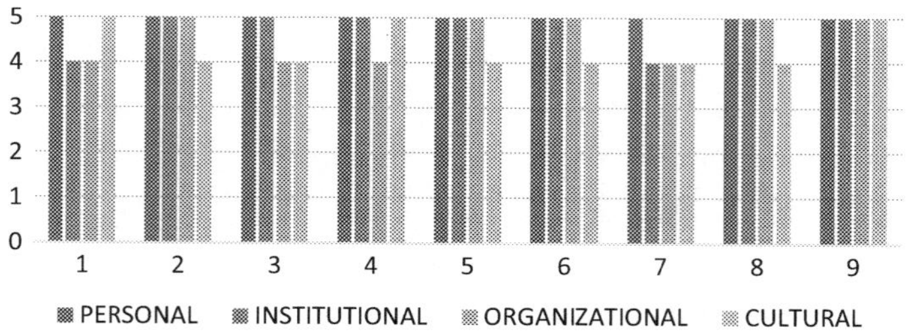

Figure 5.2 Assessment 2 Desired.

visible, not only on those best qualified, high-potential women should expand their network of peers and enhance their visibility through proximity to senior executives. Aspiring women leaders can leverage their best talents and their professional relationships with allies and mentors to ensure successful outcomes.

Reclaim your self-confidence. Recognize that success correlates just as closely with confidence as it does with competence. As studies show, women tend to have lower confidence than men with similar or lesser levels of competence (Cech, et al., 2011). Impostor syndrome can be overcome by recognizing its existence and reinforcing individual value. Regain professional role confidence by focusing on specialized knowledge and by realigning interests and expectations with career opportunities. Pay forward by leveraging success to advocate for or coach early-career women. And if you can, mentor an aspiring male leader to signify the view that women's talents are perceptible and add value to individual and organizational performance (Anderson, 2020).

Participate in a leadership development micro-credential for impact. Many schools of business offer workshops or leadership micro-credentials that emphasize strategic thinking and acting, talent development, and building self-confidence. Aspiring women executives will learn to promote themselves and move successfully towards the highest levels of corporate leadership.

Most employers will also benefit from sponsoring women in these micro-credentials.

Focused leadership development programs combine instruction by faculty and seasoned corporate leaders with interactive lessons and experiential learning activities aimed at improving women's leadership behaviors.

Tools may include:

- Assessment of strengths and weaknesses
- Conceptual frameworks of thinking
- Analysis of case situations
- Sharing of best practices
- Applications and takeaways

Critical emotional intelligence (EI) skills include:

- Developing self-awareness
- Identifying personal traits
- Reviewing personal strengths and weaknesses
- Assessing the relationship between personal traits and leadership styles
- Exploring the alignment between leadership roles and organizational goals
- Learning to adjust roles and skills during organizational transitions
- Discovering the power of understanding paradoxes
- Learning to overcome judgmental biases in executive decision-making processes

Functional and strategic skills include:

- Discovering the fundamentals of business strategy
- Identifying and exploiting opportunities to create value
- Using methods for marketing segmentation, targeting, and positioning
- Learning to review financial statements critically
- Learning how to interpret the balanced scorecard strategically
- Understanding the relationship between finance and the broader business strategies

Critical social intelligence (SI) skills

- Discovering your networking skills
- Practicing strong EI and SI skills to enhance personal confidence
- Increasing your visibility
- Learning to work with active mentors and identifying effective sponsors
- Practicing negotiation and influence skills

- Exploring sources of power and methods for resolving conflicts
- Analyzing team composition to discover the value of high-performing teams

Dyads and triads, action pathways for change, create a clinical leadership development pipeline, which facilitates the development of aspiring healthcare leaders. These co-leadership structures are also congruent with the growth strategy of integrated health systems that rely on teamwork and interprofessional collaboration to deliver services across the continuum of care. Team-based design supports the development of leaders, builds social capital, grows employee engagement, fosters collaboration, nurtures collegiality, and engenders trust (Swensen, *et al.*, 2016).

Co-leadership is transformational and supports the growth and development of inclusive cultures and women leaders. A recent study of leadership styles in health systems found a statistically significant positive link between transformational leadership and higher organizational performance and employee engagement (Žibert & Starc, 2018).

Conclusions

Research shows that through assessment, learning, and development in key leadership areas, the combined "profile" of the dyad can be further expanded for optimal performance (Belasen, 2019). To determine the most important area for improvement, the co-leaders can initiate a review of the self-assessment findings, discuss, and compare their individual and overlapping roles, identify weak spots and sweet spots for further development, and mutually agree on improvement efforts to optimize their collaborative efforts. Of course, prioritizing the co-leaders' development plans, skill building, and improvement efforts should preferably align with the strategic goals and future directions of the health system. Through a shared vision, the co-leadership model encourages systems thinking and aligns clinical and operational resources to improve outcomes and efficiency.

Dyad leaders at all levels can reduce variation and the propensity for failure by promoting interprofessional cooperation, linking partners, and cherishing mutual respect, trust, and teamwork. Leadership thrives on making employees feel safe, creating an atmosphere that supports innovation and that integrates safety and quality care narratives into daily activities and meetings. Promoting a culture of safety is reinforced through a commitment to transparent communications in response to adverse events, near misses, and unsafe conditions. Good leaders model the way by rounding for outcomes and by giving employees access to the right tools to be successful.

The co-leadership model with a focus on gender parity sends a strong signal to health stakeholders that women leaders are indispensable for *both* the clinical and administrative sides of the business. As indicated earlier in this chapter, studies have shown that companies with more women on their boards and on their senior management teams also reap greater financial rewards. Fortune 500 firms with a high number of women executives consistently outperform their industry's median firms on all measures of profitability. By increasing the number of women in senior management and corporate leadership, health systems can build diversity as a sustained competitive advantage and achieve win–win outcomes.

References

Anderson, R. H. (2020). Challenging Our Gendered Idea of Mentorship. *Harvard Business Review*, January 06, Retrieved from https://hbr.org/2020/01/challenging-our-gendered-idea-of-mentorship

Belasen, A. (2017). *Women in Management: A Framework for Sustainable Work-Life Integration*, New York, NY: Routledge.

Belasen, A. (2019). *Dyad Leadership and Clinical Integration: Driving Change, Aligning Strategies*, Chicago, IL: Health Administration Press.

Belasen, A. T., Belasen, A. M., Belasen, A. R., & Belasen, A. R. (2021). A win-win for health care: Promoting co-leadership and increasing women's representation at the top. *Gender in Management*, 36(6), 762–781. https://doi.org/10.1108/GM-06-2020-0176

Boyle, P. (2019). More Women than Men are Enrolled in Medical School. *Association of American Medical Colleges*, December 9, https://www.aamc.org/news-insights/more-women-men-are-enrolled-medical-school

Cech, E., Rubineau, B., Silbey, S., & Seron, C. (2011). Professional role confidence and gendered persistence in engineering. *American Sociological Review*, 76(5), 641–666.

Chen, J., Leung, W. S., Song, W., & Goergen M. (2019). Why female board representation matters: The role of female directors in reducing male CEO overconfidence. *Journal of Empirical Finance*, 53(C), 70–90.

Definitive Healthcare. (2016). Dynamic duo to lead CHRISTUS Santa Rosa Hospital Medical Center, November 22, https://www.definitivehc.com/resources/news/dynamic-duo-to-lead-christus-santa-rosa-hospital-medical-center

Fontenot, T. (2012). Leading ladies: Women in healthcare leadership. *Frontiers of Health Services Management*, 28(4), 11–21.

Hauser, M. C. (2014). Leveraging women's leadership talent in healthcare. *Journal of Healthcare Management*, 59(5), 318–322.

Health Research and Educational Trust. (2014, April). *Building a Leadership Team for the Health Care Organization of the Future*, Chicago, IL: Health Research and Educational Trust, Retrieved from www.hpoe.org

Highfield, R. (2008). We Prefer People We Think are Similar to Ourselves, 17 Mar, *Telegraph*, Retrieved from http://www.telegraph.co.uk/news/science/science-news/3336375/We-prefer-people-we-think-are-similar-to-ourselves.html (Accessed on 15 April 2020).

Hoffmann, A., & Musch, J. (2018). Prejudice against women leaders: Insights from an indirect questioning approach. *Sex Roles*, pp. 1–12.

Korn Ferry (2019). No Room at the Top: 80 Percent of Healthcare Workers are Women, But Few Make It to Leadership Roles: Korn Ferry Executive Survey Examines Reasons Behind Gap, May 23, Retrieved from https://ir.kornferry.com/node/16051/pdf (Accessed on 15 May 2020).

Korn Ferry Hay Group (2016). New Research Shows Women are Better at Using Soft Skills Crucial for Effective Leadership and Superior Business Performance, March 07, Retrieved from https://www.businesswire.com/news/home/20160307005205/en/ (Accessed on 15 February 2020).

LaPierre, T. A., & Zimmerman, M. K. (2012). Career advancement and gender equity in healthcare management. Gender in Management, 27(2), 100–118.

Larson E. (2017). New Research: Diversity + Inclusion = Better Decision Making at Work. *Forbes*, Retrieved from https://www.forbes.com/sites/eriklarson/2017/09/21/new-research-diversity-inclusion-better-decision-making-at-work/#108b486b4cbf. September 21.

Mangurian, C., Linos, E., Sarkar, U., Rodriguez, C., & Jagsi, R. (2018). What's Holding Women in Medicine Back from Leadership? *Harvard Business Review*, Retrieved from https://hbr.org/2018/06/whats-holding-women-in-medicine-back-from-leadership (Accessed on 30 May 2020).

Moss-Racusin, C. A., Dovidio, J. F., Brescoll, V. L., Graham, M. J., & Handelsman, J. (2012). Science faculty's subtle gender biases favor male students. *Proceedings of the National Academy of Sciences*, 109(41), 16474–16479.

MSCI. (2016). The Tipping Point: Women on Boards and Financial Performance, Retrieved from https://www.msci.com/documents/10199/fd1f8228-cc07-4789-acee-3f9ed97ee8bb, December.

Oostra, R. D. (2016). Physician leadership: A central strategy to transforming healthcare. *Frontiers of Health Services Management*, 32(3), 15–26.

Petty, K. (2019). Interview with Dr. Charles Hankins and Cris Daskevich: Leadership Team at the Children's Hospital of San Antonio Says it's Poised for Growth, https://www.sanantoniomag.com/dr-charles-hankins-and-cris-daskevich/

Roth, V. R., Theriault, A., Clement, C., & Worthington, J. (2016). Women physicians as healthcare leaders: A qualitative study. *Journal of Health Organization and Management*, 30(4), 648–665.

Silvera, G. A., & Clark, J. R. (2019). Women at the helm: Chief executive officer, gender andpatient experience in the hospital industry. *Health Care Management Review*, Jun 6. Epub 2019, Retrieved from https://www.pubfacts.com/detail/31180934/Women-at-the-helm-Chief-executive-officer-gender-and-patient-experience-in-the-hospital-industry (Accessed on February 15, 2020).

Swensen, S., & Mohta, N. S. (2017). Leadership Survey Ability to Lead Does Not Come from a Degree. *NEJM Catalyst*, August, https://www.primarycareprogress.org/wp-content/uploads/2017/11/Insights-Council-August-2017-Leadership-Survey-Report-Ability-to-Lead-Does-Not-Come-from-a-Degree.pdf

Swensen, S., Gorringe, G., Caviness, J., & Peters, D. (2016). Leadership by design: intentional organization development of physician leaders. *Journal of Management Development*, 35(4), 549–570. doi:10.1108/JMD-08-2014-0080

Wyman, O. (2019). Women in Healthcare Leadership, Retrieved from https://www.oliverwyman.com/content/dam/oliverwyman/v2/publications/2019/January/WiHC/Women-In-Healthcare-Leadership-Report-FINAL.pdf

Young, R. (2017). It Takes Two: Can Dyad Leadership Provide a Durable Pathway in Healthcare's Brave New World? *Cardiovascular Business*, January 30. https://www.cardiovascularbusiness.com/topics/practice-management/it-takes-two-can-dyad-leadership-provide-durable-pathway-healthcares

Žibert, A., & Starc, A. (2018). Healthcare organizations and decision-making: Leadership style for growth and development. *Journal of Applied Health Science*, 4(2), 209–224.

Chapter 6

Resilience from the Middle Out

This chapter focuses on the vital role of middle managers in transitioning healthcare systems and their special contributions to building resilience in healthcare leadership. More specifically we (a) discuss the dynamics associated with traditional and transitional roles of middle managers in healthcare systems; (b) describe the emergence of the hyper-effective manager; (c) identify where and how middle management in healthcare organizations creates value; (d) suggest the important role of physicians in middle management positions; (e) explore ways and offer strategies to avert the potential for leadership failure in healthcare organizations; and (f) offer suggestions for succession planning and leadership development.

According to the Bureau of Labor Statistics, in the healthcare industry, the 422,000 middle managers are an important part of the organizational resources, with most working in state, local, and private hospitals (39%); ambulatory healthcare services (26%); group medical services and outpatient healthcare centers (16%); nursing and residential care facilities (11%); and government (8%).

In hospitals, middle managers convert strategic goals into SMART goals: Specific, measurable, assignable, reasonable, and timely. These goals are aligned with actionable improvement plans at the work unit or care team, guide employees who are engaged in safety and quality assurance efforts through CQI and Kaizen, and identify processes for continuous improvement. Middle managers may manage an entire facility, a specific clinical area or department, or a medical practice for a group of physicians. They focus on improving efficiency and quality in delivering healthcare services, develop departmental goals and objectives, represent the facility at investor meetings or on governing boards, and communicate functional plans to members of the medical staff and department heads.

Middle managers are centrally located within the chain of command and typically perform or directly influence three interrelated responsibilities: (a) operational tasks linked to

DOI: 10.4324/9781003190929-6

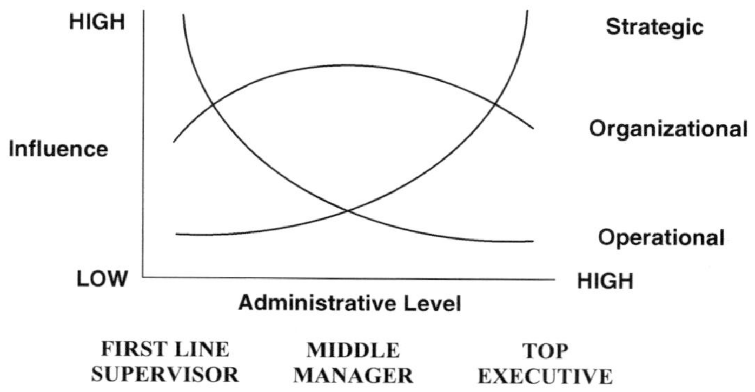

Figure 6.1 Intersecting roles.

systems, structures, and processes; (b) organizational leadership involving motivating and facilitating the work of individuals and teams; and (c) strategic goals associated with financial reports, analysis, stakeholder communication, and boardroom discussions (Figure 6.1).

Knowing when to provide structure and direction and when to "let go" through delegation and trust requires a subtle balance between transactional and transformational roles vital for running healthcare organizations effectively. Middle managers can accomplish this task through synthesizing information as well as championing and executing plans. Synthesizing information consists of gathering intelligence on the feasibility of new programs, communicating the activities of competitors and suppliers as well as assessing changes in the external environment. Championing involves justifying and defining new programs, evaluating the merits of new proposals, searching for new opportunities, and proposing programs or projects to higher level managers. Middle managers' duality of operating experience and proximity to top executives makes their roles critical for building and strengthening relationships with stakeholders.

Mollick (2011) found that it was middle managers' execution skills, more so than innovators or organizational strategy, that explained variation in firm performance. Managers accounted for 22.3% of the variation in revenue among projects, as opposed to just over 7% explained by innovators and 21.3% explained by the organization itself—including firm strategy, leadership, and practices. The strong presence of effective middle managers in innovation implementation can support the transformation of hospitals into integrated health systems and the flow of key strategic and clinical information across practice sites and units. Given the relatively high CEO turnover in hospitals and health systems (18%), are middle managers well regarded or groomed for upward mobility in a succession planning process?

Recently, however, the value of middle managers has come under attack. Middle managers are viewed as an expendable commodity that adds complexity and hinders executives' ability to understand what's "really going on" at the front line. Evidence suggests that executives increasingly prefer to get closer to their operating core. As a result, some middle managers "slide out" or lay low while others choose to becoming "hypereffective" with considerable loss of discretionary time and feelings of being overwhelmed (Belasen & Belasen, 2016). How do healthcare organizations improve if middle managers, responsible for knowledge transfer and innovation implementation, are removed from the decision-making process? Have middle managers been de-skilled as top executives rationalize resources and capabilities?

Transitional Roles

De-layering, or the process by which senior executives become more directly connected with lower levels, has led to an increase in executive *span* and at the same time to a decrease in *depth*—through the elimination of intermediate positions, typically middle managers. Evidence shows that the number of lower managers reporting to the CEO has increased (span) steadily over time, from an average (median) of 4.4 (4) in 1986 to 8.2 (7) in 1998; at the same time, the number of positions between the CEO and department managers (or division heads) has decreased (depth) by more than 25% (Rajan & Wulf, 2006). Evidently, these two trends have continued to dominate other industries as well (Neilson & Wulf, 2012).

> In today's health care environment, integrated delivery networks are growing rapidly—for good reason. These models are providing the framework for the creation of operational synergies and increasing scale for improved bottom lines. In line with these trends, hospital financial and clinical leaders continue to identify opportunities to consolidate various clinical and operational functions into centralized service centers. For example, Sharon Boggio, RHIA, enterprise director of HIM with Bon Secours Hospitals in Virginia, says the consolidation of the HIM departments at hospitals in Richmond and Hampton Roads led to nearly $2.4 million in savings from 2013 to 2014. Despite potential downsides to HIM centralization, industry professionals agree that the trend is not likely to slow down, although they caution that these complex initiatives are not for the faint of heart and require well-thought-out planning. "Consolidating HIM departments from individual facilities into a centralized corporate HIM department clearly impacts people, processes, and technology, but there can be significant benefits," says Brooks Tingey, senior marketing manager of revenue cycle solutions at 3M Health Information Systems. "Success is achieved when centralization efforts are founded on the principles of transparency, communication, and change management".
>
> **(Chavis, 2017)**

More recently, as technology advances and social media allow hospital executives and senior managers to know more about the patient experience and its impact on hospital ratings (Belasen, et al., 2021) or interact directly with stakeholders (Belasen & Luber, 2017), one trend is becoming clear: The traditional responsibilities of middle managers have begun to shift dramatically. In the healthcare field in which social media helps healthcare providers to manage relationships with patients, filter, or transfer important sources of information, middle managers are not judged simply on results as before, but also on process, but the process has increasingly become heavily controlled or centralized.

Take for example the Veterans Health Administration (VA) where primary care is organized as a Patient Centered Medical Home (PCMH) supported by interdisciplinary care teams ("teamlets") consisting of primary care providers, nurses, and clerical associates. These teams report directly to middle managers within their respective disciplines who are responsible for daily functioning, clarifying roles and responsibilities, setting expectations, providing coverage strategies, resolving conflicts, and facilitating innovation. Teamlet members were faced with challenges when middle managers' involvement was lacking especially in solving interdisciplinary issues, setting role-specific schedules and expectations, and fostering innovation. In the absence of such involvement, interfunctional collaboration was affected, requiring greater focus on the structure and training of middle managers for participation in PCMH models (Giannitrapani, et al., 2019).

Becoming Hyper-Effective

As more and more organizations become flat with an empowered workforce, the reduction in hierarchical layers creates spillover effects with a larger span of control to executives but with added responsibilities to the remaining middle managers who are expected to deal with tactical, operational issues. The combination of greater span with less depth creates a dual effect of narrower expertise or de-skilling and decrease in autonomy, so important for morale and personal motivation. Middle managers work more and produce more with the same pay and, often, without recognition. Others inherit more tasks but with technical responsibilities that require monitoring, not necessarily decision-making. They feel increasingly isolated from the management team, lose confidence in their cognitive and judgmental abilities, and, uncertain about their roles, respond often by shifting commitments.

It is the diminished role in decision-making, the freedom to determine "how to get there," the making of the decision, not the execution, that is demoralizing. Are middle managers well prepared for these challenges? Systemic barriers and stereotypical biases may inhibit or slow down their motivation to raise the bar higher (Belasen & Belasen, 2016).

To survive, many middle managers choose to perform a variety of tasks and assume many roles in meeting new expectations, in effect becoming hyper-effective. On the surface hyper-effective managers appear more efficient and have a greater desire to develop success for their organizations. On the negative side, a great deal of personal time is traded to maintain or achieve the goals of the organization. Downsizing, reorganization, and organizational transitions exacerbate these conditions. While managers may be making greater strides in achieving organizational goals, areas of management that were once deemed important are often overlooked or completely delegated. There is a trade off in that hyper-effective managers find fewer opportunities to diminish the performance of some tasks to increase their attention to others.

Notably, middle managers often had clinical duties on top of their managerial duties. Thus, implementation typically required taking on extra work although still performing their other roles. Most middle managers had clinical expertise, often required for their manager position. However, without formal training in human resources, project, or change management, they were constantly trying to learn new knowledge and skills that would help them succeed in their multiple roles. This learning was typically self-directed. Due to performing many roles, many participants felt their engagement in so many activities meant they were unable to perform all of them optimally. This was compounded by the need for additional learning. One participant stated:

> The role is so broad in the clinical area ... and the expectation is almost to program manage and program plan while at the same time be at the front line and be aware of all the clinical practices that are happening. The span is too big.

Participants described the status quo as one where they have limited decision-making power about decisions to implement innovations as well as the overarching parameters related to implementation goals and strategies. Senior managers and administrators typically make the adoption decisions, although middle managers provide information to assist in making these decisions and are subsequently expected to work within the set parameters. This was illustrated by one participant when discussing interactions with senior management:

> I don't always see eye to eye with, with the ideas that may be coming down the chute but it's sort of, um, try to explain your position and in the long run it's going to be their decision that is going to either move the car ahead or put it on park. So I mean, as far as I'm concerned, my job ends at having given them all the facts and figures that are important to make an appropriate decision.

The limited decision-making authority meant that participants were expected to implement innovations even when they perceived the innovations to be a poor fit with the implementation setting or to have limited impact on patient care. At the same time, poor fit and limited impact on patient care both impacted, in negative ways, participants' personal level of support for an innovation (Urquhart, et al., 2018).

While hyper-effectivity may sound good, it tends to transform managers into conservative and overworked individuals who are pushed to the limits by the expectations of those above them who demand nothing short of better results. In industries that experienced downsizing, the movement towards the efficiency frontier was not singularly conclusive, but the pattern of change in the tasks and responsibilities underlying the roles performed by the hyper-effective middle managers suggested a severe loss of discretionary time and an increase in the sense of powerlessness among the affected managers (Belasen & Frank, 2004).

Research findings showed that increased organizational efficiencies have come about in part due to changes in work processes and in traditional managerial roles. Pressure to increase hours at work comes from the need to perform better the ambidextrous roles of management and leadership but also from the need to pick up the slack left from those who remained uninvolved or were laid off. The larger source of productivity gain was most likely the result of the vastly increased allocation of managerial attention to activities which enhance organizational effectiveness and in some cases with little or no support from HR systems and with added stress that typically magnifies personal weaknesses (Belasen & Frank, 2004).

In hospital settings, at times of cutback and downsizing, frustrated middle managers appear to slide out to isolated, out-of-reach positions, in effect choosing an avoidance strategy (Garcia, 2006). Unable to respond to cross-over pressures, they tend to downplay their traditional responsibilities. Sliding out can be either self-initiated or forced when senior executives shun middle managers. Middle managers flee their tasks by staying away or by laying low (Carlstrom, 2012). When the emotional impact of the work middle managers perform is not acknowledged, they might feel lonely and abandoned, and become frustrated and resistant to change (Kuyvenhoven & Buss, 2011). Middle managers reportedly fear missing relevant information and not remaining informed of important projects or decisions, and suffer from a mixture of boredom and anxiety, further making it difficult to prioritize and move projects forward.

Meanwhile, employees at lower levels point fingers at middle managers whom they believe over-manage their units or excessively monitor their performance. Top executives, on the other hand, worrying about failures in meeting strategic objectives, poor financial results, stakeholder dissatisfaction, or consumer disapproval, increasingly turn to the middle manager as a convenient scapegoat. Refusing to recognize the problem, hospital administrators, for example, may react unfavorably to this behavior, typecasting middle managers as abdicators and low performers that must be further monitored or re-evaluated.

Affected middle managers become confused and demoralized, and without trust, so essential for building relationship, they gradually become less committed and less involved. Indeed, in healthcare organizations middle managers are regularly viewed as "forgotten practitioners" (Hayes, 2005). This self-reinforcing process is prime for conditions of failure in which middle managers are blamed for organizational mishaps. This is because the organizational "work" they are charged with carrying out depends on many moving parts and is often too complex to understand. Healthcare organizations often have a limited ability to learn from failures due to overemphasis on independent work units, slack resources that breed inefficiency, and removal of managers from daily work activities, which, in turn, reduce the opportunities for a broader perspective and synergy.

Veteran middle managers are viewed corporate dinosaurs who will always offer a reason why something does not work or cannot be achieved. They are perceived as mediocre or weak performers, who, in turn, tend to live down to the low expectations that their senior managers have set out for them, in effect perpetuating a vicious cycle of perceived incompetence (Manzoni & Barsoux, 2002).

The way executives relate to their middle managers is subtly influenced by what they expect of them. If their perceptions of mediocrity lead to setting up low expectations or ignoring middle managers altogether, the productivity of the affected middle managers is likely to be poor, which, in turn, reinforces the initial perception of uncommitted middle managers. This self-fulfilling prophecy creates exclusive "clubs" of winners (in-group) and losers (out-group) with members in the out-group being treated with rules, policy guidelines, and authority while the members of the in-group enjoy greater feedback, interactions, and proximity to decision makers.

The sustained attack on middle management to focus on operational effectiveness away from strategic circles and putting them in a sink-or-swim predicament would suggest that middle management is an occupation whose autonomy is systematically diminishing (Osterman, 2009).

As noted below, with rising CEO turnover rates, hospitals need to develop adequate programs to identify and train new leaders. Moreover, these programs should build a strong talent pipeline with those already fully engaged in broad-based leadership development. A crisis in healthcare leadership can be averted if leadership development programs and succession planning exist along with the motivation by senior managers to promote successful middle managers and support their upward mobility with active sponsoring, coaching, and mentoring. These observations point to a critical area where succession planning practices can and should be improved—the CEO and the board need to initiate the selection of internal candidates and ensure their preparation.

Succession Planning

Succession planning involves evaluation of organizational current capabilities and future needs and identification of suitable candidates who could assume key positions within the organization. While many middle managers in healthcare organizations may have the skills and knowledge to become effective top executives, most healthcare organizations do not have a formal succession planning process. This is surprising considering the continuing turnover of top executives which represents a high-risk situation for healthcare settings.

According to the American College of Healthcare Executives (ACHE) hospital CEO positions turned over at a rate of 17% in 2019. This represents a small decrease from turnover rates over the last five years, which have held steady at 18%. With rising CEO turnover rates, health systems need to develop adequate succession programs to identify and train new leaders. Moreover, these programs should include a robust talent pipeline with an emphasis on appropriate selection and development strategies.

Promotion from within can ensure that investments in leadership development and succession planning are linked with the strategic direction of the organization and that strategic and operational initiatives during leadership transition are not lost. Middle managers have a solid understanding of the culture, strategic realities, resources and capabilities, structures, and functions that support the alignment of the healthcare setting with its mission, vision, and values.

Healthcare leaders who can map their futures to a blueprint for actualizing their organizations' missions are more likely to succeed. At the same time, the work of the organization must get done, amid an extremely high level of scrutiny by outside regulatory authorities that examine the quality of care, operational processes, and institutional financial soundness. Operational failures are not tolerated, and the financial penalties for errors—not to mention the costs to patients who entrust their well-being to providers—are severe.

Talented middle managers can establish a balance between the forces of stability and transformation. Healthcare institutions will not be able to sustain themselves if excessive emphasis is placed on the former. Conversely, too much change, or change which is not managed and implemented effectively, can prove destabilizing to an institution that must carry out its duties with zero tolerance for medical errors. Healthcare organizations will transition successfully when they are led and managed by individuals who can define, embrace, and execute their roles in the context of this delicate balance. With resilient leaders who can integrate innovation and operations, planning and coordination, adaptability, and reputation management, these organizations will have a more prosperous and enduring presence during transitions or crises.

Competency Development for Middle Managers

Healthcare leaders operate in a complex environment with many moving and interrelated parts characterized by a constant need to deliver the most reliable, safe, and high-quality patient care. Middle managers are key to leading and coordinating administrative processes and clinical teams while effectively managing resources. In transforming healthcare with shifting regulations, rapidly evolving technological and clinical advancements, rising costs, and growing ethical concerns, middle managers' core skills and knowledge are critical for the success of healthcare settings.

Transitioning towards value-based care and an increased focus on cutting costs and improving the overall patient experience is causing a shift in healthcare delivery from inpatient to outpatient facilities (ambulatory surgery centers, primary care medical homes, urgent care centers, imaging facilities, and emergency departments). Middle managers are expected to coordinate teams across the continuum of care; track clinical and administrative processes to assess, mitigate, and prevent risks; monitor compliance with CMS regulatory requirements and financial incentives that are tied to improving quality of care and clinical outcomes; implement electronic health records (EHR), expand the use of telemedicine, employ analytics to trace patient demographics and preferences, and review HCAHPS satisfaction trends.

The complexity of the healthcare environment requires a combination of transformational and transactional roles and activities which enable middle managers to support the attainment of the triple aims of healthcare: Improving the patient experience of care (including quality and satisfaction); improving the health of populations; and reducing the per capita cost of healthcare. To support board and executive decision-making, middle managers participate in collecting and reviewing data related to market positioning and support merger and acquisition strategies with data and analysis. These strategies are key to optimizing economies of scale, reducing cost of care, and identifying the best partners to improve outcomes across the continuum of care.

Transformational roles contribute to greater employee motivation, satisfaction, and results. Transactional roles, on the other hand, focus on the orderly accomplishment of tasks and work activities, largely with an immediate or short-term focus. They provide correction when necessary and offer rewards for positive behavior. Compliance, sometimes by rules and procedural specifications is what matters most and structures and processes are reviewed for streamlining or even reengineering to maximize value. Simply put, what is most important to the transactional manager is getting things done reliably and efficiently. Transformational leaders inspire confidence and drive change. They communicate loyalty through a shared vision, focus on members' self-efficacy and emotional intelligence to create and sustain a culture of safety, an essential component of building trust in the workplace, preventing errors, and improving overall health care quality.

The key to successful middle managers is recognizing the competing tensions between the two sets of roles and balancing them based on expectations of stakeholders. These stakeholders could be internal (e.g., direct reports, executives, trustees) or external (regulators, patient advocates, investors). To see this diagrammatically, we use an assessment tool to identify strengths and weaknesses of managers performing a variety of transformational and transactional roles (Table 6.1). This tool, the Competing Values Framework (CVF), distinguishes eight critical roles that managers assume (Quinn, 1988).

The innovator and broker roles rely on creativity and communication skills to bring about change and acquire resources necessary for change management. The facilitator and mentor roles are responsible for developing individuals and groups, providing social support, and motivating team members to increase the level of their engagement and commitment to organizational goals. The monitor and coordinator roles are more relevant for system maintenance and integration and require project management and supervision skills. The director and producer roles are geared towards achieving performance outcomes and alignment with strategic plans.

The upper part of the framework focuses on transformational roles and reflects an orientation towards flexibility while the lower part focuses on transactional roles and projects an orientation towards control. The framework is also helpful in facilitating shared understanding across hierarchical levels in healthcare settings (Belasen, et al., 2015). Figure 6.2 illustrates the responses by middle managers and others about the choice and extent of the behaviors they use in performing the two sets of roles. The ratings are based on survey questions adapted from Quinn's (1988) competing values leadership.

The diagram in Figure 6.2 shows the reactions of employees (direct reports) and bosses (top executives) to a self-assessment profile of middle managers. While middle managers believe that, on balance, they perform all the roles quite evenly, their bosses think that they need to focus more on internal operations (people, processes, structures, coordination). Meanwhile, direct reports would like to see a greater emphasis on innovation, change leadership, and communication. The mixed results between how middle managers perceive themselves versus how others perceive them exemplify their complicated status within the organizational hierarchy. It could also be that middle managers make valuable contributions that often go unnoticed by most senior executives who frequently favor non-affective task focus.

Effective middle managers direct communication flow at the intersection of multiple information channels. They are responsible for communicating organizational goals and objectives, making sure executive-level directives and internal processes are understood by direct reports. At the same time, they are the voice of their employees, protecting their needs and securing resources for the effective execution of functional and strategic goals. For decades middle managers have been required to take tacit knowledge (personal, difficult to formalize) relating to strategic levels and convert it to explicit knowledge (codified

Table 6.1 Assessment: Transformational and Transactional Roles

Thinking about your roles, behaviors, attitudes, and beliefs when working with individuals and teams, reflect on each statement by indicating the response that best matches your beliefs. Direct reports and supervisor(s) can provide their ratings, too, for validation purposes. Calculate a simple average for each column, then use an Excel spreadsheet to create a chart from the data.

1—*Very untrue of what I believe*
2—*Untrue of what I believe*
3—*Somewhat untrue of what I believe*
4—*Neutral*
5—*Somewhat true of what I believe*
6—*True of what I believe*
7—*Very true of what I believe*

Dimensions	**Roles**	**Behaviors**	**Self**	**Supervisor**	**Employees**
Transformational	Innovator	Think innovatively			
		Initiate change			
		Experiment with new ideas			
		Develop creative solutions			
	Avg				
	Broker	Develop external relationships			
		Pursue proximity to higher powers			
		Persuasive			
		Influence strategic direction			
	Avg				
	Mentor	Listen actively			
		Sensitive to others			
		Show empathy			
		Supportive			
	Avg				
	Facilitator	Bridge gaps			
		Facilitate conversations			
		Encourage participation			
		Promote teamwork			
	Avg				

(*Continued*)

Table 6.1 (Continued) Assessment: Transformational and Transactional Roles

Transactional	Director	Initiate strategic planning			
		Set broader goals			
		Clarify priorities			
		Define boundaries			
	Avg				
	Producer	Clarify performance targets			
		Improve productivity			
		Results oriented			
		Motivate to meet objectives			
	Avg				
	Monitor	Track performance metrics			
		Monitor compliance			
		Detail oriented			
		Establish quality control			
	Avg				
	Coordinator	Streamline processes			
		Integrate activities			
		Synchronize workflow			
		Clarify important milestones			
	Avg				

Adapted from: Quinn, R. (1988). *Beyond Rational Management*.

and transmittable) for the front-line levels (Beck & Plowman, 2009). It is no wonder the front-line employees in Figure 6.2 showed preference to informal channels of communication when it comes to corporate goals and strategy.

Development Strategies

Middle managers' familiarity with the workings of the organization and proximity to decision makers make their "clutch roles" during transitions critical for organizational success.

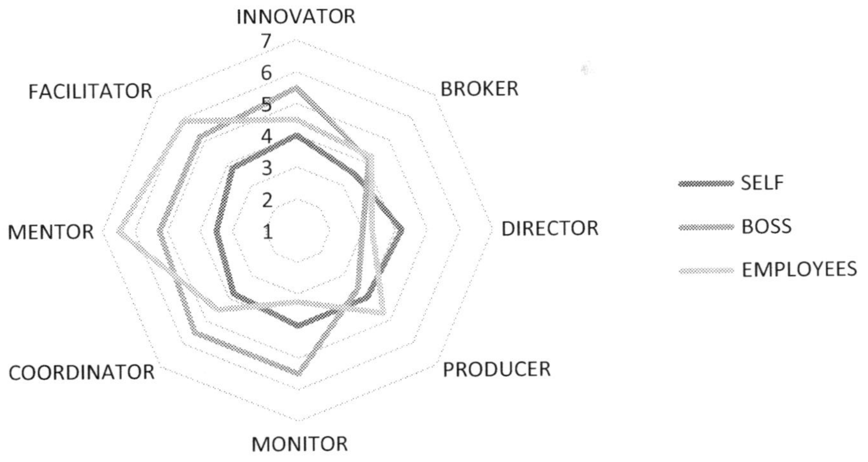

Figure 6.2 Assessing middle managers.

They search for new opportunities, align strategies and operational activities, evaluate the merits of strategy execution, and propose new projects. The duality of having strategic awareness with operating experience often requires ambidexterity with both explorative and exploitative activities essential for implementing patient safety culture as well as sustaining disruptive change (Gutberg & Berta, 2017).

The concept of sliding up (governance role) and down (advocacy role) was used by Hales (2006) to describe how middle managers move between supervisory to employee advocacy roles. Down the hierarchy, they may demonstrate a willingness to share power by creating meaningful opportunities for staff involvement as well as taking an active interest in their career development. Regaining employees' trust after off-putting or disappointing results can become quite challenging, especially during transitions. Demonstrating their value by becoming resilient and shifting the focus to influencing processes and decisions, not controlling them, is vital for their success.

Although a manager may primarily exhibit behaviors of transformational leadership to inspire employees, it is sometimes necessary to assert a transactional leadership style depending on the nature of the task. Successful strategies for middle managers include:

1. Take responsibility for your success, and your career. Discover what you are good at and in which roles you excel. Set goals and challenges and go for them. Get outside your comfort zone by communicating your goals to senior executives and soliciting their feedback towards achieving your goals. Identify gaps in your competencies and roles. Then, take ownership by seeking out the knowledge you need to improve.
2. Seek out an active mentor. Find someone in your organization or in your industry who can provide you with coaching or direction on how to achieve your goals. Check

in with your mentor at least once a month for feedback. Listen to the feedback and self-improve where needed.

3. Be a self-starter. Do you wait to be assigned projects or new responsibilities, or do you seek them out proactively? Self-starters do not wait for others to tell them how to achieve a goal. They identify opportunities, propose new projects, and improve work processes and systems. They believe in continuous improvement and self-development. They constantly seek new challenges and ways to improve their work and departmental activities.
4. Achieve more results than others. If you are not consistently achieving more results than expected, identify one or two areas within your position or department where you can make a positive impact within a short period of time. Look for at least one improvement you can make on a weekly basis. It does not have to be big. Small improvements accomplished consistently create long-term results.
5. Know how to facilitate team interactions. Every team is charged with tasks and follows certain interpersonal dynamics. This requires skills that transcend a range of leadership qualities including understanding and managing transitions, initiating structure, resolving conflict, and managing interpersonal relationships.
6. Be a problem-solver. Every work team and department can benefit from further improvements. Set an intention to become aware of problems in your work area. Talk with people informally about the problems before you bring up the issue in a meeting. Initiate conversations with peers or direct reports about how the problem might be solved. Once you have some solutions, present them to senior executives and make sure to give credit to those who contributed solutions and ideas. Bring up these solutions in team meetings to discuss implementation, offer support, and generate commitment.
7. Adopt a positive and enthusiastic attitude. Successful people show high levels of energy when they approach a task. They do not dwell on problems or failures. They take a learning approach by reflecting on what they learned when they make a mistake, so they can improve their performance in the future. Most importantly, high performers are highly motivated and have a passion for what they do.
8. Think and act strategically. Have an outside-in perspective by incorporating the goals of external stakeholders in your thinking and decisions.
9. Practice empathy by paying attention to others' words and nonverbal cues and by recognizing their emotions nonjudgmentally.

Conclusions

It is very important that executives know how to appropriately judge middle managers in ways that are fair and just to avoid undue bias. Coaching or mentoring programs have also been known to help cultivate middle managers. Executives that sponsor middle managers make themselves available and accessible. Active sponsors are good listeners and use the Socratic method to allow others to reason their way to answers. They facilitate action plans as challenges arise and encourage engagement. By embracing transformational leadership and supporting mentoring and self-coaching programs, senior executives provide middle managers the support they need to succeed as healthcare leaders.

Middle managers that are also hyper-effective managers need to recognize and respect their own limits, both professionally and personally. Placing realistic boundaries on their own capabilities while continuing to strive for success might prove useful. A manager's personal life needs to have equal balance as well. Organizations with policies that support work-life balance, (e.g., telehealth that prevents employees from feeling overworked), experience improved satisfaction and job performance. By effectively leveraging the knowledge developed from learning about their own strengths and weaknesses, middle managers can continue the path of becoming resilient leaders while still achieving a high level of personal satisfaction.

A crisis in healthcare leadership can be mitigated if a leadership development program and succession planning exist along with willingness by senior managers to support the leadership potential of successful middle managers. Healthcare senior executives and boards of directors can initiate the selection and development of middle managers to ensure leadership continuity and to respond effectively to the strategic and structural challenges presented in healthcare environments.

References

Beck, T., & Plowman, D. (2009). The role of middle managers in animating and guiding organizational interpretation. *Organization Science*, 20(5), 909–924.

Belasen, A. T., Oppenlander, J., Belasen, A. R., & Hertelendy, A. (2021). Provider-patient communication and hospital ratings: Perceived gaps and forward thinking about the effects of COVID-19. *International Journal for Quality in Health Care*, 33(1), 1–7. doi:10.1093/intqhc/mzaa140.

Belasen, A., & Luber, E. (2017). Innovation implementation: Leading from the middle out. In N. Pfeffermann & J. Gould (Eds.), *Strategy and Communication for Innovation: Integrative Perspectives on Innovation in the Digital Economy* (pp. 229–243), Germany: Springer.

Belasen, A. T., & Belasen, A. R. (2016). Value in the middle: Cultivating middle managers in healthcare organizations. *Journal of Management Development*, 35(9), 1149–1162.

Belasen, A., Eisenberg, B., & Huppertz, J. (2015). *Mastering Leadership: A Vital Resource for Healthcare Organizations*, Boston, MA: Jones & Bartlett Learning.

Belasen, A. T., & Frank, N. M. (2004). The perceptions of human resource managers of the shifting importance of managerial roles in downsizing organizations. *International Journal of Human Resources Development and Management*, 4(2), 144–163.

Chavis, S. (2017). HIM consolidation on the upswing. *For The Record*, 29(1), 12. https://www.fortherecordmag.com/archives/1117p12.shtml

Giannitrapani, K. F., Rodriguez, H., Huynh, A. K., Hamilton, A. B., Kim, L., Stockdale, S. E., Needleman, J., Yano, E. M., & Rubenstein, L. V. (2019). How middle managers facilitate interdisciplinary primary care team functioning. *Healthcare (Amsterdam, Netherlands)*, 7(2), 10–15. doi:10.1016/j.hjdsi.2018.11.003

Garcia, V. C. (2006). Putting conflict management into practice: A nursing case study. *Journal of Nursing Management*, 14, 201–206.

Gutberg, J., & Berta, W. (2017). Understanding middle managers' influence in implementing patient safety culture. *BMC Health Services Research*, 17, 582. doi:10.1186/s12913-017-2533-4

Hales, C. (2006). Mowing down the line, the shifting boundary between middle and first-line management. *Journal of General Management*, 32(2), 31–55.

Hayes, D. (2005). New effort to boost middle manager skills is under way. *Community Care*, 1559, 1–2.

Kuyvenhoven, R., & Buss, C. (2011). A normative view of the role of middle management in the implementation of strategic change. *Journal of Management & Marketing Research*, 8(1), 1–14.

Manzoni, J. F., & Barsoux, J. L. (2002). *The Set-up-to-fail Syndrome: How Good Managers Cause Great People to Fail*. Boston, MA: Harvard Business School Press.

Mollick, E. R. (2011). People and Process, Suits and Innovators: The Role of Individuals in Firm Performance, Retrieved from SSRN http://ssrn.com/abstract=1630546 or http://dx.doi.org/10.2139/ssrn.1630546

Neilson, G. L., & Wulf, J. (2012). How many direct reports? *Harvard Business Review*, 90(4), 113–119.

Osterman, P. (2009). *The Truth About Middle Managers: Who They are, How They Work, Why They Matter*. Boston, MA: Harvard Business School Press.

Quinn, R. E. (1988). *Beyond Rational Management*. San Francisco: Wiley.

Rajan, G. R., & Wulf, J. (2006). The flattening firm: Evidence from panel data on the changing nature of corporate hierarchies. *The Review of Economics and Statistics*, 88(4), 759–773.

Urquhart, R., Kendell, C., Folkes, A., Reiman, T., Grunfeld, E., & Porter, G. A. (2018), Making it happens: Middle managers' roles in innovation implementation in health care. *Worldviews on Evidence-Based Nursing*, 15, 414–423. doi:10.1111/wvn.12324

Chapter 7

Building a Culture of Resilient Care Teams

Leadership is critical for the success of teamwork, which, in turn, helps shape a more positive and engaging culture of collaboration. Studies demonstrate a positive association between empowered team leadership and cross-functional synergies (teamwork and interprofessional cooperation) and clinical patient outcomes including lower rates of errors and patient mortality.

Creating a safety culture of interprofessional collaboration and cross-functional synergies reinforces the implementation of strategic goals across the continuum of care. Safety culture is vital for the success of healthcare organizations coping with the COVID-19 pandemic. Leaders can build safety cultures by readily and willingly participating with care team members in initiatives designed to develop safety culture characteristics. They see safety issues as problems with organizational systems, not their employees, and see adverse events and close calls ("near-misses") as providing "information-rich" data for learning and systems improvement.

Assessment instruments and strategies for diagnosing and analyzing organizational culture including key techniques for managing cultural change are described in this chapter with examples and key takeaways. Since a culture of collaboration draws on strengths of empowered teams, the dimensions of teamwork are also explored through assessment and development tools.

POSITIVE CULTURE PROVIDES A STRONG FOUNDATION

During the pandemic when everyone was overwhelmed and staff were stretched thin, "The whole premise of our culture is that we treat everyone with respect and dignity,"

DOI: 10.4324/9781003190929-7

says Paul Gerharter, RN, vice president of clinical services for Caraday Healthcare. "We make it clear that it's okay to talk about family and life away from work."

When staff feel like their managers understand what they're going through and are empathetic, they are more likely to be engaged and embrace the organization's vision. "It's important for everyone to understand there will be bad days," Gerharter adds. "We need to own up to mistakes, forgive people, learn, and move forward."

One thing that has been crystal clear during the pandemic is, "You have to set up a culture of safety before a crisis hits," says Dallas Nelson, MD, CMD, associate professor of medicine at the University of Rochester School of Medicine and Dentistry. "You need a system that shows you value employees, that they can bring up questions, fears, and concerns and be respected."

She suggests that when this culture doesn't exist, trust can suffer, and staff are hesitant to believe management has their best interests at heart. "You have to make staff feel safe before they can make other people feel safe," she says.

In a culture of safety and trust, it is much more difficult for conspiracy theories, rumors, and misinformation to gain traction. This certainly doesn't mean that management is always right or that leadership has all the answers. "Those homes that have really transformed their culture to be more resident-centered and resident-directed had systems in place that helped them during the pandemic," says Penny Cook, MSW, president and chief executive officer of the Pioneer Network. As a result of their cultures, they already had consistent staffing, effective ways to interact with families, and other elements that promoted engagement, transparency, teamwork, and empathy (Kaldy, J., 2021).

Building a Culture of Safety and Reliability

Resilient leaders in health systems influence the mission, clarify the strategic vision for their organizations, employ evidence-based best practices to improve patient quality and safety, and enhance the overall efficiency and effectiveness of the organization. They visibly and consistently support the narratives of interprofessional collaboration and engage in ongoing dialogue with staff and clinicians during important transitions and strategic deployment of care teams. Employees are inspired to change their way of thinking about patient care and the culture of the organization, avoid confusion during transitions, and are open to collaborative behaviors.

Health systems with a strong culture of safety use transparent communications to build trust and promote joint accountability. According to *The Joint Commission Center for Transforming Healthcare* (2017), safety cultures are based on:

- Sufficient support of patient safety event reporting
- Meaningful feedback and positive support to staff who report safety vulnerabilities
- Prioritizing and implementing safety provisions
- Addressing staff and clinician burnout
- Establishing teamwork and building relationships

THE ESSENTIAL ROLE OF LEADERSHIP IN DEVELOPING A SAFETY CULTURE

In an organization with a strong safety culture, individuals within the organization treat each other and their patients with dignity and respect (The Joint Commission, 2017). Individuals within the organization respect and are wary of operational hazards, have a collective mindfulness that people and equipment will sometimes fail, defer to expertise rather than hierarchy in decision-making, and develop defenses and contingency plans to cope with failures.

These concepts stem from the extensive research of James Reason on the psychology of human error (Reason, 1990). Among Reason's description of the main elements of a safety culture are:

Just culture—people are encouraged, even rewarded, for providing essential safety-related information, but clear lines are drawn between human error and at-risk or reckless behaviors.

Reporting culture—people report their errors and near misses.

Learning culture—the willingness and the competence to draw the right conclusions from safety information systems, and the will to implement major reforms when their need is indicated.

Creating a culture of safety which is also patient-centered requires the mindset of a high-reliability organization (HRO). HROs are characterized by a collective mindfulness that transcends specialized areas and that empowers staff members to collaborate in identifying possible failures and tackling them proactively, timely, and responsibly. Applying HRO concepts in healthcare systems begins with leaders at all levels who initiate a discourse about how to improve the process and outcomes of care. They imbed the five hallmarks of HROs throughout the health system:

Sensitivity to operations. Preserving constant awareness by leaders, frontline nurses, patient care attendants, technicians, and support staff of the efficacy of systems and processes that affect patient care. Having situational awareness is key to identifying risks, closing loopholes in processes where there is potential for medical errors, and taking proactive steps for preventing them.

Reluctance to simplify. Simple processes are good, but simplistic explanations for why things work or fail are risky. Avoiding overly simple explanations of failure (e.g., unqualified staff, inadequate training, miscommunications) is essential for preventing medical errors. It is important to ask "why" and "what if" questions, solicit expert advice, swap the dominant thinking with perspectives from others with diverse experience, and capitalize on new thinking to get to root causes of problems.

Preoccupation with failure. Examine near misses to avoid reoccurrence and learn from them to reduce potential harm to patients. Attention to detail is crucial. Identifying and fixing problems is everyone's responsibility and is encouraged and supported by leadership.

Deference to expertise. Leaders who trust frontline teams and experts also accept their insights and suggestions about how to identify risks and make decisions with quick follow-up actions.

Resilience. Leaders and staff need to be trained to respond quickly and effectively to deal with system failures (Hines, et al., 2008).

BECOMING A HIGH-RELIABILITY ORGANIZATION

In HROs, senior leaders conduct frequent walk-rounds to reinforce safety behaviors, and find and fix critical safety issues. They also meet in daily operational briefs where they look back to learn from failures and look forward to predict and lessen risk or harm.

Frontline leaders (for example, unit charge nurses) round with staff every day, give 5:1 positive to negative feedback, conduct daily huddles, and model the expected safety behaviors.

HRO leaders manage by anticipation and prediction rather than reaction. Frontline leaders focus on predicting events in the next 24 hours and making real-time adjustments to keep patients, families, employees, and visitors safe. We also focus on several principles of reliability science:

- Designing reliable, standardized systems that support staff decisions, opportunities for feedback, ongoing learning, and change
- Learning to be more mindful of decisions and actions using HRO theory
- Improving situational awareness—the concept of reliably identifying at-risk patients, lessening their risk, and escalating risks until the patient is safe
- Managing by prediction and having robust plans in place for the expected and the unexpected
- Looking at human factors—how we relate to the world around us and how learning more about how we work and interact, and designing systems that take human factors into account, can help us better keep patients, families, employees, and visitors safe

(James Anderson, *Center for Health Systems Excellence*)

In 2004, as part of its goal to support a culture of patient safety and quality improvement, the Agency for Healthcare Research and Quality (AHRQ) sponsored the development of the *Hospital Survey on Patient Safety Culture*™ for hospitals, nursing homes, ambulatory outpatient medical offices, community pharmacies, and ambulatory surgery centers. In 2019, AHRQ released a new version, the SOPS Hospital Survey 2.0. The purpose of the survey is to assess hospital staff opinions about patient safety issues, medical errors, and event reporting. The 2019 survey included multiple items categorized in ten composite measures of patient safety culture (Table 7.1). The AHRQ Surveys on Patient Safety Culture (SOPS™) program enables healthcare organizations to use these tools to:

- Raise staff awareness about patient safety
- Diagnose and assess the status of patient safety culture
- Identify strengths and areas for patient safety culture improvement
- Examine trends in patient safety culture change over time
- Evaluate the cultural impact of patient safety initiatives and interventions
- Conduct internal and external comparisons

An earlier study (Famolaro, et al., 2016) showed that the areas of strength or the composites with the highest average percent positive responses were teamwork (within 82% and across units 61%), supervisor/manager expectations and actions (78%), promoting patient safety (72%), and organizational learning—continuous improvement (73%). The areas with the potential for improvement or the composites with the lowest average percent of positive responses were nonpunitive response to error (45%), handoffs and transitions (48%), and staffing (54%).

The survey also included 2 questions that asked respondents to provide an overall rating on patient safety for their work area/unit and to indicate the number of events they reported over the past 12 months. Event reporting was identified as an area for improvement for most hospitals because underreporting of events means potential patient safety problems may not be recognized or identified and therefore may not be addressed. Famolaro, et al. (2016) noted that on average, 45% of respondents within hospitals reported at least one event has occurred in their hospital. It is likely that this represents underreporting of events, as respondents naturally are reluctant to report their own mistakes. In comparison, on average, 76% of respondents within hospitals gave their work area or unit a grade of "Excellent" (34%) or "Very Good" (42%) on patient safety.

When healthcare settings are engaged in continuous improvement processes, the composite measures in Table 7.1 can be used as quality metrics to help track progress towards achieving desired outcomes. Over time, a trend can be traced, and quality improvement teams can review the results, explore gaps, and brainstorm ideas and action plans for achieving desired outcomes. Figure 7.1 depicts the results of a quality improvement team

Table 7.1 Assessment: AHRQ Patient Safety Culture

Composite Measures	**Scale:** 1. Strongly Disagree 2. Disagree 3. Neither Agree nor Disagree 4. Agree 5. Strongly Agree
1. Teamwork	• In this unit, we work together as an effective team • During busy times, staff in this unit help each other • There is a problem with disrespectful behavior by those working in this unit (negatively worded)
2. Staffing and work pace	• In this unit, we have enough staff to handle the workload • Staff in this unit work longer hours than is best for patient care (negatively worded) • This unit relies too much on temporary, float, or PRN staff (negatively worded) • The work pace in this unit is so rushed that it negatively affects patient safety (negatively worded)
3. Organizational learning and continuous improvement	• This unit regularly reviews work processes to determine if changes are needed to improve patient safety • In this unit, changes to improve patient safety are evaluated to see how well they worked • This unit lets the same patient safety problems keep happening (negatively worded)
4. Response to errors	• In this unit, staff feel like their mistakes are held against them (negatively worded) • When an event is reported in this unit, it feels like the person is being written up, not the problem (negatively worded) • When staff make errors, this unit focuses on learning rather than blaming individuals • In this unit, there is a lack of support for staff involved in patient safety errors (negatively worded)
5. Supervisor, manager, or clinical leader support for patient safety	• My supervisor, manager, or clinical leader seriously considers staff suggestions for improving patient safety • My supervisor, manager, or clinical leader wants us to work faster during busy times, even if it means taking shortcuts (negatively worded) • My supervisor, manager, or clinical leader takes action to address patient safety concerns that are brought to their attention

(*Continued*)

Table 7.1 (Continued) Assessment: AHRQ Patient Safety Culture

6. Communication about error	• We are informed about errors that happen in this unit • When errors happen in this unit, we discuss ways to prevent them from happening again • In this unit, we are informed about changes that are made based on event reports
7. Communication openness	• In this unit, staff speak up if they see something that may negatively affect patient care • When staff in this unit see someone with more authority doing something unsafe for patients, they speak up • When staff in this unit speak up, those with more authority are open to their patient safety concerns • In this unit, staff are afraid to ask questions when something does not seem right (negatively worded)
8. Reporting patient safety events	• When a mistake is caught and corrected before reaching the patient, how often is this reported? • When a mistake reaches the patient and could have harmed the patient, but did not, how often is this reported?
9. Hospital management support for patient safety	• The actions of hospital management show that patient safety is a top priority • Hospital management provides adequate resources to improve patient safety • Hospital management seems interested in patient safety only after an adverse event happens (negatively worded)
10. Handoffs and information exchange	• When transferring patients from one unit to another, important information is often left out (negatively worded) • During shift changes, important patient care information is often left out (negatively worded) • During shift changes, there is adequate time to exchange all key patient care information

Adapted from: Agency for Healthcare Research and Quality (AHRQ), 2019, https://www.ahrq.gov/sites/default/files/wysiwyg/sops/surveys/hospital/hospitalsurvey2-items.pdf

with the desired outcomes established as benchmarks. Action plans can be used to prioritize the objectives with milestones to help monitor progress towards measurable improvement in healthcare services.

Teamwork and Culture of Collaboration

Communicating the value of clinical integration, employing innovative care delivery models, and tracking of clinical quality outcomes create incentives for a culture of collaboration, mutual commitment, teamwork, and engagement across the continuum of care.

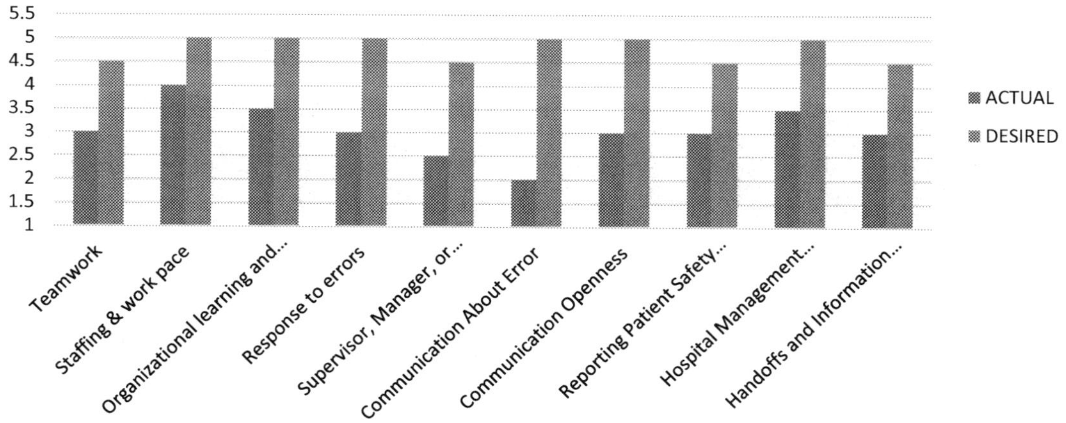

Figure 7.1 Patient safety culture: Actual and desired outcomes.

Organizational culture influences the operating conditions (e.g., norms, communication patterns, commitment, and joint accountability) that promote the effectiveness of teamwork. Teamwork expands the traditional roles of clinicians and staff members to share in the decision-making process. It involves shared responsibility, mutual trust, and enhanced communication. It can take place across units when members cooperate and coordinate with one another to provide the best care for patients over prolonged periods.

Teamwork can also take place within units where members coach and mentor each other professionally and with mutual respect. When clinical and nonclinical staff collaborate effectively, healthcare teams can improve patient outcomes, prevent medical errors, improve efficiency, and increase patient satisfaction. When healthcare settings promote a culture of collaboration *and* interprofessional collaboration, they also create incentives for cultural synergy and teamwork.

A top-down approach to building company culture no longer works for several reasons. For one, COVID-19 has upended how leaders interact with employees and how coworkers connect with each other. Next, company culture has grown in importance, thanks to recent high-profile crises at big name companies. A new culture-building approach is already in place at some organizations, one in which everyone in the organization is responsible for it. Importantly, this model doesn't relegate culture-building to an amorphous concept that everyone influences but no one leads or is accountable for. And it weaves in perspectives from employees to customers, from middle managers to the CEO ... Culture has become a strategic priority with impact on the bottom line. It can't just be delegated and compartmentalized anymore ... Shared responsibility for culture throughout an organization involves different people and functions within the organization playing different roles in developing and maintaining the culture.

(Yohn, 2021)

Increasing safety through interprofessional collaboration, breaking down silos, identifying innovative ways of care delivery, and leveraging resources and capabilities across the health systems are important areas of focus for resilient leaders. The foundation for successful clinical integration includes shared governance with strong physician leadership focusing on transforming the hospital culture and achieving clinical outcomes as key drivers towards value-based care. This requires a mindset of cross-functional synergy, sharing information, transferring best practices, managing utilization, and providing proactive care. Interprofessional or multidisciplinary teams in the acute care settings involve clinical problem-solving and planning episodes (e.g., such as teamwork during surgical procedures) among physicians, nurses, pharmacists, and caregivers where shared awareness and positive communications are crucial for the success of care delivery.

Four architypes of purposeful cultures exist in most organizations (Figure 7.2):

Culture of change and innovation reflects a dynamic, entrepreneurial, and creative health system, which creates opportunities for transformation and alignment of organizational and community goals. Leadership is visionary, innovative, and risk oriented. Commitment to innovation is the value that bonds members and partners together. Mitigating resistance is critical since typically innovation is viewed as an add-on activity to members' regular jobs, potentially reducing their focus and energy for innovation. Partners who fear reporting errors or experience perceived insecurity may also resist innovation or display risk-averse behaviors. Furthermore, financial resources and analytics may also be insufficient to support experimentation and testing.

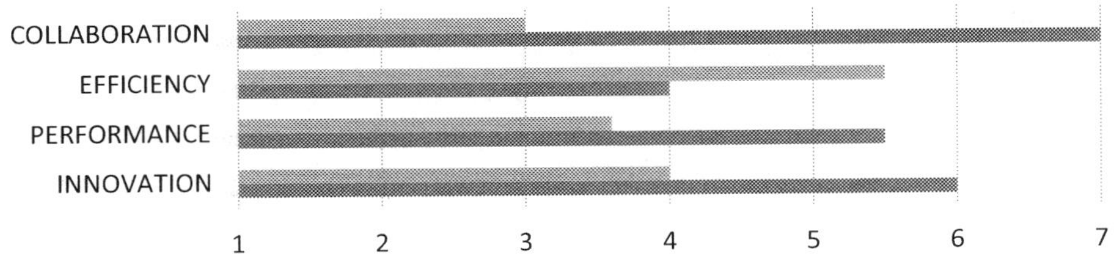

	INNOVATION	PERFORMANCE	EFFICIENCY	COLLABORATION
Actual	4	3.6	5.5	3
Desired	6	5.5	4	7

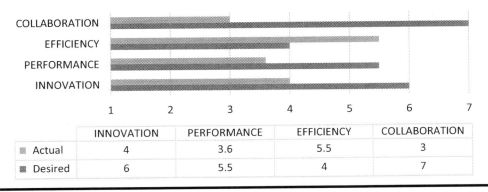

Figure 7.2 Actual and desired cultures.

Leaders must show support for clinicians and personnel who initiate new ideas to realign clinical processes with reasonable precautions to avoid harm to patients or the organization. While innovation is implemented incrementally through modifications of existing processes, rather than reconfiguration of existing structures through fundamental redesign, it is viewed as a deliberate process.

Hospital administrators prioritize formal training about innovation and encourage clinicians and staff to develop their skills and expertise in areas such as problem-solving, brainstorming, and creative thinking. As discussed in Chapter 6, this is also where the role of middle managers in innovation implementation is critical in planning and facilitating execution plans.

Culture of efficiency is characterized by a structured and disciplined workplace, extensive rules and procedures, and regulatory requirements that govern members' behaviors and actions. Managers are good coordinators and monitors who help to synchronize operations. Value is placed on stability, consistency, optimizing resource utilization, analytics, and operating efficiency. Information that might help stimulate new thinking is obtained from a variety of sources, both within and outside the organization. Potential barriers may include limited transfer of knowledge and insufficient sharing of best practices across specialized units that are discipline-bound, or because information is shared on a need-to-know basis only.

Benchmarking activities are not supported because of a belief that "we know everything" or "we are different, and it won't work here." To reduce disagreements, members prefer homogeneous teams with highly specialized knowledge, skills, experiences, and orientations. Interfunctional collaboration, of course, alters the fabric of these interactions, with behaviors and outcomes that are often incentivized externally.

Culture of performance is characterized by a focus on the external environment and managing transactions with external constituencies including payers, partners, and regulators. Hospital leaders are value strategists who drive results through strategic positioning, expansion through partnerships and mergers, and achieving economies of scale. The organization is a results-oriented workplace. Value is placed on competitive actions and meeting strategic goals with predetermined performance targets. The strong presence of effective middle managers in innovation implementation can support the transformation of hospitals into integrated health systems and the flow of key strategic and clinical information across practice sites and units.

Culture of collaboration focuses on teamwork and interprofessional collaboration by promoting transparency, honesty, and trusting relationships. Information is shared freely and rapidly, without filters or censors, to help foster innovation. Communication is clear and teamwork is trustworthy. Team members are diverse and jointly approach the issue from different perspectives. People honor ideas from each other and from nontraditional sources. There is mutual respect and honesty within teams. The collaboration culture is supportive and interactive like an extended family to members. Leaders are mentors and coaches. Individual development, high cohesion, morale, teamwork, and consensus are valued. Success is defined in terms of trust, mutual respect, and engagement. Individuals and teams are recognized and praised for initiating innovation and for enhancing the patient experience across the continuum of care.

Assessments of organizational culture are useful because they help managers and organizations adapt to the demands of external environments and enhance organizational performance. The survey in Table 7.2 allows respondents to identify their organizational culture twice—first, as they see the culture of the hospital ("actual"); and second, as they would like to see their culture manifest in the future ("desired"). The gap between the responses (i.e., current vs. desired) provides important clues about prioritizing training and development needs.

Figure 7.2 provides an example that illustrates potential gaps between actual and desired expectations. Of course, these cultural types are not exclusive in the sense that they are viewed as binary. Instead, organizational and team leaders can look at the tradeoffs between the different types, recognize their inherent tensions, and revise or shape the culture based on the desired trajectory. When the updates to organizational culture are conducted on an ongoing basis, the hospital culture becomes adaptive and, on balance, aligns well with the hospital's strategic direction.

Improving Teamwork

Despite the incentives provided by the Affordable Care Act and the Centers for Medicare and Medicaid Services to expand coverage, boost the effectiveness and efficiency of processes and outcomes, and increase the quality of care, the achievement of a comprehensive clinical integration in healthcare settings has remained somewhat elusive. With limited coordination across multiple specialty groups or settings, patients continue to be likely to receive duplicate diagnostic tests, have adverse prescription drug interactions, and get conflicting care plans. Studies show that patients receiving care with poor teamwork exhibited among care teams are nearly five times as likely to experience complications or death. On the other hand, patients receiving care from empowered teams (i.e., greater role clarity, mutual trust, and open communication) reported higher levels of satisfaction.

The Institute of Medicine (IOM) indicated that teamwork has a direct effect on patient safety and treatment outcomes. As early as 2003, its report identified the capacity to "work in interdisciplinary teams … to cooperate, collaborate, communicate, and integrate care in teams to ensure that care is continuous and reliable" as an essential competency that care providers should have regardless of specialty.

Table 7.2 Assessment: Cultural Types in Health Settings

Thinking about your healthcare setting, reflect on each statement by indicating the response that best matches your beliefs, first in terms of the actual culture (i.e., current beliefs, expectations, views, behaviors) and then in terms of desired culture.

My beliefs:

1—Very untrue of what I believe
2—Untrue of what I believe
3—Somewhat untrue of what I believe
4—Neutral
5—Somewhat true of what I believe
6—True of what I believe
7—Very true of what I believe

Cultural Type	Expectations and Behavioral Indicators	Actual	Desired
Innovation	We focus on the human experience to identify design needs		
	We invest time and energy resources in connecting with our patients		
	My hospital incentivizes innovative approaches to healthcare delivery		
	We promote innovation using interfunctional collaboration		
	We value problem-solving, brainstorming, and creative thinking		
	We create custom solutions that advance population health		
	My hospital leadership embraces disruptive innovation		
Performance	**Avg**		
	Quality ratings are an important strategic focus of our health system		
	To grow, we need to compete as an integrated health system		
	The importance of performance measurement and reporting is high		
	Hospital performance measures are viewed through the lens of value		
	Assessing my hospital financial risk position is vital for our success		
	We focus on financial ratio analysis to evaluate hospital performance		
	Operating margins are vital for meeting patient and community needs		
	Avg		

(*Continued*)

Table 7.2 (Continued) Assessment: Cultural Types in Health Settings

Efficiency	The hospital leadership uses bureaucratic control to achieve integration		
	Our administrative costs are very high		
	We rely on bureaucratic lines to maximize efficiencies		
	Managerial decision-making in my hospital is top-down		
	Hospital leaders draw on positional power (centralized control) to drive goals		
	My hospital leadership is more transactional than transformational		
	Work units are highly specialized		
Collaboration	**Avg**		
	We rely on interfunctional collaborative teams		
	We focus on interprofessional cooperation to improve patient care		
	Healthcare teams interact dynamically to deliver quality services		
	Our care teams pursue performance excellence through shared goals, shared leadership, collaboration, and open communication		
	We measure the hospital's commitment to quality care by what leaders do		
	Teamwork in our hospital positively affects patient safety		
	Teams are effective in reducing errors and improving quality care		
	Avg		

ACOs and patient-centered medical homes (PCMHs) with a strong focus on preventive and post-discharge care benefit from cross-setting collaboration. This involves coordination among physicians, social workers, nurses with various roles, others with clinical and/or diagnostic roles, and case managers as part of empowered multidisciplinary teams. These teams integrate care for targeted populations and communicate medical and social issues to patients' medical care teams. In addition, transitions of care (i.e., between care areas or shift changes) in acute care settings require strong attention to teamwork due to high-risk interactions and the potential for communication failures about the patient's status, plan of care, or treatment.

When clinical and nonclinical staff collaborate effectively, healthcare teams can improve patient outcomes, prevent medical errors, improve efficiency, and increase patient satisfaction.

Successful team leadership requires a mindset of interfunctional collaboration, sharing information, managing utilization, and providing proactive care. Communicating the value of clinical integration, employing innovative care delivery models, and tracking clinical quality outcomes create incentives for joint accountability, mutual commitment, teamwork, interprofessional cooperation, and active engagement across the continuum of care.

Studies demonstrate positive association between empowered team leadership and cross-functional synergies (teamwork and interprofessional cooperation) and clinical patient outcomes including lower rates of errors and patient mortality. Improving communication across teams helps to increase members' commitment, boost employee morale, improve processes, and create greater efficiencies in the workplace. Improved communication and cross-functional integration promote the sharing of best practices and knowledge transfer that make a positive difference in organizational growth, collaboration, brand, and productivity.

A study of medical practices by O'Malley, et al. (2015) found that a team approach to primary care was fostered by delegating more to other staff, soliciting staff input on workflow modifications and feeding back data to the team, expanding the roles of medical assistants and nurses, and holding regular team "huddles." Suggestions for managing team dynamics included using data to show the team how patient care improves with teamwork and incremental delegation of nonclinical tasks by physicians. Delegation increases staff engagement in workflow redesign and establishes a safe culture for feedback and questions. Other advantages of teamwork include:

- Physicians are more willing to delegate when team staffing is stable and when delegation is introduced incrementally, starting with routine tasks to medical assistants and licensed practical nurses.
- Assigning roles to team members helps increase their job satisfaction as well as allowing physicians more time to focus on patients' complex needs.
- Facilitation strategies involve huddles for clarifying the day's game plan; co-locating the physician, nurse, and medical assistant; promoting a culture in which staff can feel comfortable providing feedback; and taking advantage of EHR functions including instant communications.
- Nurse care managers' roles are central because of their work with patients between visits to help them manage chronic conditions and to develop care plans in partnership with patients and physicians.

- Patients are recognized as partners in identifying health goals, carrying out care plans, self-managing chronic conditions, and making decisions about their care.

The researchers observed that when teams lack formal authority to alter external system challenges (e.g., fee-for-service payment, resources, regulations), they naturally defer to the clinical leadership. Therefore, offering cross-training to physician leaders in how to change care processes may help PCMHs enhance performance, reduce errors, and improve patient safety.

Cross-training allows members to coach one another or even substitute each other's role. For example, both the nurse and respiratory therapist on a team know how to clear a patient's airway and both share similar levels of competence and confidence in performing this task. They anticipate and support one another's goals and seek each other's unique expertise and perspectives. Team members are open to feedback about errors and near misses. They listen respectfully to criticism when a member of the team challenges the safety of a plan or a process of care. It means that team members coordinate their work and jointly accept responsibility for outcomes.

HOW CORONAVIRUS SPARKED INDUSTRY COLLABORATION, TEAM-BASED CARE

The practice of team-based care is not a new concept, even if it is only emerging as a perfected science in this COVID-19 world. Industry leaders have long hailed team-based care as one of the keys to the value-based care puzzle, arguing that it leads to more efficient care, treatment access, and patient satisfaction. When doctors, nurses, advance practice providers, caseworkers, and others involved in patient care collaborate, outcomes improve. But it's not always that easy.

"Almost everybody is really good at working in a defined team," Dudley said.

> The majority are able to say, this is my team. And we can work well as a team. The challenge of that was in a hospital or clinic setting, you can't just be on one team, because there's so much integration that happens.

> Everyone working in an ambulatory clinic might work great together, which Dudley acknowledged is essential to quality patient care.

But that ambulatory clinic team needs to be able to work well with other teams that cut across them, like the social services that help patients get access to healthy food or follow-up with home-based care. "We've got to engage with those home-based care providers, whether they are part of our health system or organization or not. That is now the new team," Dudley explained. "That's traditionally where healthcare has holes. When it's not the clearest team that we're on, we're not great at creating, for example, teams of teams." But all of that has changed since the coronavirus hit US hospitals and health clinics. Providers and clinical leaders are foremost focused on getting patients better, on testing those who are displaying symptoms, and flattening the curve.

It doesn't matter if a clinic is a part of a hospital's health system when a patient displays concerning COVID-19 symptoms. Right now, things are so dire that they are all on the same team against the virus. "I have been blown away by how people are creating teams of teams," Dudley said.

> This goes to this removing of silos, and recognizing that everybody's on the team, and the team's going to follow the patient. So when the patient moves from being diagnosed, or coming to be tested, then there's another group that's going to ultimately have to engage and connect with that patient and there has to be something that continues to tie it all together.

(Patient Engagement, 2020)

Strategies and Tools

Gratton and Erickson (2007) studied teams that demonstrated high levels of cooperative behaviors despite the complexity of their structures. These researchers identified eight best practices that correlate with team success:

1. *Investing in signature relationship practices.* Health leaders can promote collaborative behavior by championing system-wide efforts and by making highly visible statements with credible communication.
2. *Modeling collaborative behavior.* Teams perform well in organizations where leaders rely on interprofessional cooperation regardless of disciplinary constraints.
3. *Creating a gift culture.* Creating incentives for collateral structures of communication and informal networks supports the social identity of members and encourages interfunctional collaboration.
4. *Ensuring the requisite skills.* HR staff that initiate teambuilding training in conflict resolution have a major impact on the success of teams.
5. *Supporting a strong sense of community.* When leaders reinforce flexible behaviors and transfer of knowledge across functional lines, organizational members feel more confident in reaching out to others.

6. *Assigning team leaders that are both task- and relationship-oriented.* These two roles are complementary, and both are important for effective team operations, especially during transitions.
7. *Building on heritage relationships.* Team members that build trust and develop common understanding help promote collaborative behavior.
8. *Understanding role clarity and task ambiguity.* When team members are familiar with their roles and tasks, uncertainty is reduced, and anxiety levels are down adding to the success of team performance.

An important tool that supports teambuilding and promotes learning and teamwork development is TeamSTEPPS™ (AHRQ, 2013). It is based on team structure and four teachable-learnable skills: Communication, leadership, situation monitoring, and mutual support. Developed for the Department of Defense Patient Safety Program in collaboration with the Agency for Healthcare Research and Quality, TeamSTEPPS is an evidence-based framework that, when used progressively with feedback sessions and improvement efforts, helps optimize team performance across the healthcare delivery system.

A shared purpose of employing TeamSTEPPS includes the reduction of clinical errors, improving the patient experience and care outcomes, improving patient and staff satisfaction, and reducing the cost of care. The TeamSTEPPS performance initiative employs an array of strategies that focus on performance feedback that is timely, accurate, specific, and respectful using the CUS, SBAR, DESC frameworks.

The team structure includes staff and clinicians with identifiable roles and responsibilities, patient advocates, and care givers or family members. Team members are accountable for communications and outcomes. The communication process is brief, clear, specific, and timely with inputs from all available sources and feedback loops to verify that updated information is communicated appropriately.

The exchange follows a structured process called SBAR by which critical information that requires immediate attention and action concerning a patient's condition is succinctly and accurately communicated among the team. Leadership ensures that team actions are understood, changes in information are shared, and team members have the necessary resources to efficiently maximize team performance.

SBAR

Situation—what is going on with the patient?

"I am calling about John Smith in room 432. Chief complaint of *dyspnea."*

Background—what is the clinical background or context?

"Patient is a 70-year-old male post-op day one from abdominal surgery. No prior history of cardiac or lung disease."

Assessment—what do I think the problem is?
"Breath sounds are decreased on the right side with acknowledgment of pain. Would like to rule-out pneumothorax."
Recommendation and request—what would I do to correct it?
"I feel strongly the patient should be assessed now. Can you come to room 432 now?"

Situation monitoring involves follow ups with team members on progress to ensure patient safety, availability of equipment, prevention of medical errors, and, if needed, revisions to the care plan. It begins with situation awareness or "knowing what's going on around you."

A shared mental model results from each team member maintaining situation awareness and ensuring that all team members are "on the same page" to support effective team functioning.

Monitoring situations in the delivery of healthcare is strengthened using a structured process called STEP with identifiable elements:

- Status of the patient
- Team members
- Environment
- Progress towards a goal

CUS, an expression of Concern, Uncomfortable, Safety—serves as an effective verbal alarm, empowering healthcare providers to "stop the line." When team members, especially in the Emergency Department (ED), speak the signal words of the CUS tool, they alert other members and cue them to clearly understand not just the issue but also its magnitude or severity. When someone says, "this is a safety issue," the current action must stop and be evaluated before continuing.

Mutual support provides task-related assistance and timely and constructive feedback to team members using accurate knowledge about their responsibilities and workload. This phase also includes advocating for the patient using the DESC script, a tool to increase the likelihood of resolving potential conflicts. Key strategies include:

- Team members jointly guard against an excess of work overload situations.
- Effective teams place all offers and requests for assistance in the context of patient safety.
- Team members foster a climate where it is expected that assistance will be actively sought and offered.

The DESC script is a constructive approach for managing and resolving conflict:

- D—describe the specific situation or behavior; provide relevant evidence.
- E—express how the situation makes you feel and outline specific concerns.

- S—suggest other alternatives and seek consensus about consequences.
- C—consequences should be stated in terms of impact on established team goals.

The ability to provide focused care for patients and improve population health at a lower cost per capita, and with higher reliability of care delivery, requires clinical integration, higher efficiency, effective EHR and shared data, and a culture of collaboration and teamwork. Resilient leaders are involved in not only planning and coordination across the continuum of care, but also in guiding and inspiring team members through transitions and challenges.

COVID-19 creates stress on multiple levels: Individual, team, organizational, and work-life. On an individual level, healthcare workers may feel concerns about their own health, or that of their families. They may also feel overworked, fatigued, or burned out.

Team-level stressors include lack of team member expertise—for example, when people must assume new roles—as well as unfamiliarity with new team members, increased consequences of mistakes that both team members and patients will experience, and new or unfamiliar processes or procedures.

On an organizational level, insufficient resources, such as PPE and ventilators, have been a major challenge. Work-life stressors, which are difficult to navigate even at the best of times, take a toll during COVID-19. These include concerns about family and friends, financial concerns due to unemployment or furlough of family members, and social isolation.

These stressors lead to both attitudinal and behavioral risk points.

Attitudes and cognitions of concern include low belief that the team can succeed (sometimes referred to as loss of collective efficacy); narrowing of attention, with excessive focus on oneself; insufficient shared mental models, such as roles and priorities; and discomfort speaking up, which creates a sense of lack of psychological safety.

Additional issues are that schisms may start to appear among team members, there may be insufficient vigilance, and people may fail to ask questions, admit concerns, or provide feedback. Perhaps most importantly when setbacks occur, they adversely affect the next tasks, creating low team resilience.

Recommendations for organizational and team leaders as well as team members to deal with these stressors and mitigate their negative impact include:

1. Celebrate all successes—big and small.
2. Make sure team members understand their roles and priorities.
3. Do not overlook anyone, including team members who work behind the scenes.
4. Encourage mutual team monitoring and support.

5. Foster psychological safety.
6. Help team members identify and address concerns within their own lives.
7. Consciously boost team resiliency.

Effective teamwork is one of the most important ways for us to continue navigating the unprecedented set of challenges posed by COVID-19 ... but also during the aftermath and going forward.

(Yasgur, B. Interview with Allison Traylor, 2020)

Assessing Teamwork

Table 7.3 outlines important criteria team leadership behaviors and skills across stages of team evolution: Team development, team leadership, promoting cooperation, facilitating meetings, resolving conflict, acting ethically, meeting team goals, and sustaining excellence. Since leadership is shared, team members take turns leading the team. The survey in Table 7.4 is designed to measure teamwork considering the eight dimensions.

Team leadership evolves through transition phases with each characterized with different needs and goals. For example, transitioning from a functional group to a highly interdependent team requires a team charter with goals and objectives, positive attitudes and team norms, clear tasks and metrics, performance strategy, effective communication, trust, and feedback. Moving towards action requires analytics, tracking systems, coordination, engagement, and maintenance of positive relationships and good team performance. To accomplish this, a driving force must be present—a resilient leader who is both task- and relationship-oriented with effective situational and teamwork skills.

Figure 7.3 shows the aggregate ratings of team members across the eight composites or dimensions of the teamwork survey. The scores are calculated by averaging composite-level percent positive scores across all dimensions. Since the percent positive is displayed as an overall average, scores are weighted equally in their contribution to the calculation of the average. The differences between the current and desired ratings are denoted in percentage points for each dimension, helpful for rank ordering the dimensions and prioritizing improvement efforts.

The assessment method helps to visually detect the differences across the eight dimensions, solicit thoughts and ideas about causes and interventions, prioritize areas for improvement, and agree on time to review results. It also helps to support the team's effort to develop a meaningful conversation about problems and brainstorm ideas for further improvement. For example, both "resolving conflicts" and "meeting team goals" reflect

Table 7.3 Behavioral Indicators

Dimension	*Boundaries*	*Priorities*	*Focus*	*Success Factors*	*Competencies*
Team development	Team leader establishes open channels of communication; the leader creates a climate where people can share ideas and feelings and begin to identify and align with common objectives	Identify team structure and team dynamics	Common goals; shared team responsibility	Obtaining external resources; shaping brand identity and image; enhancing reputation	Persuasion, effective presentation; negotiating skills
Team leadership		Employ situational leadership approaches to managing team performance	Innovation; flexibility	Identifying important trends; facilitating change	Creative thinking; intuition; innovation skills
Promoting cooperation	Team leader emphasizes common purpose and establishes acceptable norms. The leader clarifies the process of communication and encourages dialogue and involvement	Clarify the goals for team members and the roles needed to accomplish these goals	Mentoring, coaching	Developing members' capacity; inspiring action; empathizing	Self-understanding; active listening; sensitivity skills
Facilitating meetings		Facilitate meetings and encourage participation in team activities	Engagement; openness	Building cohesion and teamwork	Facilitation; problem-solving communication
Resolving conflict	Team leader encourages interdependence and reduces tensions and conflicts; promotes ownership and commitment; integrity and transparency	Recognize sources of conflict and means to resolve them	Stability; control	Maintaining the structure and flow of information; promoting consistency	Scheduling, organizing, coordinating; managing crises
Acting ethically		Distinguish ethical from unethical group decisions and behaviors	Integrity; quality; improvement	Tracking non-compliance; evaluating facts and details	Handling data and forms; reviewing behaviors and outcomes

(Continued)

Table 7.3 (Continued) Behavioral Indicators

Dimension	*Boundaries*	*Priorities*	*Focus*	*Success Factors*	*Competencies*
Meeting team goals	Team members are committed to team shared goals and have a clear understanding of expectations and responsibilities; team leader provides guidance for continuous improvement; team members are given opportunities to assume leadership	Recognize the importance of synergy and integrative solutions	Direction; goal clarity	Clarifying expectations; defining roles and responsibilities	Critical thinking; execution
Sustaining excellence		Support the team goals and the need for joint accountability	Outcome; evaluation	Motivating to accept joint accountability	Managing time and stress; working productively

Table 7.4 Assessment: Teamwork

Instructions: Rate how strongly you agree or disagree with each of the following statements by placing your responses twice: One for current, the other for desired.

Level of Agreement 1—Strongly disagree
2—Disagree
3—Neither agree nor disagree
4—Agree
5—Strongly agree

		Current	Desired
Team Development			
	I am knowledgeable about the dynamics of team development		
	I help team members establish trusting relationships		
	I help the team work more efficiently and productively		
	Avg		
Team Leadership			
	I initiate action to accomplish team goals		
	I have a good sense of the team's trajectory		
	I understand the value of synergy in inspiring team members		
	Avg		
Promoting Cooperation			
	I inspire group members to achieve common goals		
	I help clarify roles and shared responsibilities		
	I promote cooperation through trust and mutual respect		
	Avg		
Facilitating Meetings			
	I develop the agenda in consultation with team members		
	I provide information and relevant material		
	I encourage participation and contributions from others		
	Avg		
Resolving Conflict			
	I suggest ways that integrate different viewpoints		
	I use active listening during disagreements		
	I offer ideas to reach consensus		
	Avg		

(*Continued*)

Table 7.4 (Continued) Assessment: Teamwork

Acting Ethically			
	I place my concern for the group ahead of my own		
	I am respectful and sensitive to the other members		
	I treat members equally and equitably		
	Avg		
Meeting Goals			
	I value group decision-making		
	I collaborate with others		
	I support the outcomes of group decision-making		
	Avg		
Sustaining Excellence			
	I create opportunities for new development		
	I recognize and reward excellent performance		
	I pursue long-term goals for my team		
	Avg		

much larger "dents" (or gaps) and should be ranked higher on the improvement list of team members. Interventions could include team building, goal setting, time management, coaching, and mentoring. Retaking the survey and plotting the results on new diagrams can help the team to review its progress over time. Resilient leaders, team coordinators, and supervisors can use similar charts to map the responses of members, discuss the

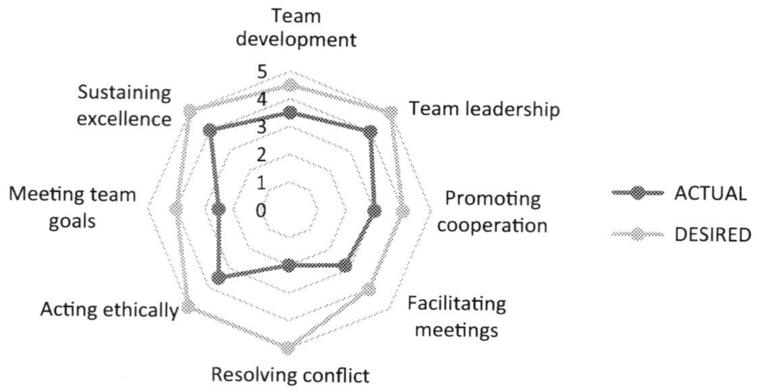

Figure 7.3 Dimensions of teamwork.

results with the team, explore the team's learning experience, and underscore the options for continuous improvement.

Conclusions

A systematic cultural assessment such as the one described in this chapter could help in identifying and implementing an effective culture of collaboration. Assessments of organizational culture are useful because they help managers and organizational leaders to target the trajectory of change and enhance the collective performance. Adaptive cultures and supportive communication practices serve as vital strategies for attracting and retaining talents in organizations and for strengthening teaming across boundaries. The first part of this chapter focused on identifying important dimensions of organizational culture that are strategically relevant, particularly with respect to the establishment of a culture of interprofessional collaboration.

Assessment instruments and strategies for diagnosing organizational cultures including key techniques for managing cultural change were described with examples and key takeaways. Organizational culture influences the operating conditions (e.g., norms, communication patterns, commitment, and accountability) that promote the effectiveness of teamwork. Therefore, the second part of this chapter explored the value of teamwork and interprofessional cooperation. Creating a culture of interprofessional collaboration and cross-functional synergies requires participative forms of leadership and communication and empowered team members. Resilient leaders who use motivational strategies that match the needs of employees and the complexity of the task environment build a culture of safety, promote teamwork, and improve patient outcomes.

References

AHRQ (2013). Team Strategies & Tools to Enhance Performance and Patient Safety, Retrieved from https://www.ahrq.gov/teamstepps/instructor/essentials/pocketguide.html#frame

AHRQ (2019). The Hospital Survey on Patient Safety Culture (SOPS), Retrieved from https://www.ahrq.gov/sops/surveys/hospital/index.html

Famolaro, T., Yount, N. D., Burns, W., Flashner, E., Liu, H., & Sorra, J. (2016). *Hospital Survey on Patient Safety Culture: 2016 User Comparative Database Report*, Agency for Healthcare Research and Quality; AHRQ, Retrieved from https://psnet.ahrq.gov/issue/hospital-survey-patient-safety-culture-2016-user-comparative-database-report

Gratton, L., & Erickson, T. J. (2007). Eight ways to build collaborative teams. *Harvard Business Review*, 85(11), 101–109.

Hines, S., Luna, K., Lofthus J., et al. (2008). *Becoming a High Reliability Organization: Operational Advice for Hospital Leaders*. (Prepared by the Lewin Group under Contract No. 290-04-0011.) AHRQ Publication No. 08–0022. Rockville, MD: Agency for Healthcare Research and Quality. April 2008.

James Anderson Center for Health Systems Excellence, Retrieved from https://www.cincinnatichildrens.org/service/j/anderson-center/safety/methodology/high-reliability

Kaldy, J. (2021). Positive Culture Provides a Strong Foundation, Retrieved from https://www.providermagazine.com/Topics/Special-Features/Pages/Positive-Culture-Provides-a-Strong-Foundation.aspx, April 1.

O'Malley, A. S., Gourevitch, R., Draper, K., Bond, A., & Tirodkar, M. A. (2015). Overcoming challenges to teamwork in patient-centered medical homes: A qualitative study. *Journal of General Internal Medicine*, 30, 183–192.

Patient Engagement (2020). How Coronavirus Sparked Industry Collaboration, Team-based Care, Retrieved from https://patientengagementhit.com/features/how-coronavirus-sparked-industry-collaboration-team-based-care, March 27

Reason, J. (1990). *Human Error*. Cambridge: Cambridge University Press.

The Joint Commission (2017). The Essential Role of Leadership in Developing a Safety Culture, Retrieved from https://www.jointcommission.org/assets/1/18/SEA_57_Safety_Culture_Leadership_0317.pdf

Yohn, D. L. (2021). Company Culture is Everyone's Responsibility. *HBR*, Retrieved from https://hbr.org/2021/02/company-culture-is-everyones-responsibility, February 8.

Yasgur, B. (2020). Interview with Allison Traylor Seven Tips for Managing Healthcare Teamwork During a Pandemic, Retrieved from https://www.empr.com/home/features/seven-tips-for-managing-healthcare-teamwork-during-the-pandemic-expert-interview/, July 16.

Chapter 8

Leveraging Strengths to Maximize Resilience in Leadership

This chapter showcases self-assessment instruments to demonstrate how to achieve balanced leadership for optimal communication relationships and alignment between leadership roles and organizational goals. Instruments for identifying and evaluating message orientations and communication strategies for clarifying expectations during organizational transitions are also included.

Knowing in advance what senior managers communicate and detecting the tone of the messages is empowering in helping managers avoid second guessing higher levels and, instead, focusing attention on messages that are consistent with the expectations of senior management and key stakeholders. This chapter begins with the shared-leadership concept that leverages complementary skills and synergistic effects that transcend organizational functions.

Keeping the organization's strategic objectives at the center of attention helps achieve the mission and goals of the integrated health system. Further, the leadership roles that C-level executives assume, and even current leadership development programs and skill-building initiatives, need to align with the strategic objectives. For example, the strategy of providing health services across the continuum of care through partnerships and alliances at the ACO level is aligned with teamwork and interprofessional collaboration at the local hospital level.

Resilient leaders model the way by walking the talk, cherishing mutual respect, trust, and teamwork, and by giving employees access to the right tools and resources to be successful.

When alignment is effective, members have a clear and shared sense of purpose; energy and inspiration run high, and cooperation is strong.

DOI: 10.4324/9781003190929-8

Members perform better when they fully understand and accept the mission and goals of their health settings, and they develop a better sense of ownership when they understand the impact they make in achieving those goals. By aligning strengths with business objectives, top executives can ensure that the investment they make in their leadership development is focused and reflects the strategic direction of the organization.

A leadership alignment strategy is explored in this chapter to help C-level executives and managers identify personal strengths and weaknesses, develop improvement plans, and realign their leadership roles with organizational goals and strategies.

Shared Leadership

The challenge to achieve better patient outcomes with increasingly limited financial resources has created an acute need for more physician leaders. However, physicians want to be led by other physicians, not administrators. They trust physician leaders to make appropriate decisions about redesigning care delivery and balancing quality and cost.

A recent study by the ABLM Foundation which engaged NORC at the University of Chicago to learn more about public and physician perceptions of trust in the U.S. health system found that 30% of physicians surveyed said the pandemic decreased their level of trust in healthcare organization leadership. Forty-one percent of physicians surveyed said the pandemic increased their level of trust in fellow physicians. In general, most physicians surveyed (94%) reported trusting fellow physicians within their practice (ABLM, 2021).

The perceptual differences between physicians and administrators often block the two sides from investing in co-leadership programs. Physicians see administrators as insulated from the real pressures of patient care—taking calls, scrambling to meet strict productivity demands. They see administrators as being paid for non-productive work. Administrators, they claim, are concerned about how much things cost, they focus on problems, and manage away from points of impact where clinicians and patients interact.

Administrators, on the other hand, claim that physicians lack a big-picture mindset. Physicians, they say, see things from their own perspective and often do not always have time or do not want to accomplish administrative tasks. However, they do not trust others to do them either. Physicians in the front lines often have a hard time coming to a group decision. There is no leadership.

Physicians, however, claim that they have a better understanding of the nature of healthcare challenges. They are unwilling to compromise quality, safety, or labor for profit and have an improved understanding of patient operational issues. Administrators see themselves as better value strategists able to anticipate change within the healthcare industry and selectively embrace or adapt to new technologies, governmental regulations, or decreasing reimbursement. They also enjoy improved interactions with other healthcare staffing (RNs, PharmDs, MDs) and are responsible for coordination with referral sources (private offices or clinics).

One response to the tension that exists between administrators and physicians is through a collaborative relationship in which the two sides can form shared-leadership structures with complementary skills called dyads.

Dyad leaders create synergistic work environments that promote mutual trust and joint accountability. Instituting a dyad management structure imbeds physician leaders into the pyramid and creates opportunities for dealing with complexity through effective collaboration and shared experiences. When operationalized, dyad leaders encourage care teams to meet broader, emerging goals through interprofessional collaboration and teamwork. While patient engagement and health advocacy are geared primarily towards care delivery in which clinicians naturally assume greater responsibilities, administrators, nonetheless, are interested in patient satisfaction, hospital ratings, CMS reimbursement, and a host of efficiency and outcome measures.

In the dyad, the equal partners bring diverse perspectives to create win–win outcomes. Administrators bring business skills essential for managing productivity and cost-effective delivery of care to health populations. Physicians bring medical expertise for determining health initiatives, providing high-value patient care, ensuring quality and patient safety, and assessing clinical outcomes. Shared leadership could operate in multiple areas of a healthcare organization, including the C-suite, divisions of care (e.g., health centers), and service lines.

In acute care hospitals, shared leadership could draw on board-level chairs and directors, chief operating officers, and clinical operations officers. In nursing homes, shared leadership could draw on facility owners, administrators, directors of nursing, and managers. These partnerships are relational methods for making inroads into a new era of quality-based, collaborative patient care. Through a shared vision, the shared-leadership model encourages systems thinking and aligns clinical and operational resources to improve efficiency and optimize outcomes.

The dyad with its focus on shared leadership allows the partners to collaborate around four important roles—the value strategist, clinical integration champion, patient advocate, and health innovator (Table 8.1). These roles span important areas of health system performance such as financial management, clinical integration, patient engagement, and population health. Shared-leadership structures provide leaders and team members with opportunities to receive recognition for their complementary competencies, gain visibility, increase breadth of knowledge by overseeing key hospital interfaces, and help support leadership development and succession programs in health systems.

The items in Table 8.1 can be used in a self-assessment survey aimed at finding out the frequency of a leader engagement in a particular role: Health innovator, value strategist, CI champion, and patient advocate.

Table 8.1 Assessment: Shared-Leadership Roles

Context	*Leadership Role*
Population Health	**Health Innovator**
	• Redesigning health system services for population health • Improving care quality and patient safety • Reducing total cost of care for a population by fostering innovation • Catering to community needs • Promoting a culture of safety and reliability • Excelling in patient care with teamwork and innovative solutions • Improving care coordination among providers and care givers • Initiating referral relationships with partner hospitals • Enhancing service line capabilities through formal partnership
Financial Performance	**Value Strategist**
	• Increasing scale by forming clinically integrated provider networks • Expanding market share for ambulatory surgery centers (ASCs) and outpatient treatments • Reducing financial risk and promoting higher rates of utilization • Creating new service lines and revenue streams to increase profitability • Recruiting physicians to support growth and patient loyalty • Managing provider productivity • Strengthening finances to facilitate reinvestment and innovation • Applying balanced scorecard to monitor performance • Conducting analysis of competitors' strategic moves • Developing and executing strategic plans • Monitoring supply chain performance • Managing human capital, staffing, and recruiting • Tracking market share performance
Clinical Integration	**Clinical Integration Champion**
	• Evaluating accounting and information systems and methods • Integrating IT systems • Implementing EHR • Promoting value-based culture • Improving interprofessional collaboration • Incentivizing teamwork among physicians and diverse care teams • Supporting the medical group practice culture • Improving cost containment and efficiency

(*Continued*)

Table 8.1 (Continued) Assessment: Shared-Leadership Roles

Context	*Leadership Role*
	• Using analytics to improve coordination of care • Using evidence-based information in patient diagnosis and treatment • Increasing rate of interoperability to improve quality and reduce cost • Evaluating clinical integration outcomes • Rewarding physician leadership and skill development • Encouraging clinical care innovation
Patient Engagement	**Patient Advocate**
	• Engaging physicians and patients in lowering clinical variation • Improving teamwork training and interpersonal skill building • Reducing readmissions • Tracking patient compliance with evidence-based practices • Increasing patient satisfaction and quality outcomes • Improving doctor-patient communication • Enhancing hospital credibility

Source: Adapted from Belasen, A. (2019). *Dyad Leadership*.

Table 8.2 provides possible responses across a seven-point Likert Scale. To find out your frequency level, indicate the response that best matches your situation next to each statement. An Excel spreadsheet with simple averages across the responses for each category in Table 8.1 can be used to create a self-assessment chart like the one in Figure 8.1.

To determine the most important areas for improvement, the subject of the self-assessment (e.g., team leader, dyad leader, division leader) can review, discuss, and compare the results of each quadrant role. They can identify weak spots and sweet spots for further

Table 8.2 Likert Scale for the Survey Items in Table 8.1

1. Never
2. Rarely, in less than 10% of the chances when I could have
3. Occasionally, in about 30% of the chances when I could have
4. Sometimes, in about 50% of the chances when I could have
5. Frequently, in about 70% of the chances when I could have
6. Usually, in about 90% of the chances I could have
7. Every time

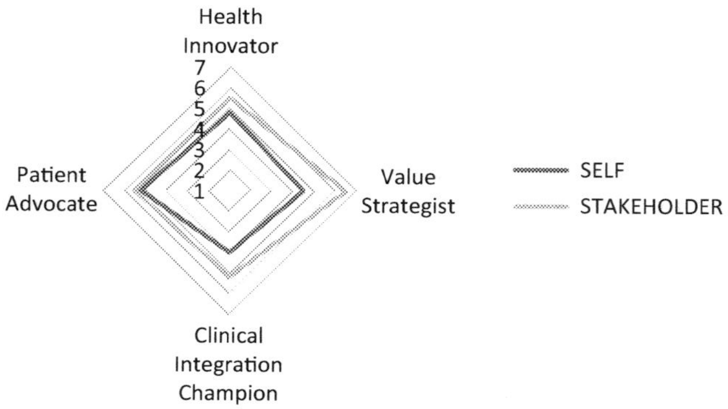

Figure 8.1 Healthcare leadership roles self-assessment.

development and discuss improvement plans with influential stakeholders (mentor, top executive, board director) to focus on key development efforts. Sometimes, however, the perceptual gap between how stakeholders view the effectiveness of their organizations and how team leaders believe they perform their communicative duties is too wide to overcome, requiring further interventions through additional mentoring, incentives, or training. Two examples with relatively larger gaps between the self-assessment ratings and those of stakeholders are the innovator role and the value strategist role (Figure 8.1).

Increasing safety through interfunctional collaboration, breaking down silos, identifying innovative methods of care delivery, and leveraging resources and capabilities across the ACO are important areas of focus of leadership in the capacity of the *innovator role*. Stakeholders such as board directors may take actions to promote the need for strengthening the culture of safety that transcends specialized areas and that empowers staff members to collaborate in identifying innovative solutions to problems.

The greatest gap in Figure 8.1, however, seems to evolve around the *value strategist* role. Stakeholders may show increased attention to expanding market share for ambulatory surgery centers (ASCs) and outpatient treatments and for creating new service lines and revenue streams to increase profitability. Stakeholders may also show vast interest in reducing financial risk, promoting higher rates of utilization, and maximizing operating efficiencies.

When leaders in the capacity of innovator role and value strategist role respond to signals and communications about perceived performance gaps in specific areas of focus, they can initiate steps to bridge these gaps and align their responses with stakeholders' perceptions and interests. Thus, the assessment serves as a powerful medium to link leadership roles and competencies with present and future organizational goals and strategies for improving the patient experience of care, enhancing the health of populations, and reducing the per capita cost of healthcare.

By aligning roles and skills with business objectives, top executives can ensure that the investments they make in leadership development and succession planning are linked with the strategic direction of the organization. When the alignment is optimal, organizational members have a clear sense of shared purpose and they understand better the scope of the organizational mission and goals.

Members develop a better sense of ownership, become more committed and accountable, and work collaboratively to achieve those goals. Moreover, energy and inspiration run high and both individual leaders and the effectiveness of their complementary skills increase.

Physician Leadership Development

The COVID-19 crisis has forced physicians to make daily decisions that require knowledge and skills they did not acquire as part of their biomedical training. Physicians are being called upon to be both managers—able to set processes and structures—and leaders—capable of creating vision and inspiring action. Although these skills may have been previously considered as just nice to have, they are now as central to being a physician as physiology and biochemistry. While traditionally only a small portion of physicians undertake management training, either through executive or joint degree programs, the challenges associated with the need to deal with the COVID-19 pandemic more holistically have reinforced the importance of interprofessional collaboration and leadership skills across the continuum of care.

Training should emphasize skills related to interpersonal communication, systems approach, planning, and coordination and align with organizational strategic objectives. For example, the strategy of providing health services across the continuum of care through partnerships and alliances at the macro level should align with teamwork and interprofessional collaboration at the micro level.

Colorado witnessed exponential growth of COVID-19 cases beginning in March 2020. As the number of acute hospitalizations increased, seven Colorado health systems came together through their chief medical officers and chief clinical officers to form a working group for the purpose of mounting a collaborative response to COVID-19. A representative from the Colorado Hospital Association was also invited. Between March and July 2020, the seven Colorado health systems cared for 6,329 (98%) of the 6,441 hospitalized patients in the state. The unique collaboration, which involved the sharing of best practices and scarce resources as well as advocating for policy to optimally address the pandemic, ultimately allowed our state to rapidly de-escalate the rates of infection, hospitalization, and mortality due to COVID-19. We share the lessons learned about the elements of this unique collaboration that allowed our state to successfully weather the first wave of the COVID-19 pandemic ... The collective goal was to bring the major health systems together to identify issues, share best practices, align on difficult decisions, and provide guidance when there was either no guidance or rapidly changing guidance on how to address these unprecedented challenges (NEJM Catalyst, 2020).

Allocating resources and championing leadership development programs and skill building that align organizational needs with broad-based leadership capability ensure successful patient outcomes. Skill building can be based on progression of learning and scope of responsibilities (Figure 8.2). Physician leaders, for example, with the capacity to move beyond their clinical task environment to lead and manage individuals, teams, or service lines often transition through several important stages of career paths with requisite skills. Technical tasks are linked to the clinical discipline, specialized knowledge, and compliance. Interpersonal tasks involve leading, motivating, and developing direct reports. Strategic tasks are associated with financial reports, analysis, and strategic communication including direct involvement in headquarter projects and boardroom discussions.

As physicians progress along the leadership pathway, the need for developing leadership and management skills and competencies to match the new task environment becomes a priority (Belasen, 2019). The practicing physicians head a care team or a project group and are often in charge of several clinicians within a specialized unit. They share common goals and understanding and most of the tasks and responsibilities require technical and interpersonal skills.

The medical group consists of several units, committees, and/or projects, and typically requires physicians with some administrative experience. Interfunctional collaboration skills and system thinking skills are vital for the success of the medical group. System-wide operations require physicians with strong strategic skills to lead hospitals, medical groups, executives, managers, and partners. Technical and interpersonal skills and to a large degree conceptual and system thinking skills are crucial for the success of the leader.

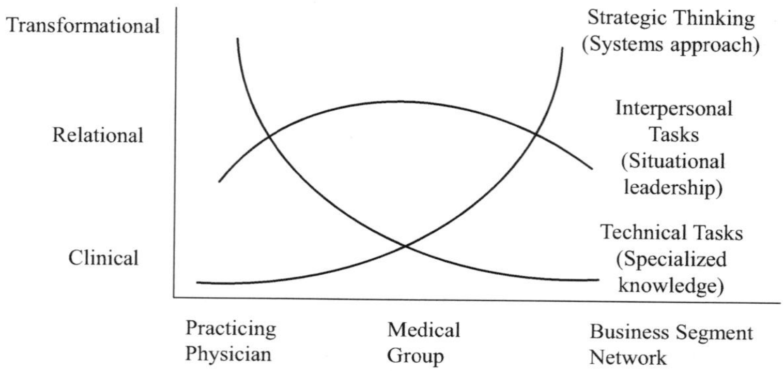

Figure 8.2 Progression of learning experience.

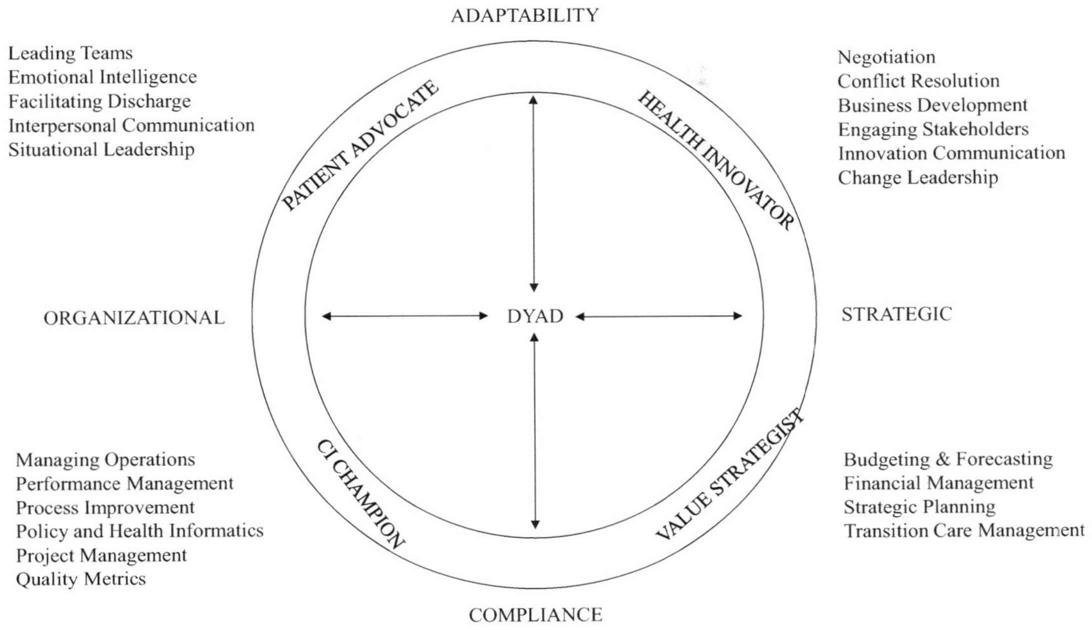

Figure 8.3 Skills and knowledge areas. *Source*: Adapted from Belasen, A. (2019). *Dyad Leadership*.

In addition to having strong clinical knowledge, physician leaders need to enhance their EI and applied management skills, analytic skills, and strategic skills to effectively lead medical groups, supervise service lines, or manage a larger hospital system. In line with the four roles described in Table 8.1, developing self-awareness and EI skills, cultivating and promoting teamwork, and championing interfunctional collaboration are always a good start. Moving forward, training in transition management and continuous process improvement helps build the foundation for developing internal business skills. At the upper middle management level, strategic decision-making, financial management, and economic analysis of healthcare markets shift the learning to the system level where visioning and strategic initiatives to drive strategic change are honed (Figure 8.3).

The progressive learning described above, and the acquisition of requisite knowledge also help to expand physicians' administrative capabilities and enhance their confidence to make informed decisions at any dyad level. As a leadership development tool, the framework in Figure 8.3 helps to identify related areas for self-development with insights about relevant training and education to meet future development and close potential gaps.

HOW TOP HEALTH SYSTEMS DEVELOP PHYSICIAN LEADERS IN-HOUSE

As the business of healthcare becomes increasingly tied to clinical outcomes, the demand for qualified physician leaders at hospitals and health systems now far outpaces the supply. With increased competition for experienced physician executives, it is more important than ever to be able to pull from an internal pool of physician talent.

However, only 47% of healthcare organizations have a development pipeline for physician leaders. If you are thinking of building a leadership development program—or optimizing your own—read on to learn about three successful programs.

BSWEEP provides emerging leaders (e.g., physician and administrative supervisors, project-leads, committee members) with the opportunity to employ their business knowledge and prepare for future leadership roles.

BSWEEP's 13-month curriculum consists of 12 required sessions that include both course work (accounting, marketing, psychology, advocacy, leadership, and finance) and team-based projects (six-person, multi-disciplinary teams), which complete one BSW specific project and several complementary exercises across each of the two semesters (Advisory Board, 2017).

Mentoring

Active mentors that guide and coach the development of key physician leaders can help accelerate the progressive learning of dyad physician leaders. Mentoring is a transformational behavior that serves aspiring physician leaders well. Mentoring can also take shape in a group setting with peer mentoring and reciprocal relationships in which everyone in the group is a mentor and a mentee. Mentoring might also help physicians overcome cultural barriers and tough workplace practices, challenge existing values and norms, and focus on the larger context rather than routine tasks. A physician mentor, regardless of setting, can empower aspiring physician leaders by fostering autonomy, personal responsibility, and problem-solving and decision-making skills.

Effective mentoring includes sponsorship, exposure, coaching, counseling, overcoming bureaucratic hurdles, and social support. Mentor transformational leadership also benefits the self-development and self-clarity of aspiring physicians, important influences on efficacy and confidence. The transformational mentor can help facilitate the attainment of physician development and growth to mastery.

LOOKING TO DEVELOP PHYSICIAN LEADERS? INVEST IN MENTORING

Hospital executives looking to find leaders among their physician ranks would be wise to invest in creating and maintaining a mentorship program. Such efforts can go a long way towards improving care and lowering costs, according to an article in *Hospitals & Health Networks*.

Mentorship programs, according to Maine Medical Center CMO Peter Bates, put into practice "abstract concepts" taught in the classroom, making retention of information a much more tangible achievement. "Having a mentor to work with someone on the application of competencies ... to a specific project is much more powerful as a learning tool than just talking about these skills," Bates says.

Designing a strong program, however, is no small feat. A recent survey conducted by the *National Center for Healthcare Leadership* shows that evidence-based leadership development is more successful at health systems and hospitals affiliated with systems, likely due to a larger pool of available resources.

Currently, Wisconsin-based Aurora Medical Group picks its physician leaders from management committees that supervise various departments throughout the hospital, according to *H&HN*. "By observing the thought processes and engagement levels of committee participants, we can obtain insights into which physicians have the interest, the fortitude ... to develop into physician leaders," says Jon Kluge, vice president of clinical operations. "The management committees give physicians an opportunity to get involved in leadership and decision-making" (Bowman, 2011).

Message Orientations

Leadership is about making employees feel safe, creating an atmosphere that supports innovation and that integrates safety messages into daily activities and meetings. Leaders must also communicate carefully to achieve positive outcomes, not merely to fill the airways. According to Clampitt, et al. (2000) executives tend to gravitate towards less effective forms of communication such as "spray and pray" (abundant communication) or "withhold and uphold" (limited communication). In fact, over-communicating can be as destructive as under-communicating.

Too much communication can cause confusion, misunderstandings, loss of productivity, and can overwhelm those on the receiving end. Withholding communication, on the other hand, can lead to distrust, uncertainty, low morale, and a lack of alignment. Instead, executives should opt for the strategy of "underscore and explore" with an articulation of a few core messages clearly linked to organizational outcomes, while actively listening for potential misunderstandings and unrecognized obstacles.

An important question is how managers select the right role to communicate different tasks and goals and use the most effective message orientation, or right approach, for each task or goal they encounter. This section focuses on the value of aligning message orientations to the type of stakeholders that healthcare leaders engage in their daily operations. It includes a self-assessment survey to help identify personal strengths and weaknesses.

Researchers suggested four different message orientations (which emphasizes style over content): Relational, promotional, transformational, and hierarchical (Belasen, 2008; Belasen & Frank, 2010; Rogers & Hildebrandt, 1993). These messages can be used situationally based on purpose, medium, focus, and audience (Table 8.3).

Relational messages are aimed at personal relationships, informal interactions, peer communications, and maintaining an awareness of the importance of the individual's role in completing the organization's mission. When leaders use the "patient advocate" role, for example, they rely on a relational approach to communication, which places emphasis on patients' insights and feedback. There is a focus on mutual respect, common understandings, commitment, and concerns for quality care.

Promotional messages relate to the mission of the organization to meet external expectations for health services, to perform productively to maximize returns on equity, and to

Table 8.3 Message Congruency

Relational **Purpose:** Establish integrity, rapport, trust, confidence, and commitment **Medium and tone:** Conversational, familiar words, inclusive pronouns, personal examples, honesty, committed **Focus:** Receiver-centered **Audience:** Employees **Example:** Informal chats, cafeteria talks, reflective	**Transformational** **Purpose:** Challenge receivers to accept mind-stretching vision **Medium and tone:** Visionary, charismatic, vivid, colorful metaphors, symbols, oral delivery, enthusiastic, emphatic, unorthodox written communication **Focus:** Idea-centered, futuristic, and rhetorical **Audience:** Customers, investors **Example:** CEO speech, written strategic plan, smart talk, communicating vision
Hierarchical **Purpose:** Providing clear directions to receivers **Medium and tone:** Neutral, precise words, controlled, sequential, standard constructions, factual accuracy, structural rigor, logical progression, realistic presentation, conventional documents, concrete examples, lists, tables, audit reports **Focus:** Channel-centered **Audience:** Regulators **Example:** Policy statements, procedural specifications, rules, standards, written documents, computer printouts, unaddressed letters, memos, directives	**Promotional** **Purpose:** Promoting an idea, selling product or service, persuading receivers, establishing credibility **Medium and tone:** Decisive, engaging, original, supported by credible evidence, prepositional, assertive, declarative, vivid examples, sense of urgency **Focus:** Argument-centered **Audience:** Partners, stakeholders **Example:** Sales presentations, recommendations to senior managers, press releases, directives, quarterly results, financial reports

Adapted from: Belasen, A. (2008). *The Theory and Practice of Corporate Communication.*

enhance performance credibility and organizational accountability. A promotional orientation fits the behaviors displayed by the "value strategist" who relies on persuasion strategies to meet hospital objectives.

Transformational messages match the styles and behaviors of the "health innovator" who excels in selling ideas effectively and in meeting future organizational and adaptation goals. There is a focus on adapting to new market requirements, branding, and reputation management to address interests of external stakeholders. Success is determined by the extent to which framing of communication is insightful, mind stretching, and visionary.

Hierarchical message orientations characterize the flow and dissemination of formal communications across organizational lines and align well with the "CI champion" who focuses on coordinating individuals and groups through work processes, metrics, and systems of control. Success is determined by whether the communication seems realistic, practical, and informative.

Message Orientation: Self-Assessment

Having a strong understanding of the frequency (amount of content), the flow (who the message is directed to), and the tenacity of the message (power of the message or the source of the message) can help mitigate communication roadblocks as well as clarify leadership expectations. When the lines of communication are clear and the messages reach their target audiences with appropriate orientation, the consistency of organizational communication increases. This should also help reduce the opportunity for miscommunication and the potential for conflict between senders and receivers.

The self-assessment tool in Table 8.4 is particularly relevant for explaining communications and message orientations in transitioning healthcare organizations. Knowing in advance what managers communicate, as well as detecting the tone of the messages, should also help managers avoid second guessing the importance of objectives and instructions, consistent with the expectations of top executives and directors (Belasen & Frank, 2010; Rogers & Hildebrandt, 1993). For each statement in Table 8.4, indicate the behavior that you will most likely use. You will have two responses: One to describe the messages as they are now; another to describe messages as they should be (preferred). These responses will be the same if the message is exactly as you think it should be for the situation.

In Figure 8.4, the manager seems to place more weight on promotional and hierarchical message orientations than on transformational and lateral, suggesting a communication orientation within the boundaries of formal logic, discipline, and credibility. This manager's profile, however, shows a clear gap between the actual and preferred modes of communication as the preferred mode seems to shift more towards transformational and relational message orientations.

Table 8.4 Assessment: Message Orientations

Frequency Level—Likert 7 Point 1—Never 2—Rarely, in less than 10% of the chances when I could have 3—Occasionally, in about 30% of the chances when I could have 4—Sometimes, in about 50% of the chances when I could have 5—Frequently, in about 70% of the chances when I could have 6—Usually, in about 90% of the chances I could have 7—Every time	**Actual**	**Desired**
When I communicate new directions, I make sure that I am discerning, and perceptive of the receivers' reactions [**aware**]		
When asked for my opinion, the tone of my messages is forceful and prevailing [**emphatic**]		
I inspire peers or team members with messages that are mind stretching and visionary [**insightful**]		
I encourage communications that are creative and original [**innovative**]		
My messages are interesting and stimulating [**engaging**]		
I am conclusive and decisive when I communicate goals to team members [**action oriented**]		
I make big efforts to use realistic and informative messages [**practical**]		
My statements and messages are focused and logical [**organized**]		
I use rigor and consistency in communicating with peers [**precise**]		
I make sure that my messages are technically correct [**accurate**]		
I use credible and believable communications with peers and team members [**plausible**]		
My communication with others is open and candid [**honest**]		

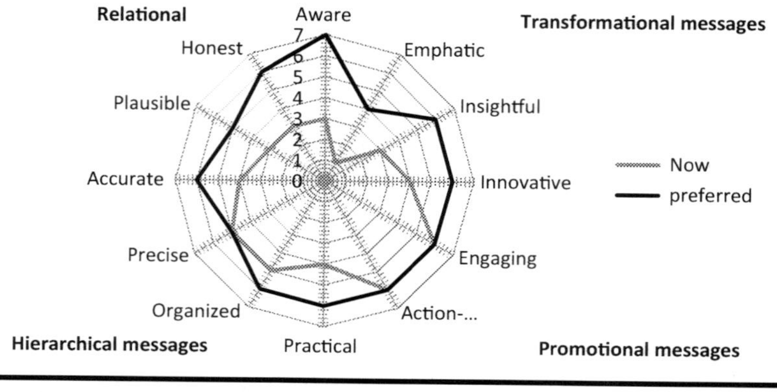

Figure 8.4 Actual and preferred message orientations.

The gap between the two charts in Figure 8.4 represents opportunities for self-improvement. When patients, employees, peers, and supervisors provide their inputs (often referred to as 360 assessments), this framework can become a powerful tool for guiding improvement efforts based on expectations from others. When communication strategies are aligned with effective EI skills, they also benefit the ability to listen and empathize with others, as well as the quality of interpersonal relationship.

EI Leader

Goffee and Jones (2000) suggest that effective EI leaders understand their weaknesses, rely heavily on intuition to gauge the appropriate timing, and display clear commitment to the course of their actions, manage employees with tough empathy, and reveal their differences. Revealing personal differences is the toughest challenge requiring a strong sense of personal integrity and moral courage. Verbalizing personal vulnerabilities demonstrates humility and honesty. It conveys confidence. When a leader admits to weaknesses, it builds trust and fuels a collaborative work environment, which promotes unity among followers and leaders.

The ability to collect and interpret relevant data requires intuition and analysis. There is an abundant amount of information that reaches leaders from multiple directions leading to unnecessary confusion and complexity. Intuition helps reduce complexity and narrows down the available options, which can then be analyzed in a logical way.

The reverse is true, too. A rational analysis may only reveal a few options for solving problems, and intuition is needed to single out the right one. Practicing tough empathy, however, requires the leader to make unpopular decisions. It prevents followers from becoming too complacent. Effective EI leaders use their differences to keep a social distance but, at the same time, they are expected not to over-differentiate to avoid the perception of being arrogant or isolated.

> I've noticed that the power of the role can blind CEOs to a lot of things, especially when it comes to themselves and their relationships at work. In essence, two key emotional intelligence competencies, self-awareness and empathy, often disappear from CEOs' tool kits.
>
> Why? There are several reasons. First, power really does corrupt us, including our judgment. Second, people treat us differently if we are powerful. Sometimes they love us more; sometimes they hate us more. Either way, it's easy to get caught up in and believe the hype.

Finally, a lot of people get to the top without doing a lot of personal introspection or growth. While they seem to have learned emotional intelligence along the way, it's often fairly superficial. What can prospective CEOs do to be better prepared to deal with our complicated and complex human responses to power in the workplace? To truly learn to be a better leader, you've got to figure yourself out. To start, ask yourself a few questions:

- How do you feel about power? How do you react to people who have power over you or who have authority and can make decisions that affect your life? Where do you think your reactions to power and authority originated?
- How do you feel about the trappings of power, things like money, cars, homes, vacations?
- Do you measure yourself with these yardsticks? How do you feel when you "measure up"? How do you treat people who don't measure up?
- What is more important to you than power? Is it family, health, well-being, happiness, ethics?

Being aware of this and letting your values guide your choices will go a long way towards helping you navigate your behaviors and thoughts at work. Most leaders have come to accept that **emotional intelligence** is key to their success. But we still have a long way to go before we realize that developing emotional intelligence is a lifelong quest, not an exercise. And for senior leaders and CEOs, who hold people's careers and livelihoods in their hands, it's a responsibility. (McKee, 2016)

EI leaders may acknowledge their weaknesses and vulnerabilities, but if a weakness involves incompetency, it may have an adverse effect on peers and followers. This is where self-assessment becomes an important tool for creating self-awareness and for developing continuous improvement plans.

Great leaders are aware of their own leadership style. Knowing your EI strengths and weaknesses helps reduce stress and promote healthy relationships. Improving your EI skills across the five components in Table 8.5 will make you a leader with the empathy and communication sensitivity skills essential for leading teams effectively.

Thinking about your attitudes and beliefs when working with teams and individuals, reflect on each statement by indicating the response that best matches your beliefs, first in terms of actual (i.e., current beliefs, views, behaviors) and then in terms of desired expectations. Calculate the averages and create a chart similar to Figure 8.5 using an Excel spreadsheet.

Table 8.5 Assessment: EI Skills

Frequency Level (Seven-Point Likert Scale) 1—*Very untrue of what I believe* 2—*Untrue of what I believe* 3—*Somewhat untrue of what I believe* 4—*Neutral* 5—*Somewhat true of what I believe* 6—*True of what I believe* 7—*Very true of what I believe*		
Emotional Intelligence Skills	**Current**	**Desired**
Self-Awareness		
I recognize immediately when I am short-tempered		
I am aware when I am happy		
I know when I feel stressed out		
I can tell when I am emotional		
I am aware when I feel anxious		
I can detect my own anger		
Avg		
Self-Regulation		
I can let go of my anger when someone hurts my feelings		
I can control my mood		
I do not hold a grudge when someone annoys me		
I can consciously alter my frame of mind		
I do not let stressful situations overcome me		
I can separate work stressors from my life		
Avg		
Motivation		
I am internally motivated to accomplish challenging tasks		
I am motivated to complete my work on time		
I always meet my personal goals		
I set my priorities and manage my time productively		

(Continued)

Table 8.5 (Continued) Assessment: EI Skills

I can challenge myself to accomplish difficult tasks		
I feel motivated when challenged		
Avg		
Empathy		
I am able to understand the other person's perspectives		
I can empathize with others		
I can tell if someone is upset with me		
I can understand if I am being unreasonable		
I can understand the effects of my decisions on others		
I can see things from others' point of view		
Avg		
Social		
I am a good listener when others communicate with me		
I do not interrupt others' conversations		
I enjoy interacting with others		
I am comfortable working with individuals and teams		
I am good at reconciling differences with others		
I know how to build trust and respect in the workplace		
Avg		

The chart in Figure 8.5 reveals a potential gap between current levels of beliefs and attitudes versus desired levels across the five skills of emotional intelligence. Moving meaningfully from the current EI skills in Figure 8.5 to the more desired level requires further development through training, practice, and even mentoring. When achieved, strong EI skills help facilitate positive interactions, build mutual trust, and enhance communication and listening skills.

Conclusions

The unique features of the pandemic have challenged leaders in an unprecedented manner. There is enormous stress due to complexity and unpredictability, and there are certain

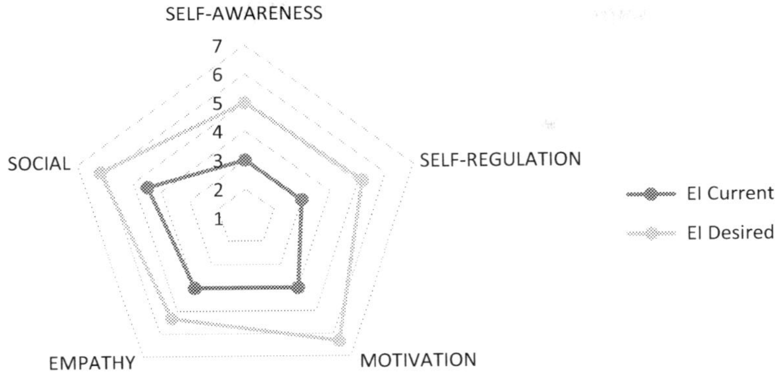

Figure 8.5 Current and desired EI skills.

characteristics leaders must exhibit to be successful. They must be calming, confident and positive, courageous, empathetic, and resilient. And, as importantly, they must express a vision, communicate, act, seek clarity, and keep things simple and purposeful.

Resilient leaders will continue to make decisions based on incomplete and conflicting information and will lead their organizations thoughtfully through a time of high anxiety, stress, and loss. In a time of crisis, a leader must leverage the power of efficient communication to protect its most important asset, its employees. The leader is tasked with establishing a communication strategy for internal information sharing, one that must adhere to a framework that is aligned with an open, accessible sharing of information.

Resilient leaders need to communicate clearly and regularly to all stakeholders and be prepared to explore and underscore important evidence and decisions during times of crisis such as the COVID pandemic. However, first and foremost, they must share information with their teams on how the organization will meet its mission and strategic goals and use empathy and the right communication orientation to motivate employees. Most leaders, indeed, have come to accept that emotional intelligence is key to their long-term success.

Mastering EI is a marathon, not a sprint. And for resilient leaders who handle the complexity of the healthcare environment, it is an important responsibility. They need to balance direction-giving—dispelling ambiguity and transparently sharing expectations; with meaning-making—giving significance and cultural guidance to employees; and empathy—demonstrating others' experiences, perspectives, and feelings. These three practices must be exercised in tangent to keep the workforce highly motivated and satisfied (Mayfield & Mayfield, 2018).

References

Advisory Board (2017). How 3 top health systems develop physician leaders in-house, March 27, https://www.advisory.com/blog/2017/03/physician-leaders

ABLM. (2021). Public & Physician Trust in the U.S. Health Care System, Retrieved from https://buildingtrust.org/public-physician-trust-in-the-u-s-health-care-system/

Belasen, A. T. (2019). *Dyad Leadership and Clinical Integration: Driving Change, Aligning Strategies*, Chicago, IL: Health Administration Press.

Belasen, A. (2008). *The Theory and Practice of Corporate Communication: A Competing Values Perspective*, Newbury Park, CA: Sage Publications.

Belasen, A., & Frank, N. (2010). A peek through the lens of the competing values framework: What managers communicate & how. *The Atlantic Journal of Communication*, 18, 280–296.

Bowman, D. (2011). Looking to develop physician leaders? Invest in mentoring, *Fierce Healthcare*, August 12, https://www.fiercehealthcare.com/healthcare/looking-to-develop-physician-leaders-invest-mentoring

Clampitt, P. G., DeKoch, B., & Cashman, T. (2000). A strategy for communicating about uncertainty. *Academy of Management Executive*, 14(4), 41–57.

Goffee R., & Jones G. (2000 Sep-Oct). Why should anyone be led by you? *Harvard Business Review*, 78(5), 62–70, 198. PMID:11143155.

Mayfield, J., & Mayfield, M. (2018). *Motivating Language Theory: Effective Leader Talk in the Workplace*, Cham: Springer International.

McKee, A. (2016). How the Most Emotionally Intelligent CEOs Handle Their Power, *HBR*, https://hbr.org/2016/12/how-the-most-emotionally-intelligent-ceos-handle-their-power, December 8.

Rogers, P. S., & Hildebrandt, H. W. (1993). Competing values instruments for analyzing written and spoken management messages. *Human Resource Management Journal*, 32(1), 121–142.

Chapter 9

Conclusion—Sustaining Resilience in Healthcare Organizations

Healthcare systems throughout the world were hard hit by the COVID-19 pandemic as hospitals were pushed to their limits in attempting to contain the virus. Most commonly, problems with resource management for ventilators, beds, PPE, and especially nurses brought emergency planning shortfalls to light.

Pandemics have occurred before and will certainly occur again (e.g., 1918's Spanish Flu, AIDS from the 1980s, and 2014's Ebola outbreak); however, the new variant has affected healthcare systems worldwide and has forced healthcare leaders to face new challenges. Issues such as limited supply chain for protective masks and sanitization supplies, critical life-saving equipment, a shortage of hospital beds, and exhausted overworked front-line staff were prevalent in the forefront of the pandemic.

The pandemic has elevated stress levels among health providers with serious implications. Chronic stress is linked to greater risk for a range of adverse health outcomes, so adopting a rigorous, evidence-based approach for identifying needs and designing interventions is critical. Nurses trained in medicine were taught how to care for critically ill patients. Ambulatory care nurses were taught how to administer countless COVID tests, and vaccinations. But even with a successful cross-training platform, mental health issues of staff continue to crop up.

A recent report in Medscape (2020) found that 44% of physicians reported at least one symptom of burnout in 2020. During the COVID-19 pandemic, early evidence suggested that this situation may be exacerbated due to shortages in ventilators, PPE, face shields, and testing kits (Ranney, et al., 2020). An earlier analysis provided evidence supporting what was feared; physician burnout was associated with increased risk of patient safety incidents (Panagioti, et al., 2018).

DOI: 10.4324/9781003190929-9

Emerging data suggests that healthcare workers treating individuals with COVID-19 are reporting significant distress and symptoms of depression, anxiety, and insomnia. Those on the front lines of responding to COVID-19 needed more focused, brief psychological interventions to enable them to cope with the highly stressful work situations. Unfortunately, current healthcare systems are not well-structured to address these problems. Many hospitals do not provide psychological support or have the resources to enable distribution of such services. Transforming them will require a combination of effective leadership from the top and workplace flexibility at the work unit level.

COVID-19 has disrupted how leaders interact with employees and how coworkers connect with each other. The need to adapt quickly and act resiliently during the pandemic has also revealed the importance of workplace flexibility, interfunctional collaboration, and the role of middle managers in innovation implementation, the topics covered in this chapter.

Leadership

Resilience is key to leading effectively during crises and transitions. Resilient leaders are analytical, adaptive, empathetic, and confident. They have the know-how to align goals, behaviors, and processes to sustain reliable operations at all levels of the healthcare organization. They rely on evidence-based practices that integrate clinical expertise with critical reasoning to analyze and make smart choices.

Resilient leaders create adaptive cultures and promote interprofessional cooperation that serves as a viable strategy for aligning partners and communities. With strong self-awareness and EI skills, they build trust with followers and team members and encourage interfunctional collaboration across the continuum of care. They meet crisis conditions head-on, identify opportunities as catalysts for long-term growth and success, track costs and risks, and move forward with confidence and resilience.

Trust is necessary in many different forms in the workplace. And organizational culture rooted in ethics is conducive to trustworthy relationships among members. Trust encourages taking risks, facilitates information sharing, increases group effectiveness, and enhances productivity. Employees need to trust in their leaders' authenticity and ability to make sound strategic and operational decisions.

To be authentic is to understand who you are and what you believe in, to practice what you preach, and to be your true self. Leaders need to reveal their vulnerabilities, build trusting relationships, demonstrate credibility, be transparent, and act ethically.

Employees' construct of authenticity influences trust, engagement, and ultimately the leader's ability to influence. Further, an employee needs to have trust that their company is treating them fairly and is articulating a mission that is both ethical and fulfilling. Leaders grow by stretching the limits of who they really are—doing new things that make them uncomfortable but that teach them through direct experience who they want to become. Authentic leaders understand that positive relationships are built on respect, openness, and trust. Acting unethically is a breakdown in the logic of an authentic relationship and may cause members to lose trust in the leader.

One open question is whether the shift towards authenticity during COVID is permanent or just a brief snapshot in time. Sheryl Miller (2020) believes that the COVID crisis has made authentic leadership more important. She observed that verbal and written exchanges between bosses and teams, service providers and clients, which were once formerly devoid of color and warmth, are becoming more *human*. The corporate masks that we are all guilty of wearing to cover up authentic elements of our personalities are slipping, almost unconsciously, as we seek comfort and reassurance in an unsettling "new normal."

Miller noted that

> if COVID marks the era of a new, trusting, more authentic form of corporate conversation, perhaps this also signifies the wake of a more congruent and empathic kind of leadership too – one that makes CEOs more relatable on a human level … A delicate balance must be struck. It is unrealistic, never mind risky, for a CEO to show complete transparency over emotive thoughts and feelings. Yet presenting oneself as *human* – that is fallible, imperfect, with quirks and idiosyncrasies – an "unfinished" article with still much to learn despite the accolades and achievements – will go a long way in communicating a sense of humanity and authenticity that fosters trust.
>
> **(Miller, 2020)**

In a time of crisis, a leader must resort to efficient communication to protect the organization's most important asset, its employees. The leader is tasked with establishing a communication strategy that is aligned with an open, accessible sharing of information. Leaders need to communicate clearly and frequently to all stakeholders in a crisis. However, first and foremost, they must share information with their teams on how the organization will meet their needs.

During periods of crises, emotions run high, and morale is low. A leader must communicate a vision of how to navigate through the crisis and what members can expect (Mendy, 2020). Openness and honesty are especially important in times of crisis. Leaders should communicate clearly, simply, and frequently. Effective leaders can not only give people what they need, but also when they need it. When communicating, a leader should choose candor over charisma. To build trust, the leader must communicate with high levels of transparency, credibility, honesty, and accountability.

Resilient leaders cannot rely on traditional decision-making strategies and tools to navigate crisis situations. However, they must activate a strategic process of collecting and analyzing data and metrics and leveraging actionable insights from key stakeholders. Good decision-making comes from effectively utilizing processes, people, and strategies. It encompasses gathering data, analyzing data, the development of solutions, debating options, implementing a strategy, and measuring performance outcomes. In dealing with the COVID-19 pandemic, for example, Australia managed to maintain some of the lowest infection and death rates, and a less pronounced economic recession than many comparable countries.

McKinsey & Company identified three themes from Australia's response to COVID that prove critical for resilient leaders: First and foremost was evidence-based decision-making followed by building trust with stakeholders and fostering effective collaboration across boundaries (Child, et al., 2020).

WHO HEALTH SYSTEMS ARE ADDING TO THE C-SUITE

Health systems are focused on having the right people with the right skills to tackle evolving issues in healthcare. This means the C-suite and leadership roles are changing.

BUSINESS TRANSFORMATION

Many health systems began focused on business transformation before the COVID-19 pandemic, especially considering mergers and acquisitions activity across the U.S. More recently, organizations are looking closely at cultural integration and business function integration with new leadership roles of chief transformation officer, and even occasionally chief integration officer. One example is BayCare Health System, a 15-hospital organization based in Clearwater, Fla., with Emily Allinder Scott as senior vice president and chief transformation officer. She is responsible for efforts around clinical variation, clinical care delivery models, value-based care, and population health.

DIVERSITY, EQUITY, AND INCLUSION

As Mr. Petros put it: "It's not just chief diversity officer anymore. I think there's a clear need, and we're seeing some of the systems put more resources behind identifying and prioritizing community-based functions as a component of population health." He said these functions may include community revitalization efforts, housing, community development, job creation, education, and/or access to high-quality internet. He has seen several titles around this work, such as chief health equity officer, president over the well-being division, chief community health officer, president over social determinants of health, and vice president of accountable communities.

CONSUMERISM

In addition to diversity, equity, and inclusion, health system C-suite and leadership roles are focusing more on patient behavior and experience. Newer titles in this area include chief consumer officer and chief consumer innovation officer.

PAYER PERFORMANCE

In April, Winston-Salem, NC-based Novant Health named Erik Helms as the health system's new senior vice president and chief payer performance officer, indicative of a larger focus on payer performance. John Gizdic, executive vice president and chief business development officer for Novant Health, said at the time:

> We recognize that cost shouldn't be a barrier for our communities to receive remarkable care. I'm confident that Erik's extensive experience in driving successful business results for multibillion-dollar reimbursement programs will enable Novant Health to work with our payer partners to keep our high-quality care affordable.

He said new price transparency rules—which took effect January 1—also may contribute to newer responsibilities or titles related to payer performance. The rules require hospitals to post a machine-readable file with the negotiated rates for all items and services, and display the prices of hundreds of services in a consumer-friendly format.

AMBULATORY SERVICES

Mr. Drometer has observed another key area of leadership: chief ambulatory officer or senior vice president of ambulatory services. He attributed the emerging ambulatory services executive role to health systems' continued shift towards more outpatient services. "They're creating more stickiness by moving out and expanding ambulatory services into the surrounding community. That is really the growth play," he said. "So, if a health system is unable to grow through acquisition, the only way they're able to grow their net revenue in a profitable way—if they do it right—is through ambulatory expansion." One example of ambulatory growth is Boston-based Mass General Brigham which is planning a roughly $2 billion project, including a $400 million ambulatory expansion. The plans have faced opposition from a coalition that includes UMass Memorial Health in Worcester and physician organization Highland Healthcare Associates IPA (Gooch, 2021).

Flexible Workplace

The trend towards increased flexibility became particularly clear just before the pandemic, when unemployment rates had dropped below 4% in the United States (Trading Economics, 2021) and companies were looking for new methods for attracting top talent. A report in 2018 found that 63% of companies were making some use of remote workers, even if they lacked defined policies (Upwork, 2018). In a 2019 survey, 80% of respondents said they would be more loyal if offered flexible work options, up from 75% in 2018 (Dunn, 2020).

Evidence shows that upskilling employees during and after periods of transition—what they should be doing, how they should be learning, and where they should be applying what they learned—helps to increase resiliency. An organization that helps its workers become more resilient can be an attractive employer indeed—one that is well positioned to compete for both existing and new talent (Volini, et al., 2020).

Other studies supported the trend towards flexible work schedules with 51% of respondents in one survey stating they can be more productive working from home due to fewer interruptions and more comfortable work environments. In addition, 73% of respondents claimed to have found a better work-life balance, allowing for more time with family, pets, and hobbies (Pelta, 2020). Other surveys found that 82% of executives agree that employees can continue to work remotely part time and 36% indicated a desire to hire fully remote employees who live anywhere, compared to just 12% before the COVID-19 pandemic (Agovino, 2020).

Flexibility in the workplace can come in different forms, ranging from minimal to more extreme options. At its simplest, a flexible work schedule might allow employees to vary their arrival and departure times as long as they work an appropriate number of hours. In other cases, employees may shift to a three- or four-day work week with longer hours on the days they work. A more drastic change would be a results-only work environment (ROWE), where employees decide their own schedule and their only obligation is to complete their work, rather than expectations to work a certain number of hours.

In a ROWE, managers evaluate team members by their performance, results, or output, not by their presence in the office or the hours that they work. Accountable members with appropriate talent are given discretion over their projects and the freedom to choose when and how they will meet their goals.

In the healthcare field, telehealth has become a key weapon in the fight against the COVID-19 pandemic. Telehealth allows patients to access essential health services from their homes and supports self-isolation and quarantine policies to reduce the risk of exposure and the spread of viruses. Advantages also include the use of informatics that leverage the clinical information captured by EHR systems to reduce physician burnout; optimized communication and operating efficiencies of care teams including physicians, nurses, and ancillary staff to produce better patient outcomes; and effective interoperability to improve care coordination and inspire innovation to alleviate stress on the current capacity.

VIRTUAL CARE

The volume of telehealth visits increased dramatically as patients sought to safely obtain outpatient care. Many physicians saw their telehealth visit volume increase by a factor of 50 to 175. This increase occurred over a very short period—often in days or at the most, weeks. Providers hastily constructed a temporary "bridge," built with digital tools and operational workarounds that are not robust enough to sustain this level of use permanently. At the same time, patients have come to expect telehealth and many providers have become comfortable delivering care via the technology.

Because virtual care is now part of the new normal, health systems must construct a sturdy, permanent bridge that includes organizational, financial, and clinical structures and processes. The health system will need to integrate telehealth technology with the electronic health record system, define clinical protocols for appropriate telehealth visits, obtain reimbursement for telehealth visits, and revamp hospital and physician practice processes to support telehealth (e.g., how should virtual waiting rooms work for telehealth visits?).

As health systems implement a permanent approach to telehealth, they should recognize that telehealth is a component of two broader digital health strategies: Ensuring that care is delivered in the right setting and creating a positive patient experience through a "digital front door" (Glaser, et al., 2021).

A shortcoming of telehealth is that there is less patient contact, as well as limited access and use of technology by older or novice patients. For most elderly and disabled individuals, learning and using patient portals and telehealth technologies is practically impossible. Involving family and/or caregivers of the older patient population in the communication and visits is therefore essential to ensure that the patient can receive the needed care safely and reliably.

Sensitivity training in paraverbal communication, change of tone, pitch, and ensuring the patient understands and can ask questions are key to successful provider-patient communication (Belasen & Belasen, 2018) and the implementation of telehealth. Employing dynamic dialogue and mutual accountability can certainly create opportunities for improved access, better patient outcomes, and lower healthcare costs.

Under the public health emergency (CMS, 2021), new or established patients can receive Medicare telehealth services and other communications technology-based services in any location. In addition, providers can waive Medicare co-payments for these telehealth services for beneficiaries in original Medicare including follow-ups, outpatient subsequent visits, and consultations.

> In any model for care, patients need to be able to trust that physicians will place patient welfare above other interests, provide competent care, provide the information patients need to make well-considered decisions about care, respect patient privacy and confidentiality, and take steps needed to ensure continuity of care (AMA, 2016).
>
> OCR will exercise its enforcement discretion and will not impose penalties for noncompliance with the regulatory requirements under the HIPAA Rules against covered healthcare providers in connection with the good faith provision of telehealth during the COVID-19 nationwide public health emergency (Notification of Enforcement Discretion, 2020).

The 2016 AMA ethical guidance notes that while new technologies and new models of care will continue to emerge, physicians' fundamental ethical responsibilities do not change. Guidelines include:

- Informing patients about the limitations of the relationship and services provided
- Encouraging telemedicine patients who have a primary care physician to inform them about their online health consultation and ensuring the information from the encounter can be accessed for future episodes of care
- Recognizing the limitations of technology and taking appropriate steps to overcome them, such as by having another healthcare professional at the patient's location conduct an exam or obtaining vital information through remote technologies
- Ensuring patients have a basic understanding of how telemedicine technologies are used in their care, the limitations of the technologies, and ways the information will be used after the patient encounter

Interfunctional Collaboration

Consistent with *disruptive innovation theory*, which places a great emphasis on the power of organizational processes and enabling technology to deliver products and services at lower costs than incumbent firms, innovative firms transform their markets by pulling in new customers (Belasen & Rufer, 2013). Key organizational functions with important synergistic effects for successful innovation include marketing, R&D, and operations/production.

However, it has long been recognized that without open communication and joint accountability, the tension among these functions, that often is also triggered by conflicting communications with external stakeholders, might lead to lower levels of organizational performance. Indeed, resources and capabilities that are not translated into well-synchronized activities, best practices, or business processes cannot have a positive impact on a firm's performance (Ray, Barney, & Muhanna, 2004). And the healthcare industry is no different.

Studies indicate that the failure to mobilize teamwork has considerable costs and that it contributes to inefficient and wasteful resource consumption, excessive lengths of stay for patients, and diminished quality of decision-making. Creating a culture of interprofessional collaboration and leveraging cross-functional synergies require participative forms of leadership and communication, empowerment, and the use of motivational strategies that match the needs of employees and the complexity of the healthcare environment.

Resilient leaders must focus on identifying characteristics of adaptive culture and innovation communication that contribute to effective interfunctional collaboration (Belasen, et al., 2015). Creating a culture of interprofessional collaboration and cross-functional synergies reinforces the execution of accountable care organization strategy and the achievement of the Triple Aim—improving the patient experience of care, improving the health of populations, and reducing per capita healthcare costs. Financially, bundled payments are well aligned with cooperative decision-making and interprofessional collaboration necessary for managing the complexity of healthcare organizations.

In healthcare organizations, which currently undergo massive transitions, reliance on interprofessional collaboration and distributed leadership has given rise to a general call to enact micro forms of leadership primarily due to integration challenges that must be met at the operational, not institutional level. At the same time, healthcare units and teams operate in environments that are largely influenced by broader organizational and institutional goals. If so, who other than middle managers with their cross-hierarchical, cross-boundary roles can better perform these roles?

Middle Managers

Positioned centrally within the chain of command, middle managers handle multiple, often contradictory roles and deal with diverse sets of internal and external stakeholders. They engage in dual lines of reporting with top-down implementation roles and bottom-up facilitation roles. Functioning as intermediaries across hierarchical levels, effective middle managers strike a delicate balance between creativity and efficiency, transformational and transactional roles. Notably, middle managers' responsibilities are likened to those of a strategist, change architect, or a communication conduit between corporate level strategy, execution, and outcomes. Communication competence is a skill most needed by middle managers as the complexity of information and number of potential interactions are greater for middle managers than for senior managers or operating-level managers.

In addition to the persuasion aspect of managerial communication and the ability to control language, gestures, and tone of voice, for managers to be perceived as competent communicators by their subordinates, they must also share and respond to information in a timely manner. Moreover, they should actively listen to other points of view, communicate clearly and succinctly to all levels of the organization, and utilize appropriate communication channels. Indeed, the strategic value of middle managers in healthcare organizations is in removing barriers to problem solving and in stimulating innovation and learning (Belasen & Belasen, 2016).

Middle managers with active involvement in the strategy process demonstrate higher levels of commitment to organizational goals and contribute to the success of strategic initiatives. They draw ideas, perspectives, and impressions from their direct reports and utilize them in their communications with top executives. In fact, evidence shows that middle managers' upward leadership and downward influence affect the alignment of organizational activities with the strategic context (Rouleau & Balogun, 2011). They help facilitate the need for change in communications with executives and implement change in interactions with lower levels (Belasen & Frank, 2010).

In the healthcare field middle managers are an important part of the organizational resources and capabilities. They support the organization through their vital know-how, experience, and internal and external networks and help strengthen the social identity and culture of the organization. In hospitals, for example, middle managers translate strategic-level goals into actionable improvement plans at the department or work unit level, engage employees in safety and quality assurance efforts, and identify and improve processes over time. In that sense, they differ significantly from senior managers, who are more concerned with the overall direction of the organization, strategic objectives, and resource allocation.

As transmitters of communication with much responsibility for day-to-day operations and internal processes, middle managers act more as negotiators and ambassadors to first-line supervisors and peer managers and are often on the lookout for tradeoffs that often escape the attention of senior managers and that are central for the performance of the organization. Effective middle managers know how to relate to lower levels and use appropriate channels of communication to respond to employees' questions or need for information and feedback.

Middle managers accomplish core tasks to ensure continuity in operations, keep the organization going, and attain positive organizational outcomes. They implement strategy, translate goals from executive level to care teams and work units, create local relevance, interpret shifting contexts, clarify words and actions of executives, and promote organizational discourse.

Middle managers' central location within the hierarchy also reinforces their mediation roles in interpreting critical events and in creating shared purpose. While senior managers are too distant, middle managers are closer to front-line employees, are familiar with informal networks and opinion leaders, and play an important role in letting employees feel valued and safe. Evidence suggests that middle managers in healthcare services support their employees by influencing their commitment to the organization and by facilitating their professional endeavors (Carlstrom, 2012).

Resilience in Healthcare Leadership

> The future of medicine will require a fundamentally different style of leadership, rooted in a willingness to decentralize authority, empower a broader network, and build processes that augment a leader's capacity for decision making and for understanding the needs of the organization and its staff and patients.
>
> **(Lobdell et al., 2020)**

The COVID-19 pandemic has been the ultimate test for leadership resiliency. Resilient leaders can sustain their intensity under stressful situations and have the confidence to take calculated risks to cope with disruptive changes and realign people with evolving operating models. They bounce back from setbacks by being thoughtful and deliberate. They promote action by asking the right questions and supporting team members to pursue common goals. Four competencies were explored in Chapter 3 and are linked in this chapter with assessment and development: Adaptive, empathetic, analytical, and confident (Figure 9.1).

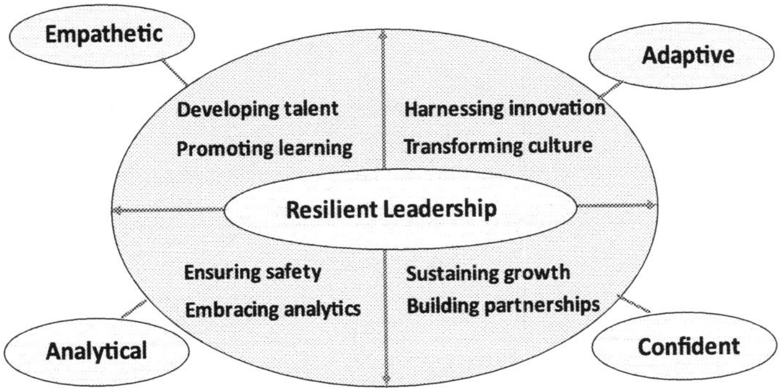

Figure 9.1 Resilience in healthcare leadership.

Adaptive—COVID-19 is an adaptive challenge that needs adaptive leadership. The COVID-19 response increasingly should be viewed as a marathon and not an infection prevention sprint to a finish line, reinforcing the need for resilience strategies and proactive measures to contain the pandemic. Operationally, it is critical to strengthen evidence-based adaptive management practices, to adjust the mix and type of interventions being implemented and pursue shared goals.

This requires adaptive leadership capacities, being open and transparent about learning, using collective decision-making processes, and building trust with communities and individuals. Resilient leaders create the capabilities that match the vision and promote supportive communication practices that serve as a viable strategy for aligning partners and communities.

Empathetic—having strong empathy can be a game changer when it comes to managing crisis such as the COVID-19 pandemic, which requires leaders who empower and trust others to carry out critical tasks. Experience shows that shifting decisions to those closest to handling COVID-19 challenges helps improve organizational agility and enhances innovation. Empathy helps leaders build trust, stay focused, and adopt a rational and intuitive decision style despite facing highly stressful situations.

Empathetic leaders must also be adept at receiving and evaluating feedback on the effectiveness of their decisions. Resilient leaders are skilled at triage, able to build trusting relationships for attracting and retaining the right talent, inspire learning, and actively encourage interprofessional collaboration. Leaders need to be sensitive, attuned, and listen nonjudgmentally and optimistically to moments of differences, and feel responsible for working with those differences. They focus on the common purpose, are inspirational, and project trustworthiness to ensure people stay calm and engaged.

Analytical—health systems must increase their analytical capacity and develop a strong foundation of informatics and systems analysis when they are tested by disruptive events such as COVID-19. In addition to aligning quality goals and incentives, harnessing innovation technology, and embracing evidence-based medicine, resilient leaders maintain a long-term perspective by engaging in pursuing value-driven strategies that may not have immediate payoffs.

Healthcare analytical leaders recognize that capital investments in health information technology, hiring, training and development, and cultural transformation often come with the risk of investing in programs that are not reimbursable under fee-for service. They believe that the programs are morally right to pursue and that in the end they will yield savings in the value-based payment. Analytical leaders combine openness, communication, and collaboration to effectively engage others and leverage existing human, financial, and technological resources, and capabilities for achieving broader organizational goals.

Confident—coping with crises is daunting. The coronavirus pandemic has been an epic test of character and determination for health leaders requiring them to be assertive and empathetic, analytical, and adaptive, lead with confidence, and emerge stronger. They are expected to balance short-term needs with courage and calm and develop long-term goals with vision and imagination.

The COVID-19 outbreak is a life-altering catastrophic event, and no preparation or previous experience can prepare leaders to deal with its unpredictability. Leaders are expected to be mentally and physically fit. Mental toughness and physical fitness help to boost personal strength and stamina and increase focus and confidence in identifying creative solutions to complex problems and in building trust with stakeholders. They use persuasion and thoughtfulness in their communications and can influence others with tact and diplomacy. They have the moral courage and integrity to speak frankly and give constructive feedback even when the implications might be negative.

Confident leaders project positive attitudes and maintain their composure despite the stress. They play the role of devil's advocate, testing the validity of arguments by asking "why" and "how" questions and by swapping dominant alternatives with ideas that organizational and team members can consider.

Profile Awareness and Self-Assessment

Profile awareness is a powerful medium which allows leaders to understand their strengths and weaknesses, what motivates them, and how they make decisions. Self-assessment tools are designed to help increase self-awareness or understanding of one's strengths and weaknesses, behavioral patterns, and motivations. Executives can use these instruments to evaluate whether gaps in the behavior of individuals have been addressed and make important decisions about their suitability to lead work units, teams, or organizations.

Profile awareness and self-assessment (Table 9.1) are the starting points in a diagnostic process aimed at identifying gaps between actual and desired behaviors and a tracking plan aimed at remedying deficiencies based on input from others. In Figure 9.2, "before and after" can represent current versus desired situations or even baseline ("before") and target ("after") levels of performance. Self-assessment gives managers a chance to see how well they master the qualities of resilient leadership (adaptive, empathetic, analytical, confident) while at the same time review their own strengths and weaknesses for further development and improvement.

Resilient Leadership: Assessment

Thinking about your attitudes and beliefs when working with teams and individuals, reflect on each statement by indicating the response that best matches your beliefs, first

Table 9.1 Assessment: Resilient Leadership

Dimension	*Current Behavior*	*Desired Behavior*
Adaptive		
I help employees and peers to get through change and uncertainty		
I see disruptions as learning opportunities		
I play devil's advocate to encourage others to think innovatively		
I encourage members to take initiatives in defining and solving new problems		
I like to experiment with new ideas and approaches		
I am open to adjusting the solution continually as new challenges emerge		
I promote learning, creativity, and adaptation in my organization		
I entice stakeholders to accept change through persuasion and diplomacy		
Avg		
Analytical		
I can evaluate information critically to support a decision or recommendation		
I integrate multiple data sources for accurate analysis		
I can analyze the current way of doing business and clinical processes		
I develop strategies to improve the effective use of comparative information		
I demonstrate critical thinking skills by identifying cause-and-effect relationships		
I examine how a system design aligns with business processes		
I am comfortable with methods of data quality and continuous improvement		
I can perform needs analysis, and identify and prioritize requirements		
Avg		
Empathetic		
I can improve my self-awareness as a leader by using good habits that become successful tendencies		

(*Continued*)

Table 9.1 (Continued) Assessment: Resilient Leadership

Dimension	*Current Behavior*	*Desired Behavior*
I solicit feedback about my strengths and weaknesses		
I recognize immediately when I am short-tempered or feel anxious		
I come across as honest and approachable		
I can understand the effects of my decisions on others' feelings		
I am a good listener when others communicate with me		
I am good at reconciling differences with others		
I embrace transparency and build trust through mutual respect		
Avg		
Confident		
I challenge people to focus on the big picture during organizational transitions		
I do not let stressful situations overcome me		
I can challenge myself to accomplish difficult tasks		
I am comfortable with emerging issues and disruptions		
I can shift priorities rapidly as business conditions change		
I see crises as opportunities for personal and organizational growth		
I evaluate my performance critically considering new challenges		
I can inspire others to achieve superior results		
Avg		

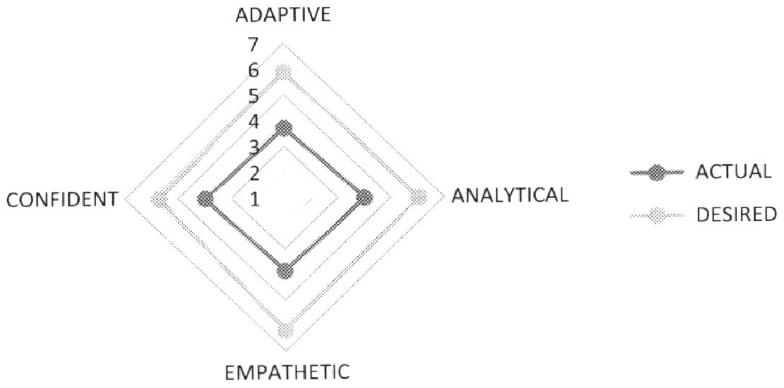

Figure 9.2 Dimensions of resilient leadership.

in terms of actual occurrences (i.e., current beliefs, views, behaviors) and then desired expectations.

1 —*Very untrue of what I believe*
2 —*Untrue of what I believe*
3 —*Somewhat untrue of what I believe*
4 —*Neutral*
5 —*Somewhat true of what I believe*
6 —*True of what I believe*
7 —*Very true of what I believe*

Methods or instruments of self-assessment which also consider responses from others (e.g., internal and external stakeholders) are particularly useful for monitoring progress towards desired goals and behaviors. They also provide executives with a dashboard to review potential gaps between actual and desired behaviors, adjust or change criteria as needed, or develop new benchmarks. Social context is important because individuals in leadership positions look to others for validation of their behavior and motivation.

There are no "ideal" scores for this survey. While it is confirming when others see you in the same way as you see yourself, it is also beneficial to know when they see you differently. This assessment can help you understand those dimensions of your resilience that are relatively strong and dimensions of your leadership you may consider for improvement. Executives and managers can use these instruments developmentally to examine how well their scores are balanced across the four dimensions, check whether important milestones have been accomplished, and revise their development plans accordingly.

In Figure 9.2, the gap between the two charts can represent an opportunity for personal development and improvement. Often the display of extreme behaviors may result in negative consequences, especially when certain qualities are used extensively without considering the other qualities. Overemphasizing activities associated with compliance and adherence (analytical role) often creates feelings of mistrust, lack of motivation, and low morale on the part of followers who may perceive these leaders as micromanagers and obsessive monitors.

Similarly, having too much empathy in the workplace can lead to burnout, especially for leaders who are overcome by their emotions or who might be perceived as too permissive or as abdicating their responsibilities. Hence, it is important that leaders consciously avoid a narrow focus or "implicit favorites" by finding ways to balance their roles and qualities across the four dimensions of resilient leadership.

Revealing personal differences requires a strong sense of personal integrity and moral courage. Verbalizing personal vulnerabilities demonstrates humility and honesty. It conveys confidence. When a leader admits to weaknesses, it creates the trust and respect conducive to a collaborative atmosphere, which promotes unity among followers and leaders. By developing self-awareness, soliciting feedback, and realigning your profile, you can gain a clear understanding of your strengths and weaknesses and unleash the potential in yourself and others.

Conclusions

Resilient leaders have the know-how to align goals, behaviors, and processes to sustain the effectiveness of healthcare teams and organizations. They can recover from adversity and manage critical disruptions with high levels of confidence and moral courage. They rely on evidence-based practices that integrate clinical expertise with critical reasoning to make smart choices.

Resilient leaders are flexible and adjust to their circumstances innovatively and proactively. With strong self-awareness and empathy skills, they can build trust with followers and team members and foster quality relationships. Resilient leaders create adaptive cultures and promote supportive communication practices that serve as a viable strategy for attracting and retaining talents in organizations and for strengthening interprofessional collaboration.

Resilient leaders inspire followers with vision and confidence, honesty, and transparency. They can build trusting relationships to meet crisis situations head-on while remaining confident about identifying opportunities as catalysts for a better future. Resilient leaders are also driven by ethical outcomes. They establish expectations based on personal integrity, credibility, and accountability. They mobilize support for a new vision of success and empower individuals and teams to stay focused on facts and data that inform long-term goals and that are also ethical and consider the broader needs of communities and stakeholders.

References

Agovino, T. (2020). *What Will the Workplace Look Like in 2025?* SHRM. Dec 12, Retrieved from https://www.shrm.org/hr-today/news/all-things-work/pages/the-workplace-in-2025.aspx

AMA (2016). AMA adopts new guidance for ethical practice in telemedicine, June 13, Retrieved from https://www.ama-assn.org/press-center/press-releases/ama-adopts-new-guidance-ethical-practice-telemedicine

Belasen, A. T., & Belasen, A. R. (2016). Value in the middle: cultivating middle managers in healthcare organizations. *Journal of Management Development*, 35(9), 1149–1162.

Belasen, A. R., & Belasen, A. T. (2018). Doctor-patient communication: a review and a rationale for using an assessment framework. *Journal of Health Organization and Management*, 32(7), 891–907.

Belasen, A. T., & Frank, N. M. (2010). A peek through the lens of the competing values framework: What managers communicate and how. *The Atlantic Journal of Communication*, 18, 280–296.

Belasen, A., Eisenberg, B., & Huppertz, J. (2015). *Mastering Leadership: A Vital Resource for Healthcare Organizations*, Boston, MA: Jones & Bartlett Learning.

Belasen, A. & Rufer, R. (2013). Innovation communication for effective interprofessional collaboration: A stakeholder perspective. In N. Pfeffermann, T. Minshall, & L. Mortara (Eds.), *Strategy and Communication for Innovation* (2nd edition, pp. 227–240), Germany: Springer.

Carlstrom, E. D. (2012). Middle managers on the slide. *Leadership in Health Services*, 25(2), 90–105.

Child, J., Dillon, R., Erasmus, E., & Johnson, J. (2020, December 15). Collaboration in Crisis: Reflecting on Australia's COVID-19 Response. *McKinsey & Company*, Retrieved from https://www.mckinsey.com/industries/public-and-social-sector/our-insights/collaboration-in-crisis-reflecting-on-australias-covid-19-response.

CMS (2021). COVID-19 Emergency Declaration Blanket Waivers for Health Care Providers, April 8, Retrieved from https://www.cms.gov/files/document/summary-covid-19-emergency-declaration-waivers.pdf

Dunn, A. (2020). 2021 Trends: Flexibility in the workplace. *Work Design Magazine*. Dec Retrieved from https://www.workdesign.com/2020/12/2021-trends-flexibility-in-the-workplace/

Gooch, K. (2021). Becker's Healthcare, Retrieved from https://www.beckershospitalreview.com/hospital-management-administration/who-health-systems-are-adding-to-the-c-suite.html, May 14.

Glaser, J., Overhage, M., Guptill, J., Appleby, C., & Trigg, D. (2021).What the Pandemic Means for Health Care's Digital Transformation, Retrieved from https://www.physicianleaders.org/news/what-the-pandemic-means-for-health-cares-digital-transformation?

Lobdell, K. W., Hariharan, S., Smith, W., Rose, G. A., Ferguson, B., & Fussell, C. (2020). Improving health care leadership in the Covid-19 era. *Nejm Catalyst Innovations in Care Delivery*. doi:10.1056/CAT.20.0225

Medscape (2020). *Medscape National Physician Burnout & Suicide Report 2020: The Generational Divide*. By Kane, L. et al., January 15, Retrieved from https://www.medscape.com/slideshow/2020-lifestyle-burnout-6012460

Mendy, A. (2020, April 7). A leader's guide: Communicating with teams, stakeholders, and communities during COVID-19. *McKinsey.com*, Retrieved from https://www.mckinsey.com/business-functions/organization/our-insights/a-leaders-guide-communicating-with-teams-stakeholders-and-communities-during-covid-19.

Miller, S. (2020). A Post-COVID World Calls for More Authentic Leadership. *CEO Today*.

Notification of Enforcement Discretion for Telehealth Remote Communications During the COVID-19 Nationwide Public Health Emergency (2020, March 30). U.S. Department of Health & Human Services, Retrieved from https://www.hhs.gov/hipaa/for-professionals/special-topics/emergency-preparedness/notification-enforcement-discretion-telehealth/index.html

Panagioti, M., Geraghty, K., & Johnson, J., et al. (2018). Association between physician burnout and patient safety, professionalism, and patient satisfaction: A systematic review and meta-analysis. *JAMA*, 178, 1317–1331.

Pelta, R. (2020). FlexJobs Survey: Productivity, Work-life Balance Improves During Pandemic. Sept 21, Retrieved from https://www.flexjobs.com/blog/post/survey-productivity-balance-improve-during-pandemic-remote-work/

Ranney, M. L., Griffeth, V., & Jha, A. K. (2020). Critical supply shortages—the need for ventilators and personal protective equipment during the Covid-19 pandemic. *The New England Journal of Medicine*, 382, e41. doi:10.1056/NEJMp200614.

Ray, G., Barney, J. B., & Muhanna, W. A. (2004). Capabilities, business processes, and competitive advantage: Choosing the dependent variable in empirical tests of the resource-based view. *Strategic Management Journal*, *25*(1), 23–37. doi:10.1002/smj.366

Rouleau, L., & Balogun, J. (2011). Middle managers, strategic sense making, and discursive competence. *Journal of Management Studies*, 48(5), 953–983.

Trading Economics. (2021). United States Unemployment Rate: 1948–2021. May, Retrieved from https://tradingeconomics.com/united-states/unemployment-rate

Upwork. (2018). *Future Workforce Report*, Retrieved from https://www.upwork.com/i/future-workforce/fw/2018.

Volini, E., Schwartz, J., Denny, B. et al. (2020). Beyond reskilling: Investing in resilience for uncertain futures. *Deloitte*, Insights, Retrieved from https://www2.deloitte.com/us/en/insights/focus/human-capital-trends/2020/reskilling-the-workforce-to-be-resilient.html

Index